The White Logic

The White Logic

Alcoholism and Gender
in American Modernist Fiction

John W. Crowley

University of Massachusetts Press *Amherst*

Copyright © 1994 by
The University of Massachusetts Press
All rights reserved
Printed in the United States of America

LC 94-14809
ISBN 0-87023-931-7
Designed by Teresa Bonner
Set in Adobe Caslon and Bitstream Cheltenham by
Keystone Typesetting, Inc.
Printed and bound by Thomson-Shore, Inc.

Library of Congress Cataloging-in-Publication Data
Crowley, John William, 1945–
    The white logic : alcoholism and gender in American modernist
fiction / John W. Crowley.
        p.   cm.
    Includes bibliographical references and index.
    ISBN 0-87023-931-7
    1. American fiction—20th century—History and criticism.   2.
Alcoholism—United States—History—20th century.   3. Drinking
of alcoholic beverages in literature.   4. Authors, American—20th
century—Alcohol use.   5. Modernism (Literature)—United States.
6. Alcoholics—United States—Biography.   7. Drinking customs in
literature.   8. Alcoholism in literature.   9. Alcoholics in
literature.   10. Sex role in literature.   I. Title.
PS374.A42C76   1994
813'.509356—dc20   94-14809
                                                              CIP

British Library Cataloguing in Publication data are available.

For Mary Anne,
who led the way

"The old long sickness, which had been purely an intellectual sickness, recrudesced. The old ghosts, long laid, lifted their heads again. But they were different and more deadly ghosts. The old ghosts, intellectual in their inception, had been laid by a sane and normal logic. But now they were raised by the White Logic of John Barleycorn, and John Barleycorn never lays the ghosts of his raising. For this sickness of pessimism, caused by drink, one must drink further in quest of the anodyne that John Barleycorn promises but never delivers."

—Jack London, *John Barleycorn*

Contents

Preface   ix

1 ▪ From Intemperance to Alcoholism in the Fiction
   of W. D. Howells   1

2 ▪ Memoirs of an Alcoholic: *John Barleycorn*   19

3 ▪ Bulls, Balls, and Booze: *The Sun Also Rises*   43

4 ▪ The Drunkard's Holiday: *Tender Is the Night*   65

5 ▪ The Infernal Grove: *Appointment in Samarra*   91

6 ▪ Transcendence Downward: *Nightwood*   115

7 ▪ After the Lost Generation: *The Lost Weekend*   135

Notes   159

Index   195

Preface

"There are no second acts in American lives." F. Scott Fitzgerald's grim pronouncement has often been cited by those who try to account for the depressing frequency of attenuated careers and imaginative diminution among the American modernists. Budd Schulberg, for instance, ponders the all-too-representative case of Ernest Hemingway: "When a man can write no better, think no better, know no more, after he is thirty-five than before, especially a man with the unique artistic equipment of Hemingway, are we not entitled, even obligated, again to ask, why? What happened?" For Schulberg, an erstwhile Marxist, the answer must lie in the noxious culture of American capitalism. The decline of Hemingway, Fitzgerald, and others can be attributed, he believes, to the cult of the bitch goddess, Success, to whom American writers have ritually been sacrificed—hyped and then destroyed by the engines of publicity.

There may, in fact, be something to this line of analysis. But it overlooks another important factor—one so conspicuous that it's almost invisible. Although Schulberg notes many other things in common to "the lives of Sinclair

Lewis, William Saroyan, Scott Fitzgerald, Nathanael West, Charles Jackson, John O'Hara, Clifford Odets, Dorothy Parker, Ernest Hemingway, Thomas Heggen, James Baldwin, Norman Mailer, James Jones, Irwin Shaw, Tennessee Williams, John Steinbeck, William Faulkner, and others whose paths have crossed with mine,"[1] he fails to observe that nearly all of these writers were alcoholics and that drinking had a crucial effect on their literary fortunes and misfortunes.

As T. S. Eliot might have said, I had not thought booze had undone so many. It is much easier to name alcoholic American writers from the early twentieth century than to think of sober ones. That the modernists—the white males especially—were a decidedly drunken lot had nevertheless escaped much notice until recent books by Donald Newlove, Thomas B. Gilmore, Donald W. Goodwin, and Tom Dardis pointed out what Goodwin deems a veritable epidemic of alcoholism.

In *The White Logic*, I owe a great deal to these pioneering studies, but I do not share completely their authors' confidence in the "disease concept" that has shaped thinking about "alcoholism" for over five decades. I am concerned here with the historical formation of this and earlier concepts of habitual drunkenness and their bearing on the social construction of gender roles. In this sense, *The White Logic* is akin to projects in "cultural studies" of the sort that have become so fashionable in English departments. But it is also a work of traditional criticism and literary history in its attention to what I have called the drunk narrative: a mode of fiction that expresses the conjunction of modernism and alcoholism in a pervasive ideology of despair.

For the time to write *The White Logic*, I am grateful to Syracuse University, which granted me a research leave for the spring semester of 1993. I owe individual debts to my editor, Clark Dougan, who encouraged this project from the outset; to Scott Donaldson, Susan Edmunds, Mary Karr, Robert Emmet Long, Michael Paller, Milton R. Stern, and my wife, Susan Wolstenholme, all of whom read one or more chapters of the draft and offered useful suggestions; and to George Wedge, who generously shared his vast knowledge of alcoholic writers. Philip N. Cronenwett, Curator of Manuscripts at the

---

[1] *Writers in America: The Four Seasons of Success* (New York: Stein and Day, 1983), pp. 27, 40.

Dartmouth College Library, extended his hospitality during my research visit there—after Carolyn Davis of the George Arents Research Library at Syracuse had kindly helped me locate the Charles Jackson Papers.

The White Logic originated in two essays I wrote for *Dionysos: The Literature and Addiction Triquarterly* (Spring 1991, Winter 1992). I thank Roger Forseth, the journal's founding editor, for permission to use revised and expanded versions of these essays as my first two chapters. "Paradigms of Addiction in Howells's Novels," yet another version of Chapter 1, appeared in the George Warren Arms memorial issue of *American Literary Realism* (Spring 1993).

Not long before I started writing *The White Logic*, George Arms, my friend and mentor, died in his eightieth year. For over two decades, George had served as my ideal reader and sounding board; he was still very much present to me as I tried to write a book I thought he would have enjoyed reading.

The White Logic

1

From Intemperance to Alcoholism in the Fiction of W. D. Howells

Drinking to excess became problematic in Western European society during the eighteenth century, when social reformers and physicians took alarm at what they regarded as an epidemic of public intoxication, especially among the lower classes. To the newly constituted United States of America, the idea of curbing drunkenness remained largely foreign until the early nineteenth century. Historians agree that there was no alcohol problem among the American colonists other than satisfying their unslakable thirst for liquor.[1]

Alcohol was integral to the colonial social order. As a "deeply entrenched economic and social interest," sanctioned by law and custom alike, drink "served in fact to maintain and promote social cohesion."[2] Home-brewed beer and cider were normally drunk at meals; wine and rum were available to those enriched by the West Indies trade; the tavern vied with the church as a focus of community life; intoxication was common during such social events as weddings, funerals, pastoral ordinations, church and barn raisings, court and militia training days; liquor was regularly rationed to farm hands and to other workers as well.[3] The general pattern in the eighteenth century was "for men and women to drink alcohol everyday, at all times throughout the day, and in large quantities on almost every special occasion."[4]

In the early republic during the final decades of the eighteenth century, there was a change in the alcoholic mix—rum was largely replaced by distilled grain spirits, mainly whiskey—but no change in the pattern of heavy drinking. Between 1770 and 1800, the annual intake of absolute alcohol from all sources dipped slightly, from three and one-half to three gallons per capita, but then it rose steadily to a staggering peak in 1830 of four gallons per capita (more than double the current level). As W. J. Rorabaugh has said of consumption during this period:

> Alcohol was pervasive in American society; it crossed regional, sexual, racial, and class lines. Americans drank at home and abroad, alone and together, at work and at play, in fun and in earnest. They drank from the crack of dawn to the crack of dawn. At night taverns were filled with boisterous, mirth-making tipplers. Americans drank before meals, with meals, and after meals. They drank while working in the fields and while travelling across half a continent. They drank in their youth, and, if they lived long enough, in their old age. They drank at formal events . . . and on no occasion—by the fireside of an evening, on a hot afternoon, when the mood called. . . .
>
> Early nineteenth-century America may not have been 'a nation of drunkards,' but Americans were certainly enjoying a spectacular binge.[5]

Americans did not, however, perceive themselves to be bingeing until temperance reform began to take hold during the 1820s. As early as the turn of the nineteenth century, the prevalence of drinking had been cause for concern among those Federalist leaders and Congregational ministers who formed in 1813 the Massachusetts Society for the Suppression of Intemperance. Implicitly, the purpose of this organization, the first of its kind, was to reassert the waning authority of an elite class through an attempt to control the drinking habits of the lower classes. But the effects of the Society were as parochial as its aims, and it soon expired. Broader-based temperance groups were meanwhile springing up locally, and they soon merged into a national organization. The founding of the American Temperance Society in 1826 is often said to have marked the inauguration of the crusade that would reach its climax a century later in the passage of the Prohibition amendment.

The true mainstream of the temperance movement consisted of middle-class "improvers": adherents of social and political change who "sanctioned the acquisitive and individualistic economic order developing in America" and who "optimistically predicted the improvement of the moral state of society on a firm basis of material progress." The leaders of the anti-drink crusade envisioned "a society of competitive individuals instilled with the virtues of sobriety and industry."[6] Excessive drinking, in other words, was incompatible with the ideology of an expansive and entrepreneurial young nation. For supporters of temperance, "the single most important negative effect of alcohol was that it weakened or destroyed self-control"; the consumption of alcohol "undermined worker discipline and productivity, and it was antithetical to the controlled, disciplined character of middle class ideals."[7] As a direct result of the temperance movement, the cultural standard of sobriety became increasingly stringent. By the 1840s, a policy of total abstinence (teetotalism) was advocated by many public figures, and hundreds of thousands of Americans had taken the pledge.

The long and complex history of temperance and Prohibition need not concern us further, for it is tangential to this study. What is pertinent is how the anti-drink crusade wrought a fundamental change in the way excessive drinking was understood. Although intoxication had always coexisted with alcohol itself, habitual drunkenness now was stigmatized by such terms as "intemperance" and "inebriation." Both words appear, for instance, in an edition from the 1840s of Noah Webster's *Dictionary*, which suggests a subtle difference between them. "Intemperance" is there defined (secondarily) as: "Habitual indulgence in drinking spirituous liquors, with or without intoxication"—a usage attributed to Lyman Beecher, the crusading minister who was one of the founders of the temperance movement. "Inebriation" is defined as "drunkenness, intoxication," and "inebriate" means an "habitual drunkard"—a usage attributed to Darwin (presumably Erasmus rather than Charles).[8] "Inebriation" is thus a likely consequence of "intemperance."

The words, which were not always used so precisely, became virtually synonymous—although "intemperance" continued to have moral and religious overtones that derived from the anti-drink advocacy of Protestant clergymen, and "inebriation" carried scientific connotations that reflected the growing involvement of physicians in the temperance cause. As the meaning of "inebriation" expanded during the nineteenth century to encompass addictions not only to alcohol, but also to other drugs (especially opiates), habitual drunkenness came increasingly to be medicalized as a clinical, as well as social, disorder. This development was reflected in the proliferation of specialized psychiatric terms. "Dipsomania" was coined in 1819 by a German doctor; at about the same time, "delirium tremens" was identified in England as a symptom of what the French were calling "*la folie des ivrognes.*"

The term "alcoholism" was introduced in 1849 by Magnus Huss, a Swedish physician, to denote the physical effects of chronic inebriation.[9] By the turn of the twentieth century, the scope of this term had widened to include behavior as well as bodily symptoms: "Whereas the word 'alcoholism' had previously been used as a medical term referring to the toxic effects of alcohol on the human system, it now came to be used with reference to the phenomenon of habitual drinking." Likewise, the paired term "alcoholic" underwent a shift in meaning. Previously limited to adjectival use in describing liquids containing alcohol, it gradually became a noun as well.[10] Neither term, however, had much currency in the United States before the modern era.[11]

Two competing concepts of habitual drunkenness coexisted, therefore, throughout the American nineteenth century. According to Harry Gene Levine, the older paradigm, dating from colonial times, held that because "there was nothing inherent in either the individual or the substance which prevented someone from drinking moderately," a person had "final control" over the intake of alcohol: "Drunkenness was a choice, albeit a sinful one, which some individuals made." This moral paradigm of "intemperance" as a sin was gradually overshadowed by the medical idea of "inebriation" as an addiction, "a sort of disease of the will, an inability to prevent oneself from drinking." The "disease" model, often traced to Benjamin Rush's influential *Inquiry into the Effects of Ardent Spirits Upon the Human Body and Mind* (1784), posited "that habitual drunkards are alcohol addicts, persons who have lost control over their drinking and who must abstain entirely from alcohol."[12]

The emergent medical paradigm, which was deeply influential within the temperance movement, fostered a sympathetic attitude toward drunkards and gave rise to reformist attempts to save them from their powerlessness over alcohol, now thought by some to be inevitably addicting. But habitual drunkenness was never entirely freed from moral stigma. In the nineteenth-century disease model, insofar as intemperance was linked to attenuated willpower, addiction was not located exclusively in the substance; it was inseparable from defective "character," for the proper building of which Victorians held each other morally accountable.[13] Of the confluence of moral and medical values in the idea of "inebriation," Virginia Berridge and Griffith Edwards observe: "Moral values were inserted into this apparently 'natural' and 'autonomous' disease entity. Addiction, clearly not simply a physical disease entity, was a 'disease of the will.' It was disease *and* vice." An addict's moral weakness, then, was an important causal element: "the disease was defined in terms of 'moral bankruptcy,' 'a form of moral insanity,' terms deriving from similar formulations in insanity."[14]

The shifting representations of habitual drunkenness in the nineteenth century may usefully be traced in the fiction of W. D. Howells, the chief American proponent of literary realism and the preeminent chronicler of commonplace American realities. Howells's life spanned the heyday of temperance. A year before his birth in 1837, the American Temperance Society was succeeded by the American Temperance Union, an even more powerful alliance of some eight thousand local chapters, with well over a million members. During the so-called petition year of 1838, pressure from these groups effected passage of several state laws (repealed soon thereafter) restricting the sale of ardent spirits.[15] The crusade to legislate Prohibition ultimately triumphed in the Eighteenth Amendment and the Volstead Act, which went into force the year of Howells's death in 1920. Although he was raised in a dry household, Howells always kept his distance from the temperance movement itself.[16] His fiction nevertheless touched on the matter of drinking, and it reflected the dominant understandings of intemperance.

In Howells's first portrayal of an inebriate—Hicks, a minor character in *The Lady of the Aroostook* (1879)—he dramatized the differences between the moral and medical models. Hicks, a former medical student whose career has been ruined by his periodic binges, has signed aboard the *Aroostook* for a sea cure by abstinence. When sober, Hicks impresses Staniford, the novel's gentlemanly hero, as "a man of some qualities . . . he was amiable, and he was droll, though apt to turn sulky."[17] Staniford, however, remains snobbishly aloof from Hicks, whom he perceives as an unworthy rival for the attentions of Lydia Blood, the innocent upcountry girl whose unchaperoned presence among the otherwise male passengers and crew poses a dilemma for Staniford's Bostonian scruples.

Allowed a shore leave at Trieste but without any money, Hicks contrives to pawn his watch and smuggle aboard a bottle of brandy, planning to drink it in the privacy of his cabin that evening and to sleep off the incriminating effects before dawn. But Hicks fails to conceal his lapse into inebriation. When he stumbles into breakfast the next morning, slurring his words and reeking of spirits, Lydia is horrified: "There seemed no scorn in her condemnation, but neither was there any mercy" (p. 197). Having grown up in Maine, the home state of the Prohibition campaign, Lydia has had no experience with men like Hicks; she apprehends his drunkenness, by the shadowless light of her "pitiless Puritan conscience" (p. 214), as simply an evil.

Howells implicitly links his characters' views of Hicks's intemperance to their class backgrounds. Similar to Lydia's repulsion is the repugnance felt by Mason, the second mate, whose sister tried futilely to tame the "tiger" of her husband's inebriation until his death at Gettysburg spared her further suffering. "Ike was a good fellow when he was sober," Mason tells Staniford. "But my souls, the life he led that poor girl! Yes, when a man's got that tiger in him, there ought to be some quiet little war round for puttin' him out of his misery. . . . I s'pose I'm prejudiced; but I do *hate* a drunkard" (pp. 154–55). Although Mason's sanguinary opinions may be justified by bitter experience, they also reveal his ignorance of the disease concept. In effect, Mason's narrow-mindedness is related to his working-class status, of which his vernacular speech is a sign.[18]

Staniford, with a worldly tolerance that seems to be an expression of upper-class cultivation, regards Hicks far more sympathetically: as the victim of a mental disease, one from which Hicks himself sees no hope of recovering. "I doubt if anything can be done," he tells Staniford. "I've studied the thing; I am a doctor,—or I would be if I were not a drunkard,—and I've diagnosed the case pretty thoroughly" (pp. 200–201). To Staniford, the drunkard's fate is pitiable, if not tragic:

Hicks was as common a soul as could well be. His conception of life was vulgar, and his experience of it was probably vulgar. He had a good mind enough, with abundance of that humorous brightness which may hereafter be found the most national quality of the Americans; but his ideals were pitiful, and the language of his heart was a drolling slang. Yet his doom lifted him above his low conditions, and made him tragic; his despair gave him the dignity of a mysterious expiation, and set him apart with those who suffer beyond human help. Without deceiving himself as to the quality of the man, Staniford felt awed by the darkness of his fate.   (Pp. 201–202)

Later, Staniford attempts to temper Lydia's severity toward Hicks, explaining that "He's a doomed man; his vice is irreparable; he can't resist it" (p. 212).

If intemperance is an irreparable vice—a view consistent with the disease paradigm to which Hicks himself subscribes as a result of his medical studies—then the inebriate cannot be held to full moral account for what is not strictly a sin. His very hopelessness, indeed, may accomplish a "mysterious expiation." Both Staniford and the narrator of *The Lady of the Aroostook* are thus in accord with the emergent Victorian model of intemperance as a "disease of the will," toward which compassionate understanding is more appropriate than moral disgust.

The degree of Howells's compassion varies, however, with his judgment of a drunkard's basic character. Hicks may be "vulgar" in Staniford's eyes, but he is also fundamentally decent.[19] Mortified by his behavior, of which he has no clear recollection because of an alcoholic blackout, Hicks stands duly contrite before Staniford and begs him to convey apologies to Lydia. Insofar as Howells reads intemperance as a sign of a more pervasive inner corruption, however, he treats it less tolerantly. The moral decay of Bartley Hubbard in *A Modern Instance* (1882), for example, is suggested subtly by his increasing consumption of Tivoli beer. Whether or not Bartley is truly a drunkard remains unclear in the novel, from which he all but disappears just at the point when his complete degeneration seems imminent. It is significant, in any case, that Howells also describes Ben Halleck, Hubbard's erstwhile friend, in terms of inebriation.

Halleck, who delivers the drunken Bartley to his wife Marcia on one occasion,[20] does not himself drink. But after pouring out the anguish of his illicit desire for Marcia to the lawyer Atherton, Ben keeps a secret vigil outside the

Hubbards's house, feeling cast into the hell of "love without marriage": "The night wind rose in a sudden gust, and made the neighboring lamp flare, and his shadow wavered across the pavement like the figure of a drunken man."[21] Months later, as Halleck passes the same house in Atherton's company, he bolts up the hill, and the lawyer must overtake him: "[L]ike a man who has attempted to rule a drunkard by thwarting his freak, and then hopes to accomplish his end by humoring it, he passed his arm through Halleck's again, and went with him" (p. 366).

Sexual longing is figured here as being equivalent to the drunkard's obsession with drink. Halleck may be a teetotaler, but he is nonetheless besotted by an emotional "freak" that renders his will dangerously diseased. The danger consists in a threat to privileged social values. According to Atherton, Halleck represents the cream of Bostonian society, and his deviation from probity would do far more harm than anything of which Bartley Hubbard and his ilk are capable. Of Ben's unconsummated desire for Marcia, Atherton asserts that if a man of such "pure training and traditions had yielded to temptation," it would have been a "ruinous blow" to the general moral order: "All that careful nurture in the right since he could speak, all that lifelong decency of thought and act, that noble ideal of unselfishness and responsibility to others, trampled under foot and spit upon,—it's horrible!" (p. 416).

The linkage of drunkenness to social disorder is even stronger in Berthold Lindau, the fiery radical in *A Hazard of New Fortunes* (1890), who becomes all the more inflamed when he is (all too often) under the influence. Lindau drinks too much at Jacob Dryfoos's dinner party—a scene parallel to the Corey dinner in *The Rise of Silas Lapham* (1885)[22]—and denounces his host as a capitalist oppressor. The result is a chain reaction of moral complications for Basil March and the other characters associated with *Every Other Week*, the literary magazine for which Dryfoos is the angel. Lindau's mixing of alcohol with socialism proves ultimately lethal, both to himself and, worse, to the innocent Conrad Dryfoos. Like Halleck's sexual desire, Lindau's political passion is shown to be destructive of the equipoise that Howells places at the center of the moral life and the good society.

For Howells, then, intemperance as a "disease of the will" is inseparable from social dis-ease. His most complex and comprehensive treatment of this connection is found in *The Landlord at Lion's Head* (1897), in which drinking is treated not merely as an individual defect of character, but also as a symptom of disorder in American culture at large.

The Landlord at Lion's Head depicts the rise of Jeff Durgin from poverty to material success as the entrepreneur of Lion's Head, the fashionable hotel he constructs on the ashes of his mother's country inn. There is no need to summarize the novel's complicated plot because only one strand of it is relevant here. As a student at Harvard, Durgin encounters Alan and Bessie Lynde, who, like Staniford and Halleck, represent the Bostonian elite. In Durgin's dealings with the Lyndes, Howells exposes the degeneration of their class and traces its roots to addiction: Alan is a drunkard, and Bessie is comparably obsessed by sexual desire.

Alan Lynde recognizes despairingly the insanity of his drinking, but he is helpless to stop. Although he submits himself periodically to a Keeley Cure,[23] Alan returns invariably to the bottle until another drunken crisis drives him to yet another cure. During one of his sober spells at home, Alan confronts his sister Bessie about her flirtation with Durgin. In the slang of the period, Jeff is a Harvard "jay," an outlander whose social inferiority makes him unfit, in Alan's eyes, for Bessie's company:

> "Then I don't understand how you came to be with him."
>
> "Oh, yes, you do, Alan. You mustn't be logical! You might as well say you can't understand how you came to be more serious than sober." The brother laughed helplessly. "It was the excitement."
>
> "But you can't give way to that sort of thing, Bess," said her brother, with the gravity of a man feeling the consequences of his own errors.
>
> "I know I can't, but I do," she returned. "I know it's bad for me, if it isn't for other people. Come! I'll swear off if you will!"
>
> "I'm always ready to swear off," said the young man, gloomily.[24]

Later in the same conversation, Bessie compares her attraction to Durgin with a taste for "some very common kind of whiskey" when "If one must, it ought to be champagne" (p. 234). She then proposes a pact to her brother: "No more jays for me, and no more jags for you" (p. 235).

Neither one can stick to the bargain. Within days, Alan gets drunk at a Bostonian ball—abetted by Durgin, who proffers more liquor to the already intoxicated Alan and then carries him home. Off on another jag, Alan cons his sister into leaving him alone with the decanters of whiskey and brandy she has threatened to smash: "That's over, now; you could put them in my hands and be safe enough . . . You can trust me, Bessie . . . I won't fail you, Bessie. I shall 'keep well,' as you call it, as long as you want me" (p. 274). By morning the decanters are as empty as Bessie's promise to swear off her jay.

Seeking the cause of her own weakness, Bessie questions the family physician about her brother's:

> "What is it makes him do it?"
>
> "Ah, that's a great mystery," said the doctor. "I suppose you might say, the excitement."
>
> "Yes!"
>
> "But it seems to me very often, in such cases, as if it were to *escape* the excitement. I think you're both keyed up pretty sharply by nature, Miss Bessie." . . .
>
> "I know!" she answered. "We're alike. Why don't I take to drinking, too?"
>
> The doctor laughed at such a question from a young lady, but with an inner seriousness in his laugh, as if, coming from a patient, it was to be weighed. "Well, I suppose it isn't the habit of your sex, Miss Bessie."
>
> "Sometimes it is. Sometimes women get drunk, and then I think they do less harm than if they did other things to get away from the excitement."
>
> (P. 267)

Here, as in *A Modern Instance*, Howells makes intemperance analogous to sexual desire, but he also distinguishes according to gender. For a lady like Bessie, the habit of drinking has been proscribed by the rules of Victorian conduct for women. As a gentlemanly vice, inebriation is hardly imaginable in a lady, as the doctor's reaction testifies.[25] Yet Bessie realizes that her own infatuation with Jeff is fundamentally no different from her brother's fascination with alcohol. In both cases nervous excitement fuels an addiction that results only in more excitement.

At the same ball at which her brother gets drunk, Bessie feels a similar agitation that induces in turn a physical craving: "The party had not been altogether to her mind, up to midnight, but after that it had been a series of rapid and vivid emotions, which continued themselves still in the tumult of her nerves, and seemed to demand an indefinite sequence of experience" (p. 255). The "sequence of experience" in her case means a renewal of her compulsive flirtation with Durgin. Such a syndrome of "excitement" was described by Lewis Cass in 1833, when he addressed a temperance convention on the habit of intoxication: "The difficulty consists in the entire mastery it attains, and in that morbid craving for the habitual excitement, which is said to be one of the most overpowering feelings that human nature is destined to encounter. This feeling is at once relieved by the accustomed stimulant, and when the result is not pleasure merely, but the immediate removal of an incubus, preying and pressing upon the heart and intellect, we cease to wonder that men yield to the palliative within their reach."[26]

In their susceptibility to "excitement," the Lyndes are recognizably "neurasthenic." As originally defined by Dr. George Miller Beard during the 1880s, "neurasthenia" was a peculiarly American disease in which exhaustion of the nerves resulted from the stress of modern living in an increasingly urban and industrial culture. In Beard's theory, "A person with a nervous tendency is driven to think, to work, to strive for success. He presses himself and his life force to the limit, straining his circuits." Like Herbert Spencer in his Social Darwinian speculations, Beard regarded neurasthenia as the price of evolutionary "progress," and he identified the condition with the "higher" classes: "persons born with a fine [nervous] organization—as opposed to those with a coarse organization—frequently associated with superior intelligence, and more often appearing in men than in women."[27] Those most vulnerable to neurasthenia were also thought to exhibit hypersensitivity to alcohol, narcotics, and even such milder "stimulants" as tea and coffee. The Lyndes, who are "keyed up pretty sharply" by virtue of their upper-class refinement, betray a tendency toward addiction that their neurasthenia ushers in. Once caught up in the compulsive cycle of excitement, however, their evolutionary advantages are nullified. The greater "harm" to which Bessie alludes is her violation of the civilized standards that constitute the claim of her class to moral (and thus social) superiority.

The Landlord at Lion's Head is primarily concerned with the erosion of

Victorian moral certainties: the decline of "civilization" under the influence of men like Durgin, who lack anything resembling a good character—at least in the view of Jere Westover, the puritanical artist who is the central consciousness of the novel.[28] Although Howells undercuts the pretensions of the Bostonian elite, the novel validates Westover's anxiety about the Lyndes's diseased wills. Who, if not the supposed pillars of society, will dependably uphold the socially binding values? The most damning effect of addiction on both Alan and Bessie is what Atherton dreads in *A Modern Instance,* the loss of upper-class identity and, therefore, the power of moral example.

When Durgin slips the drunken Alan out of the ball and pours him into his carriage, such discretion is lost on the working-class attendants who stand in the cold outside to await the bidding of the social elite. "The policemen clapped their hands together, and smiled across the strip of carpet that separated them, and winks and nods of intelligence passed among the barkers to the footmen about the curb and steps. There were none of them sorry to see a gentleman in that state; some of them had perhaps seen Alan in that state before" (pp. 247–48). The strip of carpet, which symbolizes the class line that ordinarily divides Alan from the barkers, the footmen, and the police, has lost its signal force under these circumstances. The leveling influence of alcohol has not merely lowered Alan in their estimation; it has negated any claim he might make to superiority. Implicit here is a derangement of the social order that threatens the gentlemanly customs for which Alan stands, however more often he may breach than observe them.

Bessie's fall from grace has similar social consequences. At the climax of her involvement with Jeff, the erotic energy that arcs between them results in a passionate kiss—which, in the euphemistic Victorian code to which Howells adheres in his fiction, is tantamount to a rape:

> He put his other large, strong hand upon her waist, and pulled her to him and kissed her. Another sort of man, no matter what he had believed of her, would have felt his act a sacrilege then and there. Jeff only knew that she had not made the faintest struggle against him; she had even trembled towards him, and he brutally exulted in the belief that he had done what she wished, whether it was what she meant or not.

She, for her part, realized that she had been kissed as once she had happened to see one of the maids kissed by the grocer's boy at the basement door. In an instant this man had abolished all her defences of family, of society, of personality, and put himself on a level with her in the most sacred things of life. Her mind grasped the fact and she realized it intellectually, while as yet all her emotions seemed paralyzed. She did not know whether she resented it as an abominable outrage or not; whether she hated the man for it or not. But perhaps he was in love with her, and his love overpowered him; in that case she could forgive him, if she were in love with him.

(Pp. 336–37)

In the use of such words as "sacrilege" and "sacred," the narrator proves himself to be "another sort of man," one who sustains the class standards that the Lyndes are incapable of upholding—standards, it is suggested, that vouchsafe nothing less than the divine order. Jeff, by contrast, is associated with the "brutality" of the lower order in his lust, which is not so much for Bessie as for the power to reduce her to his level. Emotionally "paralyzed," Bessie instantly loses her identity; stripped of her "defences," she becomes indistinguishable in her own mind from the maid.

Feeling degraded both socially and morally, she attempts to reclaim her accustomed self by rationalizing the incident in terms of the civilized code: Jeff must be in love with her, or else she must be in love with him. But Bessie immediately senses the falsity of this reasoning in her guilty awareness that she can "never tell any one, that in the midst of her world she was alone in relation to this; she was as helpless and friendless as the poorest and lowliest girl could be. She was more so, for if she were like the maid whom the grocer's boy kissed she would be of an order of things in which she could advise with some one else who had been kissed; and she would know what to feel" (p. 337).

Bessie does not know what to feel because, as a lady, she is supposedly devoid of any sexual feeling, except as it may be sublimated into "love." Although she is a prisoner of the repressive gender codes of her class—epitomized in the cult of True Womanhood—Bessie's illicit flirtation, like Alan's drinking, nevertheless diminishes the moral authority of their class. For Howells, the disturbing prospect is that the corruption of the Lyndes will only hasten the cultural domination of those, like Jeff Durgin, who scoff at the Victorian ideal of character and who disclaim the power of will to affect human motives.

In his most sympathetic thoughts about Jeff, Westover muses that "this earth-bound temperament was the potentiality of all the success it aimed at. The acceptance of moral fact as it was, without the unconscious effort to better it, or to hold himself strictly to account for it, was the secret of the power in the man which would bring about the material results he desired; and this simplicity of the motive involved had its charm" (p. 281). Such a charm exists, however, only because at this very moment Westover himself is under the influence of the alcoholic punch he has been imbibing as a remedy for his cold. The narrator remarks that in "the optimism generated by the punch," Westover temporarily suspends his strict accounting of moral facts and indulges "in the comfort we all experience in sinking to a lower level." The effects of alcohol, then, are linked by Howells to a devolutionary loss of "moral elevation" (p. 282).[29]

Rather than a cultivated (and therefore "unconscious") power of will to improve on "moral facts," Jeff embodies a simpler will to power in which nothing matters but "material results." Like the Dreiserian characters he anticipates, Durgin exemplifies what Jackson Lears has called a new and "ever more chimerical" type of "self-made manhood" ascendant at the turn of the century, in which "'personal magnetism' began to replace character as the key to advancement." As "conventional definitions of 'will power' began to seem oversimplified and familiar feelings of selfhood began to seem obsolete," the disintegration of "character" produced the modern sense of unreality—the "weightlessness" that, as Lears argues, was symptomatic of the anxiety felt by civilized Victorians in the face of the modern.[30]

As the chimerical modern man, Durgin does not, significantly, betray any weakness for alcohol. Although he is rusticated from Harvard for a semester as the penalty for a single drunken escapade, he otherwise holds his liquor well. Matching Alan drink for drink, Jeff shows no effects: "It was as if his powerful physique absorbed the wine before it could reach his brain" (p. 239). His "brutality" renders Durgin resistant to the vices of the civilized Lynde, with his sharply pitched sensibility and attenuated physique. In terms of the Social Darwinian discourse within which the novel operates, Jeff is an atavism. Lower on the evolutionary ladder than the Lyndes, Durgin is commensurately less vulnerable to neurasthenic excitement and thus to addiction.

Durgin, however, may be seen to prefigure a new, modern type of addiction. Whereas Bessie and Alan are undone by their lack of willpower, Durgin is animated by unbounded willfulness. If he does not share Alan's obsession with alcohol, he also lacks Bessie's susceptibility to sexual passion. For Durgin, who takes no more deeply to women than to drink, excitement is associated only with material desire. The object of his addiction, then, points toward a new paradigm.

Like Beard and Spencer, Howells sees addiction as over-refinement leading to compensatory decadence. The evolutionary "progress" of mental sensitivity has produced a disabling disjunction of mind from body, of "nerves" from the nervous system. Addiction, particularly in Bessie's case, is figured as a return of the (bodily) repressed: a drag upon spiritual aspiration from the inexorable claims of the "lower level"; a sign of an enfeebled capacity to choose the good within a cultural discourse that defines "character" as the accretion of such choices.[31] For Howells, any addiction, including intemperance, presupposes a pernicious weakness of will that tips the mental balance essential to moral stability. Howells also implies that a lack of willpower, insofar as it may be attributed to the workings of evolution/devolution, may obviate human agency and thus individual moral responsibility. If, as their physician speculates, the Lyndes are "keyed up pretty sharply by nature"—that is, by the Lamarckian inheritance of "civilized" nervous systems—then how much are they really to blame for needing "to *escape* the excitement" (p. 267)?

This question recalls a famous passage in Dreiser's *Sister Carrie* (1900) in which the narrator meditates on the imperfect state of human evolution:

> Our civilisation is still in a middle stage, scarcely beast, in that it is no longer wholly guided by instinct; scarcely human, in that it is not yet wholly guided by reason. On the tiger no responsibility rests. We see him aligned by nature with the forces of life—he is born into their keeping and without thought he is protected. We see man far removed from the lairs of the jungles, his innate instincts dulled by too near an approach to free-will, his free-will not sufficiently developed to replace his instincts and afford him perfect guidance. . . . In this intermediate stage he wavers—neither drawn in harmony with nature by his instincts nor yet wisely putting himself into harmony by his own free-will. He is even as a wisp in the wind, moved by every breath of passion,

acting now by his will and now by his instincts, erring with one, only to retrieve by the other, falling by one, only to rise by the other—a creature of incalculable variability.[32]

Although Dreiser goes on to prophesy that the "jangle of free-will and instinct" will be "adjusted" when the former gains the power to supplant the latter, such faith in evolution also seems to demand a suspension of moral judgment until the future arrives. Despite the Victorian sentiments of this passage, *Sister Carrie* is largely free of Howellsian anxiety. In fact, Dreiser seems to mitigate Carrie's "immorality" and to celebrate the vitality of her "instincts."

Carrie may be regarded as a combination of Jeff Durgin and Bessie Lynde, as if she were the offspring of an unholy union between them. (The pairing of Jeff with Bessie is a possibility away from which Howells carefully steers the plot of *The Landlord at Lion's Head*—as if such a coupling, however logical, were finally too monstrous to conceive.) Like Bessie at the moment when she has devolved to the level of the maid, Carrie is unbound by civilized constraints; her feelings, about which she knows no more than Bessie, derive from an uncorseted desire not merely for "excitement," but also for Jeff Durgin's "material results." In Carrie, Bessie's desire has been desublimated; the field of desire, moreover, has enlarged to embrace the vast material accumulation of Carrie's world.

In his provocative reading of American naturalism, Walter Benn Michaels deconstructs the nineteenth-century model of addiction by inverting its underlying assumptions. Michaels argues that in Dostoevsky, for example, addiction to gambling is represented "as a disease of the will, not because the gambler's will is weak but because his commitment to the power of his will (understood in *The Gambler* as absolute self-control) is total. . . . The gambler's mistake is thus to imagine that his fate is entirely within his control."[33] The illusion of control derives, in fact, from the Victorian idea of "character" as a product of willed acts, of deliberate choices.

In both Howells's and Dostoevsky's fiction, the function of character is to maintain a positive balance within what Michaels calls an "economy of scarcity" in which "power, happiness, and moral virtue are all seen to depend finally on minimizing desire." The threat to "the humane values of equilibrium and moderation" is located in an "economy of desire": "a conception of desire as disrupting this equilibrium, desire that, exceeding and outstripping any possible object, is in principle never satisfied."[34] It is in the passage from the economy of scarcity to the economy of desire that Michaels sees the key difference between Howells and Dreiser.

This difference also marks a modernist revision of the Victorian paradigm of addiction. Within the economy of scarcity, which also informed Victorian medicine—as in Beard's idea that good health depended on the conservation of precious life force—"addiction" named an insatiable desire that outstrips its object. As Levine puts it, "In the nineteenth century, the concept of addiction was interpreted by people in light of their struggles with their own desires. The idea of addiction 'made sense' not only to drunkards, who came to understand themselves as individuals with overwhelming desires they could not control, but also to great numbers of middle-class people who were struggling to keep their desires in check—desires which at times seemed 'irresistible.'"[35] If, as Michaels suggests, such desires were part and parcel of a "more general economy of excess" inherent to a later stage of industrial capitalism and the structures of "self" produced within it, then it follows that addiction in post-Victorian culture might, as Howells feared, spread pandemically.

The shift from the economy of scarcity to the economy of desire at the turn of the century corresponds to what historians have perceived as the rise of cultural modernism:

> Where Victorianism preached thrift, industry, and sobriety, cultural modernism exalted consumption and display, identified self-expression as the key to the good life, and sought fulfillment in leisure. The orientation was consistent with the changing needs of an industrial economy that produced more goods than it could sell, an economy that relied increasingly on advertising to foster new needs and thereby to create fresh markets for its surplus. "Men must enjoy," a leading economist proclaimed. "The new morality does not consist in saving but in expanding consumption."[36]

This "new morality" undermined Victorian ethics while it blurred Victorian class distinctions. Whereas the traditional elite had justified its social authority by its stricter accounting of desire, the newly rich, as Thorstein Veblen observed, defined themselves through "conspicuous consumption," a material desire in excess of its object that created a hierarchy not of restraint but rather of excess.[37] Within an emergent culture of conspicuous consumption, addiction would become, in effect, the sign of modernity itself. "Alcoholism" and literary "modernism" emerged together in a dialectical relationship that produced, in the drunk narrative, both a portrait of the modernist as an alcoholic and a portrait of the alcoholic as a modernist.

2

Memoirs of an Alcoholic:
John Barleycorn

A generically indeterminate narrative on the border between fictional autobiography and autobiographical fiction, Jack London's account of his drinking career was written ostensibly in support of Prohibition. *John Barleycorn* (1913) differed strikingly, however, from Victorian temperance novels in its psychological and sociological modernity.[1] Although London died before the crest of the Freudian tidal wave that would engulf American culture during the 1920s, he was an early and avid reader of Carl G. Jung; and in *John Barleycorn*, he showed a psychoanalytic understanding of inner conflict and unconscious motivation. His approach to the ethos of drinking was likewise modern in its calculated detachment. In the role of participant-observer, London as narrator abstracts general patterns along class and gender lines from the details of his own case.

London wrote *John Barleycorn* at his California ranch soon after he had cruised around Cape Horn aboard the *Dirigo* in 1912. This voyage, much like Hicks's sea cure in *The Lady of the Aroostook,* was motivated by a need to dry out. For years, London's drinking had become ever more destructive of his health and marriage; and despite his promise to quit, he went on a binge, perhaps the worst bender of his life, during the weeks before sailing from New York. But after five months at sea, beyond the bottle's temptation, London felt renewed. "When the alcohol passed from his system," observes a biographer, "he was triumphant and claimed that he did not need it at all. 'I have learned, to my absolute satisfaction,' he declared, 'that *I am not an alcoholic* in any sense of the word.'"[2]

True believers in Jack London have steadfastly taken him at his word. The mere suggestion that their hero was an alcoholic is fiercely resisted by the London cult, a band of literary devotees both inside and outside the academy. Clarice Stasz, who has written with admirable enlightenment about London's drinking, reports that nothing in her work "drew more extensive and impassioned criticism from London experts." The pressure was so powerful, in fact, that in the early drafts of her book Stasz reluctantly toed the party line: that London's "enormous productivity" and his "ability to go for periods at a time without drinking at all" prove that he could not have had "a drinking problem." Such evidence is inconclusive at best, and it is controverted by the testimony of London's wife, Charmian, whose anguished entries in her unpublished diaries finally convinced Stasz that the experts' "objections are no longer credible."[3]

It is astounding that they *ever* seemed credible to any reader of *John Barleycorn*, which has rightly been judged "one of the most moving and dramatic histories of the making of an alcoholic in the literature of drinking."[4] But, then, *John Barleycorn* has also been recognized as "a classic study of the drinker in denial."[5] London convinced himself that those dry months on the *Dirigo*, when he did not drink because he did not desire a drink, had proven that "among all my bodily needs not the slightest shred of a bodily need for alcohol existed" (p. 340). Any desire for alcohol was rooted in mental and social, rather than organic, need. No harm, then, in an occasional nip for the sake of good fellowship: "I would drink—but, oh, more skillfully, more discreetly, than ever before."[6] Surely, the results would be different: "Never again would I be a peripatetic conflagration. Never again would I invoke the White Logic," which "now lies decently buried alongside the Long Sickness" (pp. 342–43). These are London's metaphors for the "cosmic sadness" (p. 309)—the agonized sense of life's hopelessness and worthlessness—that he attributed to his drinking. The

"White Logic" and the "Long Sickness" were soon disinterred, however, when he picked up the bottle again. Within three years London was dead—under ambiguous circumstances, including a possible overdose of prescription morphine. Although the question of suicide has been debated by his biographers, exactly what happened will never be known. Drinking, in any case, had undoubtedly hastened London's bodily and mental deterioration; and although he had developed multiple addictions by the end of his life, alcohol had always been his primary drug.

London was inspired to write *John Barleycorn,* he reports in the opening chapter, on the day he rode into town from his ranch in order to vote on various amendments to the state constitution, including one for women's suffrage. "Pleasantly jingled" by drink (p. 4), he found himself voting "yes" despite his previous opposition to the cause. As he later explained himself to Charmian, women are the ultimate victims of drinking—"They have paid an incalculable price of sweat and tears for man's use of alcohol" (p. 336)—and women are therefore more likely than men to vote, if given the chance, for stemming its flow. Only Prohibition will slay the dragon of drink; and women, as "the true conservators of the race" (p. 336), must act to save men from themselves and to insure a more civilized future in which the rising generation will never miss drinking because it will never have encountered alcohol. London envisions Prohibition, from a Social Darwinian perspective, as a step in evolutionary progress: "The only rational thing for the twentieth century folk to do is to cover up the well . . . and to relegate to the nineteenth century and all the preceding centuries the things of those centuries, the witch-burnings, the intolerances, the fetiches, and, not least among such barbarisms, John Barleycorn" (p. 158).

Charmian urges Jack to write down his thoughts for the benefit of the young and of prospective women voters:

> "The 'Memoirs of an Alcoholic.'" I sneered—or, rather, John Barleycorn sneered; for he sat with me there at table in my pleasant, philanthropic jingle, and it is a trick of John Barleycorn to turn the smile to a sneer without an instant's warning.
>
> "No," said Charmian, ignoring John Barleycorn's roughness as so many

women have learned to do. "You have shown yourself no alcoholic, no dipsomaniac, but merely an habitual drinker, one who has made John Barleycorn's acquaintance through long years of rubbing shoulders with him. Write it up and call it 'Alcoholic Memoirs.' " (Pp. 9–10)

London, in fact, called it neither one, choosing instead a title that invokes the hoary folk legend of John Barleycorn, a personification of the grain used in brewing beer, whose godlike death and regeneration are figured symbolically in the annual cycle of harvest and replanting. But London adds to the legend a modern psychological twist. John Barleycorn names not only alcohol, but also the doppelgänger of John (Jack) London. As John Barleycorn gives voice to the sinister wisdom unveiled by drinking, he insidiously takes possession of London himself, seeming to talk "through me and with me and as me, my adopted twin brother and *alter ego*" (p. 51).

"Memoirs of an Alcoholic" or "Alcoholic Memoirs"? The shade of difference between these titles matters rhetorically in *John Barleycorn* because London wants to present himself as an ordinary man writing for the average reader. Whereas the first title marks London himself as "an alcoholic," the second applies the term only to the written recollections of his "habitual drinking," which is presented as normal—or at least not diseased in the sense suggested by the term "dipsomaniac." Thus although John Barleycorn sneers his approval of "Memoirs of an Alcoholic," London favors "Alcoholic Memoirs." He later refers to his "alcoholic reminiscences" (p. 333), and he insists that "mine is no tale of a reformed drunkard" because "I was never a drunkard, and I have not reformed" (p. 338).[7] He also distances himself from the "genuine, chemical dipsomaniac," whose disorder is said to be exceedingly rare, afflicting "not one man in ten thousand, or in a hundred thousand" (p. 339). Although London admits that he "always was an extremist" (p. 240), he has "no word to say for or about the microscopically unimportant excessivist, the dipsomaniac" (p. 11).[8]

London's understanding of the "genuine, chemical dipsomaniac" derived from the medicalized model of "inebriation" that was constructed by psychiatrists and physicians during the nineteenth century. "Inebriation" (or "inebriety") covered addiction both to alcohol and to other drugs as well. "Alcoholism," the strict connotations of which were more narrowly clinical in Victorian than in modern usage, referred to the long-term physical consequences of alcohol addiction. "Alcoholism" in this sense was more or less synonymous with "dipsomania," another medical term. By the early twentieth century, however, "alcoholism" was being used more loosely to refer to habitual drunkenness; and in this sense it was more or less synonymous with "intemperance," a term with moral and religious overtones.

The idea of dipsomania as a congenital, "chemical" form of insanity was widely disseminated throughout the later nineteenth century, mainly through the mandatory drug education programs that were initiated in public schools during the 1880s under the aegis of the Women's Christian Temperance Union (W.C.T.U.) and other anti-drink organizations. A definition from an 1883 textbook designed for such classroom use—the sort of book London himself might have studied as a schoolboy—may be taken as typical of the prevailing view. "Certain writers on diseases of the mind allude especially to a form of insanity called *dipsomania,* in which state a man has a maddening thirst for alcoholic drinks." Dipsomania describes the extreme case of an "appetite for alcoholic liquors" that, according to "some of the best medical authorities," may be "inherited, just as people inherit such diseases as scrofula, gout, or consumption."[9] Within the Social Darwinian framework of such textbooks, the drunkard (or dipsomaniac) is regarded as clinically insane: the defective offspring of degenerate stock. By definition, such a creature is radically different from a "normal" person.

These views still had currency early in the twentieth century.[10] In a popular book published just two years after *John Barleycorn,* for example, a journalist identified two different types of drunkards: "one is morally defective from the start—a moral imbecile of a sort; that was the cause of his taking to drink. The other drunkard had to set up a pathological process which would bring him to the same state of moral imbecility. The one was born to his drunken inheritance, the other prepared himself for it. The one was diseased at the start; the other took his self-appointed way, through vice, to the identical degenerative condition of disease."[11] The first type is recognizable as the Victorian "dipsomaniac"; the second as the "alcoholic" in the broader modern sense of the habitual drinker who devolves into a dipsomaniac. Although both ultimately attain the same "condition of disease," the alcoholic seems more normal; and because he is more normal, he is also held more responsible for his "self-appointed way," his choice of an avoidable vice.

In the Victorian paradigm, "inebriation" was disease *and* vice, dipsomania *and* intemperance. In the modern paradigm, "alcoholism" became less a vice than a disease—and less degrading a disease than dipsomania had been thought to be. Insofar as the idea of the drunkard as a degenerate still prevailed upon London, however, he had cause to insist on his being no drunkard—an insistence that was complicated by his wish to conceal his drinking problem, even from himself. In *John Barleycorn*, the conflation of Victorian and modern paradigms and their accompanying terminologies results in some confusion in London's depiction of the "alcoholic." This term is used inconsistently: sometimes in the clinical Victorian sense as a synonym for dipsomaniac (a drunkard through bad heredity), and sometimes in the modern sense (a drunkard through bad habits). London is "no hereditary alcoholic," he says, because he was not born with any "organic, chemical predisposition toward alcohol" (p. 6). He considers himself, therefore, to be "a normal, average man" who drinks "in the normal, average way, as drinking goes" (p. 11). He also regards his drinking as fundamentally different from an addiction to opiates or tobacco: "Drinking, as I deem it, is practically entirely a habit of mind" (p. 339).

John Barleycorn traces the incremental progression of this "habit of mind" into a mental obsession—and, in effect, reveals the subtle transformation of a "normal" person into an alcoholic. "A left-handed man, by long practice, can become a right-handed man," the narrator observes. "Had I, a non-alcoholic, by long practice, become an alcoholic?" (p. 277). The answer is clear even to London in his denial; but as he explains how prolonged acquaintance with John Barleycorn did finally induce "the alcoholic desire" (p. 200), he continues to argue, somewhat desperately, that his need for drink differs from the organic need of the dipsomaniac.

London recalls that he was initiated into drinking at the tender age of five, when, as he carried a pail of beer to his stepfather in the fields, he sipped enough to become dizzy and nauseated. Two years later, at a neighbor's ranch in San Mateo County, the boy was induced by adults, incredulous at his capacity, to drink so much wine that he collapsed into a drunken delirium from which he narrowly escaped with his life. The effect of these childhood incidents, especially the nearly fatal once, was not merely to instill a guilty fear and physical loathing of drink—"No mad dog was ever more afraid of water than was I of alcohol" (p. 35)—but to foster a perverse pride in the boy for having done "something heroic" (p. 36).

London also learned a powerful association between drinking and manliness. As a newsboy at the age of ten, he burned with curiosity about the saloons of San Francisco: "Here was a child, forming its first judgments of the world, finding the saloon a delightful and desirable place" (p. 39). Life in these places held a special mystery and excitement; although the saloons may have been, in fact, terrible dives, veritable dens of iniquity, they were "terribly wonderful, and it is the terribly wonderful that a boy desires to know" (p. 43). Men seemed more fully alive somehow as they clinked their glasses and shuffled their feet in the sawdust. They "talked with great voices, laughed great laughs, and there was an atmosphere of greatness" (p. 42).

Since the saloons functioned as "poor men's clubs" (p. 93), the "atmosphere of greatness" compensated for the brutal hardships of working-class life.[12] From his own childhood poverty and his later working experience, London understood why it seemed better "to reign among booze-fighters, a prince, than to toil twelve hours a day at a machine for ten cents an hour" (p. 112). He also perceived a resemblance between wage slavery and slavery to the bottle. As a "work-beast" in the steam laundry, London felt just two overwhelming desires: to sleep and to get drunk. "John Barleycorn makes his appeal to weakness and failure, to weariness and exhaustion. . . . He offers false strength to the body, false elevation to the spirit, making things seem what they are not and vastly fairer than what they are" (p. 228). The saloons will remain ubiquitous, London argues, either until the needs it meets are removed or until some other institution satisfies them better.

Some of these needs were material and practical. As Roy Rosenzweig points out, "public toilets, food, warmth, clean water, meeting space, check-cashing services, newspapers—often otherwise unavailable to workers in the late nineteenth century city—could be found free of charge in the saloon."[13] But intangible needs were also met: primarily a desire for male fellowship that alcohol seemed to heighten. In London's view, the saloon would never be replaced by such bourgeois alternatives as the Young Men's Christian Association unless society evolved into a future free of alcohol; then "it will be the Y.M.C.A., and similar unthinkably better and wiser and more virile congregating places, that will receive the men who now go to saloons to find themselves and one another" (p. 172).[14]

Saloon life secures its virility through the exclusion of women and the domestic sphere. All ways lead to the saloon, in fact, because the young man can escape there "from the narrowness of women's influence into the wide free world of men" (p. 7). Although the hearts of some women—such as the Queen of the Oyster Pirates, who flirts with young Jack aboard the *Razzle Dazzle*—may apparently be won by a man's drunken swagger, the real purpose of drinking is not to impress women, but to render them superfluous.

Rosenzweig argues that the men who patronized saloons implicitly questioned and sometimes explicitly rejected "the goals and values of industrial society, such as home-ownership, thrift, social mobility, and punctuality." Because of public drunkenness, "by far the most common late nineteenth century 'crime,'" they often clashed directly with police authorities. In general, the culture of the saloon "operated outside of, if not against, the formal legal system." The power of this system ultimately resided, of course, with men in the upper classes; but the interests of the dominant culture, in which "family-centered recreation was becoming the middle-class norm," were also advanced by women of the upper classes, who had become more active and influential in the temperance movement.

Fear and loathing of women were part and parcel of saloon culture. As a site for male drinking, the saloon displaced unlicensed kitchen barrooms, often operated by women, which had been home-centered and sexually integrated. Rosenzweig, who wishes to make the most of the ways in which working-class men resisted and subverted the bourgeois hegemony, concedes that in "its maleness and gender segregation, the saloon both challenged and affirmed the dominant culture." By mandating subservient roles for women, the saloon was no different from the middle-class family. Thus although working-class saloongoers "apparently departed from some of the basic values of industrial America, they nevertheless shared some of its deepest patriarchal assumptions."[15]

As the influence of alcohol supplanted the influence of women, men escaped the moral rigor that women were seen to represent. Thus London can justify squandering his money in the saloon instead of repaying his loan from Mammy Jennie, the black woman who nursed him as a child. The voice of John Barleycorn tells him: "You 're a man and you 're getting acquainted with men. Mammy Jennie does n't need the money as promptly as all that. She is n't starving" (pp. 89–90). London professes to deplore the behavior of his younger self, offering it as an example of how alcohol inhibits morality: "Wrong conduct that it is impossible for one to do sober, is done quite easily when one is not sober" (p. 69). But the incident also exemplifies a contempt for women that is inseparable in *John Barleycorn* from the representation of drinking and the gendering of alcoholism itself as exclusively and homosocially male.

Although London claims he has learned to be cautious "when casting sociological generalizations," he does not hesitate to affirm Kipling's misogynous maxim—which he labels a "biological rather than sociological" generalization—that the " 'Colonel's lady and Judy O'Grady are sisters under their skins' " (p. 177).[16] As part of his convalescence from the Long Sickness, London had to depend on "the love of woman to complete the cure and lull my pessimism asleep for many a long day, until John Barleycorn again awoke it" (p. 256). As he later relapsed into melancholy, he found that without the numbing effect of alcohol in social situations, "it was a torment to listen to the insipidities and stupidities of women, to the pompous, arrogant sayings of the little half-baked [i.e., feminized] men." The "silly superficial chatterings" of women cannot conceal their covert menace; for beneath their softness, they are "as primitive, direct, and deadly in their pursuit of biological destiny as the monkey women were before they shed their furry coats and replaced them with the furs of other animals" (pp. 259– 60).[17] As if in answer to Freud's notorious question, London knows what women really want. Their "biological destiny" is ruthlessly to seduce men.

Within late Victorian gender codes, the nightmare of woman as atavistic sexual predator coexisted with the daydream of woman as sexless angel on a pedestal. Woman was often portrayed contradictorily as both morally superior to man and also profoundly amoral: simultaneously as more and less than "human." In recirculating these stereotypes, *John Barleycorn* registers the anxiety that accompanied a radical transformation at the turn of the century in the cultural understanding of what it meant to be a man or woman. Feminist critics such as Sandra M. Gilbert and Susan Gubar have suggested that "the literary phenomenon ordinarily called 'modernism' is itself—though no doubt over-determined—for men as much as for women a product of the sexual battle" that erupted from "the late nineteenth-century rise of feminism and the fall of Victorian concepts of 'femininity.'"[18]

The resurgence of a more aggressive model of "masculinity" was a major element in the post-Victorian reformation of gender roles, and the consumption of alcohol was integral to the rugged ideal of manliness that arose in reaction to the perceived enervation and "feminization" of American life. To London, nothing is more potent a male sign than drinking: "John Barleycorn is everywhere the connotation of manliness, and daring, and great-spiritedness" (p. 158). In his youth, London envied Nelson, the Herculean young oyster pirate, for his credit at the saloon. To have his own page in the account book seemed "the final badge of manhood" (p. 85), and there was no higher "commendation as a man" imaginable than the barkeeper's "magic words": "*He's been sousin' here with Nelson all afternoon*" (p. 87). Irony plays lightly across this passage, calling into question the true worth of an "accolade delivered by a barkeeper with a beer glass!" (p. 87). But irony does not ultimately diminish London's ardor for saloon culture as a male preserve, the very hypermasculinity of which is proof against gender confusion.

The underlying logic of *John Barleycorn* holds that if drinking is *the* badge of manhood, then the manliest of men, because he stands at the farthest remove from women and their domestic regime, is the alcoholic. The alcoholic, moreover, enjoys a homosocial intimacy with other men that exists nowhere outside the world of the bottle.

Throughout *John Barleycorn*, drinking is represented as a primal means to bonding among men, who huddle in saloons just as their ancestors once "gathered about the fire of the squatting-place or the fire at the mouth of the cave" (p. 7). Within the safe bounds of a male environment, men express their mutual devotion and even display physical affection. On the occasion when young Jack drank himself unconscious, he witnessed, with eager dread, a tussle between the two big-fisted giants with murderous reputations:

> Maybe I would see that wonderful thing, a man killed. Anyway, I would see a man-fight. Great was my disappointment. Black Matt and Tom Morrisey merely held on to each other and lifted their clumsy-booted feet in

what seemed a grotesque, elephantine dance. They were too drunk to fight. Then the peacemakers got hold of them and led them back to cement the new friendship in the kitchen.

Soon they were all talking at once, rumbling and roaring as big-chested open-air men will when whiskey has whipped their taciturnity. And I, a little shaver of seven, my heart in my mouth, my trembling body strung tense as a deer's on the verge of flight, peered wonderingly in at the open door and learned more of the strangeness of men. And I marveled at Black Matt and Tom Morrisey, sprawled over the table, arms about each other's necks, weeping lovingly.   (Pp. 23–24)

When London later got drunk in the company of two other adolescent sailors, the young men emulated these elders in the ritual of using alcohol to attain intimacy through conflict. "Scotty and I flared and raged like young cockerels, until the harpooner poured another round of drinks to enable us to forgive and make up. Which we did, arms around each other's necks, protesting vows of eternal friendship—just like Black Matt and Tom Morrisey, I remembered, in the ranch kitchen in San Mateo" (p. 52). In the saloons, too, London discovered that nearly every fight, once resolved by rounds of drinks, led into a love feast of mutual embraces and pledges of "undying friendship" (p. 103).

The emotional excess here—friendship based on drunken camaraderie never seems less than "eternal" or "undying"—suggests the economy of desire that governs the culture of drinking in *John Barleycorn*. At the moment when London makes a "grave decision" to embrace saloon life, he knows that the choice is "between money and men, between niggardliness and romance." He must either "throw overboard all my old values of money and look upon it as something to be flung about wastefully" or else forsake his comradeship "with those men whose peculiar quirks made them care for strong drink" (pp. 83–84). Money has no value for such men except as a token of exchange for what is invaluable. "There was more in this buying of drinks than mere quantity," London observes. "There was a stage when the beer did n't count at all, but just the spirit of comradeship of drinking together" (pp. 84–85). The culture of (literal) consumption in the saloon promises to fulfill a desire for such intangible blessings as inner peace and good will among men.

The "code" that men learn "along with all the other things connected with

John Barleycorn" (p. 207) demands a vast consumption of alcohol through the custom of treating. A man is expected to buy a round of drinks for every round he has received, and London is mortified to realize that his ignorance of this custom has caused him to lose face with "Young Scratch" Nelson, who bought six rounds at the bar while he waited in vain for London to reciprocate. "I have blushed many times in my life, but never have I experienced so terrible a blush as that one" (p. 80). The rule of treating must be observed even when nineteen shipmates from the *Sophie Sutherland* come into port together; no less than nineteen rounds are duly consumed!—with the result that most of the men roll "out of the saloon and into the arms of the sharks and harpies," who quickly snatch what is left of their pay (p. 167). London escapes this fate only because he has "a home and people to go to" (p. 168).

The ritual of treating, which apparently derives from Irish peasant custom, is interpreted by Rosenzweig as a form of working-class resistance to "the transformation of social relationships into 'commodities'—a means of preserving reciprocal modes of social interaction within a capitalist world" that advocated individualism and acquisitiveness.[19] Insofar as London was a socialist (as he often claimed he was), his appreciation of treating may also be read as part of his own protest against the alienation of labor under capitalism.

In *John Barleycorn*, London asserts that his conversion to socialism in 1904 was directly responsible for his recovery from the depression and confusion of his Long Sickness: "It was the PEOPLE, and no thanks to John Barleycorn, who pulled me through" (p. 256). He goes on to claim that his radicalism in the cause, which he had taken up with the zeal of his "extremist" temperament, was "so strenuous, so unsafe and unsane, so ultra-revolutionary, that I retarded the socialist development in the United States by five years" (p. 256). It has long been recognized, however, that London's socialism contained an alloy of Nietzschean elitism and nihilism as well as of ordinary bourgeois values.[20]

The custom of treating, in the sheer extravagance it encouraged, rubbed against the grain of London's boyhood experience of a strict economy of scarcity. When he was young, the chronic "pinch of poverty" (p. 80) had taught him to place the highest value on hard work and material accumulation, and he became "famous as a trader" and "notorious as a miser" (pp. 82–83). Thus in London's conversion from an economy of scarcity to an economy of excess, as he turns himself "loose with a more lavish disregard for money than any of them" (p. 110), his repudiation of the work ethic involves nothing less than a Nietzschean "transvaluing of values" (p. 80).[21]

Through the necromancy of John Barleycorn, London's values undergo a comprehensive transvaluation as he gains an occult knowledge undreamt of in the philosophy of his conventional upbringing. Drunk aboard the *Idler*, he catches "enticing and inflammatory hints of a world beyond my world. . . . I had got behind men's souls. I had got behind my own soul and found unguessed potencies and greatnesses" (p. 60). To some extent, these hints are an illusion produced by the duplicitous John Barleycorn, who is both "the king of liars" and "the frankest truth-sayer." "He is the august companion with whom one walks with the gods. He is also in league with the Noseless One. His way leads to truth naked, and to death. He gives clear vision, and muddy dreams. He is the enemy of life, and the teacher of wisdom beyond life's vision" (pp. 4–5). What eventually becomes clear is that the wisdom beyond life's vision is inimical to life itself. "Alcohol tells truth, but its truth is not normal. What is normal is healthful. What is healthful tends toward life. Normal truth is a different order, and a lesser order, of truth" (p. 305). The quest for a "higher" order of (unhealthy) truth is recounted in the most memorable chapters of *John Barleycorn*, in which London, with merciless self-scrutiny, relives his gradual but inexorable descent into alcoholic hell.

Thanks to the "gorgeous constitution" (p. 132) of his youth, London was immune for a while to the damage that alcohol inflicted on his drinking companions. As he realized that "habitual drunkards" have "a way of turning up their toes without apparent provocation" (p. 143), he was able to moderate his own consumption, hoping to avoid "the death-road which John Barleycorn maintains for his devotees" (p. 142). On one terrifying occasion, however, he followed this road himself, when, "drunk-maddened to lunacy" (p. 119), he yielded to a suicidal urge and nearly drowned off the coast of Benicia. Another time, he got so drunk at a political rally that he experienced his first alcoholic blackout.

London ignored such warnings because in "years and years of heavy drinking, drinking did not beget the desire" (p. 96). But he reached a turning point when he was cramming for his college entrance examinations. His acute "brain-fag" prompted a spontaneous and imperative craving for alcohol: "For the first time in my life I consciously, deliberately desired to get drunk. It was a new, a totally different manifestation of John Barleycorn's power. It was not a body need for alcohol. It was a mental desire" (pp. 213–14). Before long, mental desire had become a physical need that led ultimately to a state of continual intoxication: "I achieved a condition in which my body was never free from alcohol. Nor did I permit myself to be away from alcohol" (p. 298). Despite strict rules he tried to impose on himself so that drinking would never encroach on his work, London found himself incapable of writing without the stimulus of alcohol.

For all the honesty of his account, however, London never fully accepts the idea that he lost all control over his drinking. "Merciful goodness!—if John Barleycorn could get such sway over me, a non-alcoholic," he exclaims, "what must be the sufferings of the true alcoholic, battling against the organic demands of his chemistry while those close to him sympathize little, understand less, and despise and deride him!" (p. 302). The remarkable strength of London's denial derives from the force of his invidious distinction between two types of drinkers:

> There is the man whom we all know, stupid, unimaginative, whose brain is bitten numbly by numb maggots; who walks generously with wide-spread, tentative legs, falls frequently in the gutter, and who sees, in the extremity of his ecstasy, blue mice and pink elephants. He is the type that gives rise to the jokes in the funny papers.
>
> The other type of drinker has imagination, vision. Even when most pleasantly jingled he walks straight and naturally, never staggers nor falls, and knows just where he is and what he is doing. It is not his body but his brain that is drunken. He may bubble with wit, or expand with good fellowship. Or he may see intellectual specters and phantoms that are cosmic and logical and that take the forms of syllogisms. It is when in this condition that he strips away the husks of life's healthiest illusions and gravely considers the iron collar of necessity welded about the neck of his soul. This is the hour of John Barleycorn's subtlest power. It is easy for any man to roll in the gutter. But it is a terrible ordeal for a man to stand upright on his two legs unswaying, and decide that in all the universe he finds for himself only one freedom,

namely, the anticipating of the day of his death. With this man this is the hour of the white logic . . . when he knows that he may know only the laws of things—the meaning of things never. (Pp. 11–13)

In the rhetoric of this passage, the second type—the one recognizable as the modernist (male) artist—is plainly superior to the clownish stumblebum. This prophet of the White Logic is a deadly serious man among men, a visionary with a tough-mindedness to match his rugged physical constitution. He wears the iron collar standing (more or less) upright. Blessed are they who roll in the gutter with pseudo-visions of blue mice and pink elephants; they enjoy some peace, at least, in the stupor of illusion. But the "imaginative man" must bear "the pitiless, spectral syllogisms" and look upon life "with the jaundiced eye of a pessimistic German philosopher. He sees through all illusions. He transvalues all values. God is bad, truth is a cheat, and life is a joke" (p. 14). He is, in short, the modernist writer as Nietzschean hero: Zarathustra in his cups.

In affirming Nietzsche, London rejects what he sees as the philosophical pusillanimity of William James in his will to believe in the "vital lie":

"And pray what is a vital lie but a lie?" the White Logic challenges. "Come. Fill your glass and let us examine these vital liars who crowd your bookshelves. Let us dabble in William James a bit."

"A man of health," I say. "From him we may expect no philosopher's stone, but at least we shall find a few robust tonic things to which to tie."

"Rationality gelded to sentiment," the White Logic grins. "At the end of all his thinking he still clung to the sentiment of immortality. Facts transmuted in the alembic of hope into terms of faith. The ripest fruit of reason the stultification of reason. From the topmost peak of reason James teaches to cease reasoning and to have faith that all is well and will be well—the old, oh, ancient old, acrobatic flip of the metaphysician whereby they reasoned reason quite away in order to escape the pessimism consequent upon the grim and honest exercise of reason." (Pp. 326–27)

London touches here on William James's famous meditation on the "healthy-minded temperament" versus the "sick soul." The former "settles his scores with the more evil aspects of the universe by systematically declining to lay them to heart or make much of them, by ignoring them in his reflective calculations, or even, on occasion, by denying outright that they exist." The latter, on the contrary, is given to "maximizing evil . . . based on the persuasion that the evil aspects of our life are of its very essence, and that the world's meaning most comes home to us when we lay them most to heart." Whereas to the sick soul the healthy-minded way "seems unspeakably blind and shallow," the way of the sick soul, to the healthy-minded, "seems unmanly and diseased."[22]

There is an important difference between the gender coding in this passage and that in *John Barleycorn*. Whereas James follows Victorian assumptions in associating "manliness" with robust and tonic healthy-mindedness, London anticipates other male modernists in appropriating "manliness" to a sick-souled vision of life (deep, muscular, dark), thereby denigrating healthy-mindedness (shallow, soft, light) by implicit association with "femininity." Thus James, with his "gelded" rationality, is figured as a philosophical castrate who has never propped his boot on a bar rail, lifted a glass with John Barleycorn, and stared down the White Logic without flinching from his deadly truths.

Although *John Barleycorn,* with its bleak determinism, may be read as an example of *fin de siècle* naturalism, it also embodies a theme characteristic of modernism: the artist as meaning-maker, the sole source of order in a deranged universe. *John Barleycorn* is finally less about its titular hero (alcohol personified) than its heroic narrator, who attains through his duel with meaninglessness a dark triumph of the will. What later modernists were to see through a glass darkly was foreseen by London; like the speaker of *The Waste Land,* he defiantly shored fragments against his ruins.

In defining "The Modern Temper" of his prematurely jaded generation, Joseph Wood Krutch outlined in 1929 a "gloomy vision of a dehumanized" new world in which "man must henceforth live if he lives at all, for all his premises have been destroyed and he must proceed to new conclusions." Painfully aware of its predicament, this lost generation has "awakened to the fact that both the ends which its fathers proposed to themselves and the emotions from which they drew their strength seem irrelevant and remote." For Krutch, the epitome of "The Modern Temper" is T. S. Eliot in his "bleak, tortuous complexities": "Here disgust speaks with a robust voice and denunciation is confident, but ecstasy, flickering and uncertain, leaps fitfully up only to sink back among the cinders." Thoreau's "quiet desperation" has become the intellectual's status quo; "and the more highly developed the reflective powers of the individual become, the more likely is that quiet desperation to become an active rebellion which expresses itself in self-regarding vices."[23]

The chief modernist vice was habitual drunkenness. As Donald W. Goodwin has convincingly argued, "[W]ell-known writers in America during the first half of the twentieth century were extraordinarily susceptible to the disease called alcoholism." Within this group, alcoholism was nothing short of "epidemic," in fact. "What is hard," says Goodwin, "is to think of *non*alcoholics among American writers of the twentieth century."[24] Robin Room, a sociologist, finds "a clear association of problematic drunkenness not only with American writers, but with a particular generational cohort that came of age in 1909–1921."[25] By Room's head count, over half of all American authors with a reputation for heavy drinking were born between 1888 and 1900.

Statistics of this sort are inevitably imprecise and questionable; but if one charts, as Room does (see table 1), the birth dates of alcoholic American writers from Poe through the 1920s, a definite pattern does seem to emerge. Table 2 is a revised version of Room's chart, in which his list has been augmented to include one hundred significant American writers, born before 1921, who were known for habitual drunkenness.[26] The pattern remains the same: drinking problems were relatively rare early in the nineteenth century; the incidence rose after the Civil War; heavy clustering occurred at the end of the nineteenth century.

The evidence does suggest that alcoholism was rampant among American writers of the Lost Generation, particularly among white, middle-class men. Of those listed in table 2, well over a third were born during Room's thirteen-year span, from 1888 to 1900; but three-quarters were born between 1885 and 1919. And if one brackets those who came of age during the Great War (i.e., those born from 1893 to 1897) and those who came of age during Prohibition (i.e., those born from 1898 to 1912), then about one quarter falls into each group—or half the total.

The attitudes of the Lost Generation, those children of the century who believed they had come too soon into a world too old, were formed as much by

■ *Table 1*

1809	Edgar Allan Poe
. . .	
1869	E. A. Robinson
. . .	
1876	Jack London
. . .	
1879	Wallace Stevens
1880	
1885	Ring Lardner, Sinclair Lewis
1888	Raymond Chandler, Eugene O'Neill
1889	Robert Benchley
1890	
1891	
1892	Edna St. Vincent Millay
1893	J. P. Marquand, Dorothy Parker
1894	e. e. cummings, Dashiell Hammett
1895	Edmund Wilson
1896	F. Scott Fitzgerald
1897	William Faulkner
1899	Hart Crane, Ernest Hemingway
1900	Thomas Wolfe
1902	John Steinbeck
1905	John O'Hara
1908	Theodore Roethke
1910	Charles Olson
1914	John Berryman, Tennessee Williams

1917	Robert Lowell
1920	
1922	Jack Kerouac
1928	Donald Newlove

---

growing up in the heyday of Prohibition as by living through the Great War. Both experiences bred deep skepticism about the wisdom and integrity of the elders and provoked rebellion against authority that exceeded the ordinary friction between generations. Simply because it became illicit, drinking possessed a singular importance; drinking in defiance of Prohibition was a sign of solidarity with the rising generation's resistance to what it called "puritanism" and to what it considered to be the oppression of bourgeois American life. As A. J. Liebling recalled, his contemporaries had felt a particular "reverence for strong drink" because, for them, liquor had been both "the symbol of a sacred cause" and a "self-righteous pleasure": "Drinking, we proved to ourselves our freedom as individuals and flouted Congress. . . . It was the only period during which a fellow could be smug and slopped concurrently."[27]

In revolt from their native villages, some of the young stormed Greenwich Village, capital of the old American Bohemia. Prohibition "altered the general decorum of the Village itself," observes Frederick J. Hoffman. Here as elsewhere, it was "responsible for a considerable increase in drinking; it also served as another excuse for the exodus to Paris during the postwar decade. Its effect upon the intellectual life was severe: from being a mild accompaniment to dining and conversation, alcohol became almost a primary and constant necessity."[28]

One suggestive sign of a generational shift in American attitudes toward drinking was the proliferation of terms for drunkenness. By 1927, Edmund Wilson had collected over a hundred of them, noting that the "vocabulary of social drinking . . . seems to have become especially rich: one gets the impression that more nuances are nowadays discriminated than was the case before Prohibition. Thus, *fried, stewed* and *boiled* all convey distinctly different ideas;

■ *Table 2*

1809	Edgar Allan Poe
. . .	
1836	Bret Harte
1837	Joaquin Miller
. . .	
1842	Ambrose Bierce
1843	Charles Warren Stoddard
. . .	
1849	James Whitcomb Riley
. . .	
1857	James Gibbons Huneker
. . .	
1862	William Sydney Porter (O. Henry)
. . .	
1867	Finley Peter Dunne (Mr. Dooley)
1868	Edgar Lee Masters
1869	E. A. Robinson, George Sterling, Booth Tarkington
1870	
1871	Theodore Dreiser
1872	Paul Laurence Dunbar
1873	George Cram Cook
1874	
1875	
1876	Sherwood Anderson, Jack London
1877	
1878	Don Marquis
1879	Wallace Stevens
1880	H. L. Mencken
1881	
1882	
1883	
1884	Damon Runyon
1885	Ring Lardner, Sinclair Lewis
1886	William Seabrook
1887	Robinson Jeffers, Alexander Woollcott
1888	Heywood Broun, Raymond Chandler, Eugene O'Neill

1889	Conrad Aiken, Robert Benchley
1890	Katherine Anne Porter
1891	Harold Stearns
1892	Djuna Barnes, James M. Cain, Edna St. Vincent Millay
1893	Maxwell Bodenheim, John P. Marquand, Dorothy Parker
1894	e. e. cummings, Dashiell Hammett, Ben Hecht, Donald Ogden Stewart, James Thurber
1895	Caroline Gordon, Charles MacArthur, Ernest Walsh, Edmund Wilson
1896	Philip Barry, Nancy Cunard, F. Scott Fitzgerald, Robert McAlmon, Marjorie Kinnan Rawlings
1897	Louise Bogan, Kenneth Burke, Bernard De Voto, William Faulkner, Dawn Powell, Thornton Wilder
1898	Malcolm Cowley, Harry Crosby
1899	Hart Crane, Ernest Hemingway, E. B. White
1900	Thomas Wolfe
1901	Granville Hicks
1902	Kenneth Fearing, Wolcott Gibbs, John Steinbeck
1903	James Gould Cozzens, Charles Jackson, Nathanael West
1904	R. P. Blackmur, A. J. Liebling
1905	Lillian Hellman, John O'Hara, Dalton Trumbo
1906	Clifford Odets
1907	
1908	Theodore Roethke, William Saroyan, Mark Schorer
1909	James Agee
1910	Charles Olson
1911	Elizabeth Bishop, Winfield Townley Scott, Tennessee Williams
1912	John Cheever
1913	William Inge, Delmore Schwartz, Irwin Shaw
1914	John Berryman, Weldon Kees
1915	Jean Stafford
1916	
1917	Jane Bowles, Robert Lowell, Carson McCullers
1918	
1919	Tom Heggen, Shirley Jackson
1920	Howard Nemerov

and *cock-eyed, plastered, owled, embalmed,* and *ossified* evoke quite different images." It was significant, Wilson thought, that as new terms were coming into vogue, some of the old ones were falling out of use. Fewer persons, it seemed, were going on "*sprees, toots, tears, jags, bats, brannigans* or *benders,*" perhaps because such words suggested "not merely extreme drunkenness, but also an exceptional occurrence, a breaking away by the drinker from the conditions of his normal life." Wilson speculated that the disappearance of these terms reflected "the fact that this kind of fierce protracted drinking has now become universal, an accepted feature of social life instead of a disreputable escapade."[29]

Writing for an audience of liberal intellectuals in *The New Republic,* Wilson was overgeneralizing. Fierce and protracted drinking—or even ordinary drinking, for that matter—was far from "universal" under Prohibition. As might have been expected, despite the wholesale failure of enforcement, the consumption of alcohol declined overall during the 1920s. At the same time, however, it likely increased among young and educated city dwellers, in whose sophisticated circles heavy drinking was not merely tolerated, but actively encouraged. As Room points out, this group came to maturity when "temperance had become a majority sentiment in the country at large and a sentiment associated by and large with conservative or reactionary political forces." In such circumstances, drunkenness could be construed as "an act of political dissent." Room also observes that drinking among some members of the Lost Generation was an act of cultural reaffiliation. Those who migrated to France tended to adopt the drinking habits of a country that had "the highest recorded per capita alcohol consumption in the world"; they also followed the French tradition in which intoxication was closely tied to political radicalism and the artistic avant garde.[30]

The commercial success of a few novels during the 1920s—notably *This Side of Paradise* and *The Sun Also Rises*—magnified the Lost Generation's influence on American culture. As Alfred Kazin says, one key element of "the great changeover from the old rural and small-town America" during the 1920s was "the triumph in the marketplace of 'advanced,' wholly 'modern' writers and books, ideas, and attitudes"—which made heavy drinking stylish and created an enduring association between modernism and alcoholism. Booze came "to seem a natural accompaniment of the literary life—of its loneliness, its creative aspirations and its frenzies, its 'specialness,' its hazards in a society where values are constantly put in money terms."[31]

London was perhaps the first American writer to drink in the modern spirit; and with *John Barleycorn,* the prototype for the modernist drunk narrative, he helped to create the cultural climate for "advanced" ideas.[32] *John Barleycorn* suggests that The Modern Temper itself may have been one byproduct of the "epidemic" of alcoholism among writers and intellectuals early in the twentieth century. For even as London celebrates an ideology of despair, in part by emphasizing the "manliness" required to espouse it, he acknowledges an epistemological dilemma. Exactly how is the White Logic visited upon the "imaginative man"? Does alcohol merely unveil what is otherwise hidden from common view? Or, rather, does alcohol itself produce the "pitiless, spectral syllogisms"? "Temperamentally I am wholesome-hearted and merry," London tells his wife. "Yet when I walk with John Barleycorn I suffer all the damnation of intellectual pessimism" (p. 8). It is the curse of the White Logic—"the argent messenger of truth beyond truth, the antithesis of life, cruel and bleak as interstellar space, pulseless and frozen as absolute zero, dazzling with the frost of irrefragable logic and unforgettable fact"—that blights the dreams of the dreamer and compels him to cry out, "as in 'The City of Dreadful Night': 'Our life's a cheat, our death a black abyss'" (p. 308). Then, in vain hope of relief from the "sickness of pessimism, caused by drink," the victim "must drink further in quest of the anodyne that John Barleycorn promises but never delivers" (p. 303).

If alcohol in its physical, psychological, and spiritual effects on so many writers was not solely responsible for The Modern Temper, it was certainly inseparable from the modernist ideology of despair—what Saul Bellow has called "The Thinking Man's Waste Land." Bellow complained in 1965 that American literature had been dominated too long and too uncritically by a tradition in which the "alienation" of the artist is "accompanied by the more or less conscious acceptance of a theory of modern civilization." According to this theory, "modern mass society is frightful, brutal, hostile to whatever is pure in the human spirit, a waste land and a horror. To its ugliness, its bureaucratic regiments, its thefts, its lies, its wars, and its cruelties, the artist can never be reconciled."[33]

The horrors of modern life may account, perhaps, for the waste-land mentality of so much modernist literature. But this ideology of despair was propagated largely under the influence of alcohol: by writers for whom writing and drinking were conjoined. London, for one, could imagine the thrill of literary success only in terms of intoxication: "A thin envelope from an editor in the morning's mail was more stimulating than half-a-dozen cocktails. And if a check of decent amount came out of the envelope, such incident in itself was a whole drunk" (p. 243). Likewise, many Americans of the Lost Generation who bellied up to the bars of Paris or frequented the speakeasies back home came to believe that ardent spirits and artistic inspiration went hand in glove. In communion with the White Logic, these writers fashioned a literature steeped in what Donald Newlove calls "the authentic rhetoric of the true drunk, its shadow and ironies, universal overcast, the last red dingdong of doom breaking ecstatically over a dying landscape."[34]

3

Bulls, Balls, and Booze: *The Sun Also Rises*

Born the same year, 1899, in which Carry Nation mounted her campaign of "hatchetation" against the saloons, Ernest Hemingway was raised in a conservative suburb of Chicago by teetotaler parents. His father, who was "adamant on the subject," summarily fired "a jolly Irish maid who was especially fond of Ernest and had always brought him presents for twice coming home drunk at night after her day off."[1] His mother was equally ferocious about temperance. Hemingway's kid sister recalled that the first time she had ever seen liquor in the house was when her brother returned wounded from the war and a grateful Italian-American club brought along some wine to a party they threw for him. She was sure, however, that Ernest had consumed "quite a few drinks when he was in the hospital in Milan."[2]

Hemingway later became a fixture in the bars of Paris. During the 1920s, no one did more to set the trends of expatriate life, including heavy drinking. Gifted with a cast iron stomach and a steely physique, he exhibited an enormous capacity for alcohol and the ability to burn it off through vigorous exercise. Hemingway simply loved to drink, and he never had much use for anyone who didn't. As he privately noted in 1923, the things he distrusted in one of his *Toronto Star* colleagues were his ignorance of sports and his sobriety: "I have never seen him drunk. . . . I like to see every man drunk. A man does not exist until he is drunk. . . . I love getting drunk. Right from the start it is the best feeling."[3]

If drinking was a litmus test of manhood for Hemingway, he also deemed it essential to his existence as a writer. He never thought of alcohol as a means to inspiration, however; drinking was an anodyne, a reward, a soporific—a way to cut the overheated engine of imagination and cool it down restoratively at the end of a good day's work. The proper use of booze, he liked to think, distinguished him from those he disdained as "rummies." Like Jack London in his contempt for "chemical" dipsomaniacs, Hemingway felt superior to F. Scott Fitzgerald, William Faulkner, and other drunken writers and rivals for whom his pity was always laced with malice. Also like London, Hemingway set himself strict rules. As he told A. E. Hotchner in 1949: "Have spent my life straightening out rummies and all my life drinking, but since writing is my true love I never get the two things mixed up."[4]

This was a self-protective lie. By 1949, Hemingway had long since discovered, like London before him,[5] that for an alcoholic there is finally no sanctuary from alcohol. Hemingway's drinking infringed upon his writing, and he became at last no different from the rummies whose more obvious problems he had used to reassure himself that his own drinking could go on and on without repercussions. That he himself was a rummy was vehemently denied by Hemingway throughout his life and curtly dismissed by his biographers until recently. The evidence is conclusive, however, and need not be rehearsed.[6] It is also clear, as Tom Dardis says, that "Hemingway's alcoholism began far earlier than is generally thought" and that, as his drinking got "mixed up with his writing," it "played a major role in the deterioration of his great talent."[7]

Unexplored so far is how drinking bears on Hemingway's first novel, written at the height of his powers, when his alcoholism was still incipient. Some form of alcohol is consumed on nearly every page of *The Sun Also Rises* (1926), the work to which Hemingway later referred as "one book about a few drunks"; yet the importance of drinking in this novel has been ignored by critics.[8] *The Sun Also Rises* is, in fact, a major example of the drunk narrative, in which alcoholism is inseparable from the modernist ethos of despair.

Robert Penn Warren observed long ago, in his delineation of the "code," that Hemingway's central characters constitute a "cult" of initiates into nada: "the little secret community of, paradoxically enough, individualists who have resigned from the general community, and who are strong enough to live without any of the illusions, lies, and big words of the herd."[9] When Brett Ashley assures Jake Barnes that Count Mippipopolous is "quite one of us,"[10] she speaks for this "secret community," all of whose disillusioned members in *The Sun Also Rises* are initiates into the White Logic.

The "general community" from which these characters have resigned receives only oblique and ironic treatment in the novel. This is the mundane world of Woolsey and Krum, whose entrapment in domesticity and the work-a-day routine leaves them too stultified for playing tennis or hitting the fashionable bistros. Their insipidly bourgeois dream is of a little car and a house in the country (pp. 36–37). Even more benighted, it would seem, are the Catholic pilgrims bound for Lourdes. It is bad enough that these "Goddam Puritans" from Dayton, Ohio, apparently believe in miracles, but they also monopolize the dining cars and force Jake and Bill Gorton to make other arrangements for lunch (p. 86)!

Aboard this train from Paris to Madrid, Jake and Bill meet an archetypally American-Gothic couple, modeled in part on Hemingway's own parents, who embody the old-fashioned values from which the jaded expatriates have run for their lives. When conversation turns to fishing, the old man drawls:

> "Well, I never cared for it, myself. There's plenty that do out where I come from, though. We got some of the best fishing in the State of Montana. I've been out with the boys, but I never cared for it any."
>
> "Mighty little fishing you did on them trips," his wife said.
>
> He winked at us.
>
> "You know how the ladies are. If there's a jug goes along, or a case of beer, they think it's hell and damnation."
>
> "That's the way men are," his wife said to us. She smoothed her comfortable lap. "I voted against prohibition to please him, and because I like a little beer in the house, and then he talks that way. It's a wonder they ever find any one to marry them." (P. 86)

Here is Hemingway's nightmare of Prohibition America: a society in which overweight wives (an enormity of smugness seems to weigh upon that comfortable lap) may feign a lenient attitude toward beer but subscribe in their hearts to the temperance cause and henpeck their husbands into submission. Despite his comradely wink, this man has nothing in common with Jake and Bill. Whereas Jake, who was genitally maimed in the War, nonetheless remains every inch a man, this evidently pathetic excuse for a man has been symbolically castrated by the W.C.T.U.[11]

On several other occasions in *The Sun Also Rises,* Hemingway uses mockery of Prohibition to sharpen the contrast between the cultists of nada and the conventional community they have left behind. "You can't get this in America, eh?" boasts a Basque peasant who once lived in California as he shares Jake's wine (p. 107). "Direct action . . . It beats legislation," quips Bill, as he watches Jake take matters into his own hands—because the punch prepared by a stingy innkeeper proves too weak—by grabbing a rum bottle off the shelf to improve the blend (p. 110). And when Bill and Jake fish the Irati River, their intimacy is attained in part through giddy hilarity at the expense of Wayne Bidwell Wheeler, general counsel and tactical genius of the Anti-Saloon League, the man popularly credited with masterminding the passage of the Eighteenth Amendment:

> "Do you know what you are?" Bill looked at the bottle affectionately.
> "No," I said.
> "You're in the pay of the Anti-Saloon League."
> "I went to Notre Dame with Wayne B. Wheeler."
> "It's a lie," said Bill. "I went to Austin Business College with Wayne B. Wheeler. He was class president."
> "Well," I said, "the saloon must go."
> "You're right there, old classmate," Bill said. "The saloon must go, and I will take it with me."[12]   (P. 123)

Roger Forseth calls the Irati River fishing episode "a supreme evocation of the culture of drink."[13] This apt phrase applies to the entire novel; for *The Sun Also Rises,* no less than *John Barleycorn,* is dominated by what London describes as "the way of the devotees of John Barleycorn":

When good fortune comes, they drink. When they have no fortune they drink to the hope of good fortune. If fortune be ill, they drink to forget it. If they meet a friend, they drink. If they quarrel with a friend and lose him, they drink. If their love-making be crowned with success, they are so happy they needs must drink. If they be jilted, they drink for the contrary reason. And if they haven't anything to do at all, why they take a drink, secure in the knowledge that when they have taken a sufficient number of drinks the maggots will start crawling in their brains and they will have their hands full with things to do. When they are sober they want to drink; and when they have drunk they want to drink more.[14]

This passage might serve as a plot summary of *The Sun Also Rises*, in which all of the main characters except Cohn are dedicated drinkers if not outright drunkards, and in which it always matters what kind of alcohol is being consumed, where, and by whom.

Consider the opening scene of the novel: a rather ordinary evening during which Jake goes from his office to the bars of the Left Bank and finally, after a disturbing encounter with Brett, to his apartment. Robert Cohn arrives while Jake is rushing to meet his deadline for the week's mail stories. In order to brush off his garrulous visitor, Jake invites him downstairs for a drink. "Aren't you working?" Cohn inquires. "No," Jake lies, explaining for the reader's benefit that because the "ethics" of journalism require "that you should never seem to be working," it is all the more imperative to practice deceit in order to get any work done (p. 11). At the bar they order whiskey and soda; then, as planned, Jake excuses himself and returns to work for a couple of hours while Cohn naps outside his office door.

At quitting time they gravitate to the Café Napolitain for an apéritif. After Cohn leaves, the prostitute Georgette solicits Jake, and he joins her in drinking pernod. This imitation absinthe, which has "a good uplift" but "drops you just as far," suits Jake's melancholy—a gloom so palpable that Georgette is prompted to ask, "What's the matter? You sick?" (p. 15). This is the first purposeful drinking that Jake has done, and the reader is meant to understand that he seeks relief from the torment of loving Brett. At dinner Jake and Georgette share "another bottle of wine" (p. 16)—the consumption of the first bottle goes unrecorded in the text—and soon thereafter, in the company of

Frances Clyne and the Braddocks, he takes coffee and liqueurs (p. 19). It's a hot night, so he switches to beer, drinking at least one glass in the doorway before Brett arrives with her escort of homosexuals. Since "they always made me angry," Jake must suppress a urge to "swing on one, any one, anything to shatter that superior, simpering composure" (p. 20).

Jake's homophobia is an essential element of the Hemingway code—and also, as we shall see, of the modernist culture of drinking. But at this moment Jake is also displacing his anger toward Brett upon her companions, and he avoids doing them any violence by moving down the block for another beer—which, unfortunately, is "not good." Before returning to the original bar, Jake drinks "a worse cognac to take the taste out of my mouth" (p. 20). Then back at the Braddocks's table, in self-defense against the naive and sycophantic Robert Prentiss, a recent arrival from the States to whom Jake has just been introduced, he has another *fine à l'eau.*

At this point, having consumed *at least* one whiskey, one pernod, half of two bottles of wine, some liqueur, two beers, and two brandies within a space of three or four hours, Jake feels "a little drunk." But only a little: "Not drunk in any positive sense but just enough to be careless" (p. 21). So, carelessly, he vents his irritation with Brett on the hapless Prentiss, until Cohn distracts him with the offer of yet another drink. When Brett joins them at the bar, Jake asks, "Why aren't you tight?" She admits to being "wonderfully sober" (as he puts it).

Whereas Jake has finished for the evening, Brett is just getting started. After they drive off in a taxi for a depressing talk about the futility of their relationship, Brett meets up with Zizi and Count Mippipopolous for some serious drinking. Jake, pleading "a rotten headache" (p. 29), declines all further offers of alcohol and retires, he thinks, for the duration of the night. In the wee hours, however, Brett arrives "quite drunk" (p. 32) but wanting more, and Jake obligingly fetches the brandy and soda, only sipping his drink as Brett drains her first one and downs another. She invites him along for a champagne breakfast—the Count is waiting in the car with a dozen bottles of Mumms—but Jake has work to do later in the day, and he is "too far behind you now to catch up and be any fun" (p. 33). After Brett's departure, he pours his own glass, still half-full of brandy, down the sink before returning to bed (p. 34).

This gesture is extremely significant because it is one of the signs by which Hemingway means to indicate that Jake Barnes, unlike Brett Ashley or Bill Gorton or Mike Campbell or Harvey Stone, is *not* a drunk. Throughout the evening, despite his steady intake of alcohol, Jake's consumption has been carefully "controlled." He is never shown drinking compulsively; instead he drinks deliberately, evidently to blunt the pain of his (forever-to-be) unconsummated desire for Brett. Despite Jake's customary restraint, the pain breaks through on occasion—as in the passage where Jake's dull recital about his mail and the exact balance of his checking account leads him relentlessly (but unconsciously) to the very thoughts of Brett that concentration on such trivia is meant to forestall, and he cries out, bewildered by his mind's treachery, "To hell with Brett. To hell with you, Lady Ashley" (p. 30). "Not to think about it": this is the "swell advice" of the Catholic church about how to renounce what is forbidden (p. 31). Jake practices such mental discipline only imperfectly, and it seems that he must rely on alcohol at times for help.

If things get too intense, if Jake finds himself pushed beyond the limits of his endurance, *then* he self-consciously gets drunk. The first such occasion occurs in Pamplona, just before the fiesta begins, when the friction among Lady Ashley, Mike Campbell, and Robert Cohn threatens to flare up. From the permeating dis-ease, Jake takes refuge in an alcoholic fog: "It was like certain dinners I remember from the war. There was much wine, an ignored tension, and a feeling of things coming that you could not prevent happening. Under the wine I lost the disgusted feeling and was happy. It seemed they were all such nice people" (p. 146). This last impression, as Jake well knows, is an alcoholic illusion; and when he reaches his room in the Hotel Montoya, he recognizes that he is "quite drunk," so drunk that he does not wish to shut his eyes "because the room would go round and round" (p. 147).

Although the flow of alcohol never ceases during the fiesta, Jake gets drunk only once more: after he has pimped for Brett and sold out Romero. Understandably, this act of betrayal leaves Jake feeling "like hell" (p. 223); and neither wine nor brandy, the usual means to drunkenness in the novel, can numb the pain. Only absinthe will do.[15] As Bill urges him on, Jake downs one glass after another, all the while sulkily acting as if Bill were somehow responsible for his getting tight:

"Don't drink it fast that way. It will make you sick."
I set down the glass. I had not meant to drink it fast.
"I feel tight."
"You ought to."
"That's what you wanted, wasn't it?"
"Sure. Get tight. Get over your damn depression."
"Well, I'm tight. Is that what you want?"
"Sit down."
"I won't sit down," I said. "I'm going over to the hotel."
I was very drunk. I was drunker than I ever remembered having been.

(P. 223)

Such excessive drinking happens only at Jake's worst moments, and he soon recovers his alcoholic balance when he stops in Bayonne after the festival. At dinner there Jake orders a bottle of Château Margaux and finds it "pleasant to be drinking slowly and to be tasting the wine and to be drinking alone. A bottle of wine was good company" (p. 232–33). With coffee he samples the local liqueur, which looks like hair-oil and smells like *strega*, and then clears his palate with two glasses of *vieux marc*. Jake's serenity lingers as he travels on to San Sebastian, but he loses his equanimity again after he receives Brett's desperate telegram from Madrid.

As he hurries there to rescue her, Jake feels overwhelmed by the old despair, and he gets drunk intentionally for the third time in the novel. At a bar in Madrid, he gulps three quick martinis as he listens to Brett's fatuous intimations—"You know it makes one feel rather good deciding not to be a bitch" (p. 245)—and then he orders a second bottle of wine after lunch:

"Bung-o!" Brett said. I drank my glass and poured out another. Brett put her hand on my arm.
"Don't get drunk, Jake," she said. "You don't have to."
"How do you know?"
"Don't," she said. "You'll be all right."
"I'm not getting drunk," I said. "I'm just drinking a little wine."
"Don't get drunk," she said. "Jake, don't get drunk."   (P. 246)

Jake is certainly *not*, as he disingenuously puts it, merely "drinking a little wine." He is getting blind drunk out of disgust with Brett and with himself. Her reiterated pleas that he *not* get tight suggest her own state of intoxication as she tries to smooth things over, as always, with alcoholic sentiment. "Oh, Jake," she sighs at the end, "we could have had such a damned good time together." To which Jake replies, in perhaps the most famous retort in American literature, "Yes . . . Isn't it pretty to think so?" (p. 247). This time, Jake neither loses "the disgusted feeling," as he did in Pamplona, nor mistakes Brett for a "nice" person. With the cold eye of irony, Jake takes the measure of his own failure of discipline: if only he were stronger about Brett, he wouldn't need to lapse into excessive drinking.

Warren says of the Hemingway code that the "discipline of the soldier, the form of the athlete, the gameness of the sportsman, the technique of an artist can give some sense of the human order, and can achieve a moral significance." This ideal also governs the culture of drinking in *The Sun Also Rises*. What sets Jake apart from the other characters, most of whom are alcoholics, is adherence to self-discipline. Even in defeat, even when he falls short of the ideal, the Hemingway hero retains, as Warren says, "some definition of how a man should behave . . . some notion of a code, some notion of honor, that makes a man a man, and that distinguishes him from people who merely follow their random impulses and who are, by consequence, 'messy.' "[16] In his drinking, as in the rest of his life, Jake tries to display manly courage without ever becoming "messy." But when he does get drunk, as when he yields to Brett's seduction, Jake loses control of himself and thus dishonors the ideal of discipline. Despite his failures—and to some extent because of them—Jake's life still is accorded greater moral significance than the random lives of his drunken companions.

Hemingway uses drinking, that is, to establish a hierarchy of moral merit for his characters. In Jake's shorthand: "Mike was a bad drunk. Brett was a good drunk. Bill was a good drunk. Cohn was never drunk" (p. 148). To put it somewhat more elaborately: Mike is not only a bad drunk, but also a bad person; Brett is a good drunk but a bad person; Bill is a good drunk and a good person, but finally less good than Jake because his goodness is less severely tested; Robert is a congenital non-drinker, incapable of becoming either a good or a bad drunk, and therefore a non-person. That leaves Pedro Romero, a non-drinker by vocational choice, who is nonetheless vulnerable to the corrupting influence of alcohol.

Aside from Harvey Stone, a minor character who appears only long enough to be established as a hopeless rummy, Mike Campbell represents the extreme of alcoholic excess in *The Sun Also Rises*. Although he has recently tried to limit himself to "one drink a day with my mother at tea" (p. 78), Mike has fallen off the wagon long before his arrival in Paris. The explanation he offers for his bloodied nose is otherwise quite improbable: he was attacked on the train, he says, by a old lady's bags, when he helped her remove them from the overhead rack. At present, as Mike confesses, he is "a little tight, you know" (p. 78); and he remains more than a little tight throughout the novel. On his first morning after, he retains no memory of what Brett calls the "disgraceful business" of his drunken night before (p. 81).

Like Jake, Mike would seem to have an excellent excuse to drink: he is driven to it by Brett's flagrant and humiliating infidelity. "I think I'll *stay* rather drunk," he tells Jake. "This is all awfully amusing, but it's not too pleasant. It's not too pleasant for me" (p. 203). It is not, of course, any more pleasant for Jake. But whereas he gets drunk only as a last resort, Mike wallows in alcoholic misery. Hemingway forgives drunkenness if, as in Jake's case, it is an occasional deviation from sober self-discipline; he condemns drunkenness if, as in Mike's case, it reflects chronic self-indulgence. Take, for example, the scene in which Romero, who has been drawn to the expatriates' table, asks Jake about Mike:

> "What does the drunken one do?"
> "Nothing."
> "Is that why he drinks?"
> "No. He's waiting to marry this lady."
> "Tell him bulls have no balls!" Mike shouted, very drunk, from the other end of the table.
> "What does he say?"
> "He's drunk."
> "Jake," Mike called. "Tell him bulls have no balls!"
> "You understand?" I said.
> "Yes."
> I was sure he didn't, so it was all right. (P. 176)

What the reader is meant to understand is that Mike's belligerence is *not* all right, whatever the provocation from Brett.

Although Hemingway was a generation younger than Jack London, his understanding of habitual drunkenness derived from the Victorian idea of intemperance as a sign of moral failure and defective willpower. Hemingway never effaced the imprint of his upbringing by strictly dry parents; and despite his contempt for Prohibition, he still believed at a deep level that every drink contained at least a dash of demon rum. *The Sun Also Rises* may be awash in alcohol, but there is more than a hint of disapprobation—and even of moral revulsion—in Hemingway's treatment of drinking.

In accord with the Victorian view that individuals should be blamed for their excesses, Hemingway holds Mike Campbell as fully accountable for his inebriation as for his bankruptcy. The two are connected, in fact. As Brett reminds him, Mike was more than "a little tight" on the day he was dragged before his creditors in court: "Tight! . . . You were blind!" (p. 136). His reckless indifference to money may seem comic at times, but it becomes a very serious matter in the context of the culture of drinking. Near the end of the novel, after Brett has eloped with Romero, Mike accompanies Jake and Bill to Biarritz; and although he has finished a bottle of brandy en route, Mike needs to find a bar. The rules of treating apply as strictly in *The Sun Also Rises* as they do in *John Barleycorn;* and when Mike quickly volunteers to buy the first round, he probably expects to receive two free drinks thereafter. If so, he is thwarted when Bill wants to roll dice for the tab and Mike loses each gamble, leaving him too broke to pay for the final round.

The severity of this breach of drinking custom is plainly visible:

> Bill's face sort of changed.
> "I just had enough to pay Montoya. Damned lucky to have it, too."
> "I'll cash you a check," Bill said.
> "That's damned nice of you, but you see I can't write checks." (P. 229)

Mike is bankrupt, this incident reveals, in both a moral and a financial sense. His violation of the bar-room code shows the depths of irresponsibility to which drinking can lead. It is not, as Mike obnoxiously and erroneously insists, bulls who have no balls; it is rummies like Mike who are truly "unmanned."

In this sense, oddly enough, Mike Campbell figures as Robert Cohn's double. Mike, who viciously goads Robert throughout the festival, likens him to a steer:

> "You came down to San Sebastian where you weren't wanted, and followed Brett around like a bloody steer. Do you think that's right?"
>
> "Shut up. You're drunk."
>
> "Perhaps I am drunk. Why aren't you drunk? Why don't you ever get drunk, Robert? You know you didn't have a good time at San Sebastian because none of our friends would invite you to any of the parties. You can't blame them hardly. Can you?" (P. 142)

Cohn does not abstain completely, but his undersized capacity—and thus his lack of true manliness—is exposed when he passes out from little more than a whiff of Manis del Mono. The novel implies that Cohn the crypto-teetotaler is the negative image of Campbell the drunkard; neither understands the discipline of drinking, which precludes the extremes of too much or too little.

Not drinking is never acceptable and scarcely imaginable to Hemingway except for a man like Romero, who consciously chooses to abstain for the sake of his art. By contrast, Cohn the pseudo-artist can neither drink nor write like a man. Any success his work may have enjoyed is accountable, it seems, to the appalling taste of the same ignoramuses who, as tourists in Pamplona, underestimate Romero as they applaud the fraudulent pyrotechnics of the aging Belmonte.

Romero is the real thing for Hemingway: a paragon not only of youthful virility, but also of artistic and moral integrity. As many critics have said, the beauty and daring of Romero's work in the bull ring set a standard in which the esthetic and the ethical are sublimely conjoined.[17] Just as Hemingway uses drinking to gauge the deficiencies of Campbell and Cohn, he uses it also to suggest Romero's superiority to the decadent expatriates. "Tell me what drunks they [bullfighters] are," jokes Brett, as she spies him in the ring, "Oh, frightful," Mike answers, immediately alert to her attraction to the young man. "Drunk all day and spend all their time beating their poor old mothers"

(p. 168). That such a description seems so ludicrous is a testament to Romero's innocence and purity. But Romero is not immune to alcoholic excess, and Jake shamefully exploits this potential weakness when he acts as Brett's pimp.[18]

The full measure of Jake's treachery is taken when Montoya enters the bar room: "He started to smile at me, then he saw Pedro Romero with a big glass of cognac in his hand, sitting laughing between me and a woman with bare shoulders, at a table full of drunks. He did not even nod" (p. 177). A true aficionado would know that Romero has no business in such company; and Jake stands convicted in Montoya's eyes, even before his actual betrayal of Pedro to Brett, of abetting the young man's corruption through alcohol.[19] Montoya's worst fears are confirmed a few pages later when, after luring Romero to join him and Brett for a round of brandy, Jake artfully excuses himself. Later he reads the "success" of his mission in the "three empty cognac-glasses" that remain upon the now unoccupied table (p. 187).

It is a critical commonplace that Brett proves herself as unworthy of Romero as of Jake.[20] But Hemingway has rigged the novel against her, of course, by portraying her as a predatory nymphomaniac—and also a dipsomaniac. "She's a drunk," Jake bluntly warns Cohn the first time he sees her (p. 38).[21] The objectivity of this claim might be questioned: Jake could be putting the worst face on Brett in order to discourage a potential rival's interest in her. But there is plenty of confirmatory evidence.[22] Probably because of a blackout, she forgets her date with Jake at the Crillon. "I must have been blind," she explains, and Count Mippipopolous confirms that "You were quite drunk, my dear" (p. 54). On the way to Pamplona with Mike, she passes out on the train (p. 126). In Spain, as in France, Brett never strays very far from the liquor supply; and Mike, with the self-interested perspicacity of a fellow drunkard, anticipates her needs. Thus when Brett grows suddenly restless during the fireworks, Mike intuits that "Her ladyship wants a drink"—to which Brett replies, "How you know things" (p. 179).

The count knows things as well; he tells Brett, "You're always drinking, my dear" (p. 58). They are visiting Jake's apartment; and while the two men discuss the finer points of champagne—"I like to drink champagne from magnums," says the count, carefully drying a bottle—Brett squirms impatiently until he opens it.

It was amazing champagne.

"I say this is wine," Brett held up her glass. "We ought to toast something. 'Here's to royalty.'"

"This wine is too good for toast-drinking, my dear. You don't want to mix emotions up with a wine like that. You lose the taste."

Brett's glass was empty.

"You ought to write a book on wines, count," I said.

"Mr. Barnes," answered the count, "all I want out of wines is to enjoy them."

"Let's enjoy a little more of this." Brett pushed her glass forward. The count poured very carefully. "There, my dear. Now you enjoy that slowly, and then you can get drunk."

"Drunk? Drunk?"

"My dear, you are charming when you are drunk."

"Listen to the man."

"Mr. Barnes." The count poured my glass full. "She is the only lady I have ever known who was as charming when she was drunk as when she was sober." (P. 59)

Oblivious to what the men alone seem able to appreciate—"That is the secret," intones the count, "You must get to know the values" (p. 60)—Brett swills her champagne because she is incapable of savoring it. For Jake, as for Count Mippipopolous, knowing the values means knowing how to maximize pleasure without falling into hedonism: abundance without excess, getting your money's worth.[23]

As an alcoholic, Brett lacks a proper sense of values. Like Mike Campbell, for whom she is the fitting consort, she subscribes to an economy of excess; Brett is addicted both to alcohol and to sexual excitement. When she confesses her desire for Romero, she parries Jake's warnings by pleading helplessness before an overwhelming force:

"I'm a goner. I'm mad about the Romero boy. I'm in love with him, I think."

"I wouldn't be if I were you."

"I can't help it. I'm a goner. It's tearing me up inside."

"Don't do it."

"I can't help it. I've never been able to help anything."

"You ought to stop it." . . .

"I've got to do something. I've got to do something I really want to do. I've lost my self-respect." (P. 183)

Brett goes on to explain, as if drunkenness were the only imaginable alternative to uncontrollable passion, "I can't just stay tight all the time." Pleading the impossibility of self-control, Brett succeeds in enlisting Jake's help to do what she believes is inevitable: "I don't say it's right. It is right though for me" (p. 184).

Drunk or (rarely) sober, Lady Ashley is not simply charming; she is deviously enchanting—a sexually ambiguous Circe who leads men spellbound to their doom by means of an androgynous allure. Curvaceous as a racing hull, Brett also sports a man's hat over a boyish haircut; and although her sexual desire is shown to be exclusively and insistently heterosexual, she, like her name, might easily be (mis)taken as "mannish," especially when she is drinking. Brett might even be described as a feminized twin to Jack London's nemesis—as John Barleycorn in drag: Jane Barleycorn.

Whereas Hemingway, like London, genders drinking as a quintessentially "masculine" behavior, he associates drunkenness with the threat of gender uncertainty. The alcoholic for Hemingway is *not*, as for London, the manliest of men; rather, the male rummy is as unmanly as Brett is unwomanly. To a point, then, the culture of drinking in *The Sun Also Rises* serves, as it does in *John Barleycorn*, to promote homosocial bonding among men and to secure them from homosexuality. But just as the supreme artist, such as Romero, has no need of drink, so the strongest bonds between men are formed less by means of alcohol than in spite of it. Drinking as a proof of manhood is ultimately motivated for Hemingway by the power and presence of women beyond the charmed male circle. If there could ever be men without women, gender would be transcended. Left alone with each other in a state beyond gender, men would have no need of drink.

This idea is implicit in the novel's pastoral moment: the fishing trip to the

Irati River. In nearly all of the criticism on *The Sun Also Rises,* as Scott Donaldson notes, "the interlude at Burguete stands in idyllic counterpoint to the sophisticated pretentiousness of Paris and the destructive passions of Pamplona."[24] This contrast is established in part by a significant difference in the characters' drinking habits. Alcohol is no less prominent in the country than in the city, but drinking is more conducive to fraternity than to fractiousness.

In Pamplona, just before the trip to Burguete, Jake is upset to learn about Brett's tryst with Cohn in San Sebastian, and he is feeling "unforgivingly jealous" (p. 99). As Jake's best friend, Bill tries to soothe him by appealing to the joys of intoxication: "We're going trout-fishing in the Irati River, and we're going to get tight now at lunch on the wine of the country, and then take a swell bus ride" (p. 102). And, in fact, their mood becomes carefree aboard the bus, as the Basques introduce the Americans to the manly art of drinking wine from skins. The customs of alcoholic hospitality are universal, it seems; and when the bus makes a stop, the treating commences in the local *posada.* "Two of our Basques came in and insisted on buying a drink. So they bought a drink and then we bought a drink, and then they slapped us on the back and bought another drink. Then we bought, and then we all went out into the sunlight and the heat, and climbed back on top of the bus" (p. 106). This last detail is not incidental: here are men who can hold their wine without staggering around under the mid-day sun, whose reflexes remain sharp enough for climbing.

Whenever they are alone together, whether drinking or not, Bill and Jake always communicate in the bluff banter of alcoholic bonhomie. Bill has the role in this novel of the comic drunkard, whose wacky wit and good-natured antics spread boozy jollity all around.[25] Typical of Bill's drunken banter is the following exchange from the Parisian section of the novel: a routine—so stagy that it might have come from vaudeville—in which Jake plays straight man to Bill's clown:

> "Well," I said, "I hear you had a wonderful trip."
> "Wonderful," he said. "Budapest is absolutely wonderful."
> "How about Vienna?"
> "Not so good, Jake. Not so good. It seemed better than it was."
> "How do you mean?" I was getting glasses and a siphon.

"Tight, Jake. I was tight."

"That's strange. Better have a drink."

Bill rubbed his forehead. "Remarkable thing," he said. "Don't know how it happened. Suddenly it happened."

"Last long?"

"Four days, Jake. Lasted just four days."

"Where did you go?"

"Don't remember. Wrote you a post-card. Remember that perfectly."

(P. 70)

And so on (did you hear the one about the stuffed dogs?) for most of a chapter. By the end of the evening, however, after they have strolled for miles around Paris and dined quietly at Madame Lecomte's restaurant (which the loathsome tourists invade only in the daytime), the men have attained such ease in each other's company that even Bill, accustomed to blackouts and four-day benders, feels no need for another drink (pp. 77–78).

This same tranquility prevails when Jake and Bill arrive at the Irati. Immersion in natural harmony has a decidedly sobering effect on both of them. Not that they don't continue to drink or to use humor self-consciously as a shield against emotional "messiness." But things are said over coffee that would be unspeakable in New York and unutterable even in Paris, except under the heavy influence of alcohol. At breakfast, Bill twits Jake for being one of those sex-crazed expatriates who, according to the papers back home, never work and drink themselves to death. Comic momentum carries Bill into a questionable joke—about impotence—that might have hurt Jake's feelings under different circumstances. But Jake is so serene as he contemplates a day of trout fishing with Bill that he overlooks the gaffe and keeps the mood light.

The affectionate chaff resumes when Jake and Bill reach the river, but they also touch on serious and personal matters, such as Jake's "technical" Catholicism and his despair over Brett. Throughout this scene the drinking remains notably moderate. Only two bottles of wine have been chilling in the river; and although Jake accuses Bill of being "cock-eyed" on wine, their normal consumption is such that neither could get drunk on a single bottle. Indeed, Bill complains about the limited supply of booze, hinting that Jake is in cahoots with the Anti-Saloon League. It seems ironic that their moment of deepest intimacy comes when Bill and Jake are nearly as sober as Wayne Wheeler himself. But Hemingway suggests that a higher order or brotherhood exists beyond the boon fellowship of the bottle; this higher order is, in fact, conspicuous for its sobriety.

During the idyll at Burguete, Jake and Bill take in a third partner: Wilson-Harris, who ties his own flies and knows how to "utilize" the local vintage. The three men are soon sharing a companionship so delightful that the Englishman gets "a little tight" and more than a little messy at the end of their "jolly good time" (p. 129). This generally hard-boiled novel has a soft spot for male bonding, and the episode with Wilson-Harris is markedly sentimental. Its purpose is apparently to show how dyadic male intimacy may become more inclusive. This manly trio prefigures the quasi-monastic brotherhood of aficionados described a few pages later, in which Jake, Montoya, Romero, and all true lovers of manly sport are joined in a homosocial union that takes expression in the slightly embarrassed laying of hands on shoulders: "But nearly always there was the actual touching. It seemed as though they wanted to touch you to make it certain" (p. 132).

As Arnold and Cathy Davidson suggest, "the whole ethos of *afición* resembles a sublimation of sexual desire."[26] Displaced in the intense preoccupation with bulls and bullfighters is a passion otherwise inadmissible to the minds of men who insist on defining their manhood heterosexually, who place "man" in binary opposition to "faggot." Yet homoeroticism suffuses the passage in which Jake and Montoya rediscover the warmth of their old intimacy. This becomes more obvious if, as in the following passage, blanks are strategically substituted for "bull-fighting" in the first sentence and thereafter for "aficionado":

> He always smiled as though [. . .] were a very special secret between the two of us; a rather shocking but really very deep secret that we knew about. He always smiled as though there were something lewd about the secret to outsiders, but that it was something that we understood. It would not do to expose it to people who would not understand.
>
> "Your friend, is he [. . .], too?" Montoya smiled at Bill.
>
> "Yes. He came all the way from New York to see the San Fermines."

"Yes?" Montoya politely disbelieved. "But he's not [. . .] like you."
He put his hand on my shoulder again embarrassedly.
"Yes," I said. "He's a real [. . .]."
"But he's not [. . .] like you are."   (P. 131)

Is Bill also privy to the "very special secret," the "very deep secret" shared by Jake and Montoya? Does it seem "lewd" to him? Does he *really* understand?

Bill may not be an aficionado, but he certainly stands closer to Jake than does any other male character in the novel. At Burguete, when Bill inadvertently mentions impotence and Jake refuses to take offense, Bill's admiration for his friend's aplomb inspires him to tell Jake how much he loves him. Needless to say, he doesn't put it that way. Such a declaration carries so high an emotional charge that it must be thickly wrapped in insulating humor.

> "And you're a hell of a good guy. Anybody ever tell you you were a good guy?"
> "I'm not a good guy."
> "Listen. You're a hell of a good guy, and I'm fonder of you than anybody on earth. I couldn't tell you that in New York. It'd mean I was a faggot. That was what the Civil War was about. Abraham Lincoln was a faggot. He was in love with General Grant. So was Jefferson Davis. Lincoln just freed the slaves on a bet. The Dred Scott case was framed by the Anti-Saloon League. Sex explains it all. The Colonel's Lady and Judy O'Grady are Lesbians under their skin."   (P. 116)

Both the depth of Bill's feelings for another man and, implicitly, the intensity of his fear of them are suggested by nonsense so extreme that it becomes desperate, burlesque so exaggerated that it becomes grotesque.[27] The rhetoric of manly love lays bare an underlying dread of otherness that conflates women with homosexuals (both male and female) and freed slaves, and that produces a virulently "virile" cocktail of misogyny, homophobia, and racism. For Bill, playing off the same Kipling lines that London cites, all women, regardless of class, are not merely sisters under their skins; they are lesbians—and, therefore, not "real" women at all.

Within the homophobic logic of the novel, the only thing apparently more dreadful than male homosexuality is female homosexuality; both threaten the code of discipline and its proscription of excess. There is, nevertheless, a recurrent pattern in Hemingway's fiction of unisex haircuts, sexual experimentation, and gender switching that points to what Mark Spilka calls "androgynous predilections." These predilections, especially prominent in the unedited manuscript version of the aborted late novel, *The Garden of Eden,* suggest that "androgyny" was both a "wounding" and a "bedeviling" condition for Hemingway. He imagined, says Spilka, "the secret muse within himself first as a devilish woman, inclined toward role reversals, lesbianism, and *ménages à trois,* whose degrading hold upon his passions and affections stirred him to manly resistance, then as a supportive woman who encouraged his recovery."[28]

In *The Sun Also Rises,* male homoeroticism has an unexpectedly "feminine" dimension. In decoding Mike Campbell's anatomically incorrect insistence that "bulls have no balls," the Davidsons claim that "Mike's body taunt readily translates, 'bulls *are* balls, cojones.' And so, as Mike also realizes full well, are bullfighters." When Mike shouts, "Tell him Brett is dying to know how he can get into those pants," (p. 176), he means, of course, "that she is dying to know how she can."[29] But Mike's taunt may be taken more literally to suggest that some bulls do *not* have balls and yet remain bulls (as opposed to steers), that cojones are not strictly necessary for manhood. Some critics have seen Jake Barnes, with his genital lack, to be a "steer" like Cohn, a man without virility. But, as Spilka recognizes, Jake is less a steer than a bullish sort of cow: a man who, identifying himself with lesbians rather than male homosexuals, desires Brett "in a womanly way." "What if Brett," Spilka asks, "is the woman Jake would in some sense like to be?"[30]

As Jake's androgynous double, Brett represents not only the woman he would in some sense like to be, but also the "unmanned" alcoholic he may very well become if he continues to relax the control of his drinking that the manly code requires. For although the booze flows freely in this novel, it nonetheless exhibits Hemingway's moral aversion to the excessivism of drunkards and teetotalers alike. Far more than his later works, *The Sun Also Rises* shows a healthy respect for alcohol's power and a healthy-minded skepticism of the alcoholic cult of nada.

In his own comments on the novel, provoked by reviews he considered obtuse, Hemingway stressed its tragic theme and moral vision. He told Fitzgerald in 1926: "It is so obviously *not* a collection of instructive anecdotes and is such a hell of a sad story—and not one at all for a child to read—and the only instruction is how people go to hell. . . ."[31] Hemingway was indicting the expatriates. As Michael S. Reynolds observes, "*The Sun Also Rises* is a study in moral failure, a jaded world of unemployed and irresponsible characters who drink too much—a fable of ideological bankruptcy." Reynolds, unlike critics who assume Jake's superiority to the others, includes him in the indictment: "Jake Barnes, who sees through the foolish aspects clearly enough, appears to himself, by the novel's end, just as foolish as the Latin Quarter crowd he despises."[32]

It might be argued that Barnes is not merely just as foolish as the rest, but just as drunken, too. Jake's "controlled" consumption could be seen as the familiar alcoholic strategy, used by Hemingway himself, of contrastive concealment—by which an alcoholic keeps company with even worse drunks in order to appear relatively "sober" and thus to prove the absence of any drinking problem. Whether or not Jake goes to hell with the Latin Quarter crowd, whether or not he truly qualifies as a drunk, *The Sun Also Rises* remains notably resistant to The Modern Temper.

In her revised version of Robert McAlmon's *Being Geniuses Together*, Kay Boyle reports an incident from the late 1920s, when Harry Crosby, the fast-living founder of the Black Sun Press, tested out a new cocktail on McAlmon, whose drinking reputation was unsurpassed among the expatriates. Although Crosby's elixir was "intended to send Bob into poetic delirium for the next twenty-four hours," he was inspired only to unleash a barrage of self-vituperation. "The God-damned, fucking, quivering pieces of me!" he screamed savagely at Boyle. "Good enough to be flushed like you know what down the drain! Stinking enough to be tacked on the barn door in warning to the young!" This outburst climaxes Boyle's treatment of McAlmon as the Lost Generation's exemplary alcoholic: a man who desperately tried to drown his "violent dissatisfaction" with himself.[33]

Elsewhere in *Being Geniuses Together*, McAlmon recalls sardonically that William Carlos Williams once ascribed to him a "genius for life": "If absolute despair, a capacity for reckless abandon and drink, long and heavy spells of ennui which require bottles of strong drink to cure, and a gregarious but not altogether loving nature is 'a genius for life,' then I have it." Boyle juxtaposes this gloomy passage to a joyous account, quoted from Williams's *Autobiography*, of the poet's youthful zeal for his artistic vocation: "My furious wish was to be normal, undrunk, balanced in everything. . . . I would not court disease, live in the slums for the sake of art, give lice a holiday. I would not 'die for art,' but live for it, grimly! and work, work, work . . . and be free . . . to write, write, as I alone should write, for the sheer drunkenness of it. . . ."[34] Whereas McAlmon voices the bleak nihilism of the White Logic, Williams invokes the transcendental ebullience of the natural high—what Emily Dickinson, echoing Emerson, celebrated as the imaginative intoxication of "a liquor never brewed": "Inebriate of Air—am I— / And Debauchee of Dew—"[35]

Hemingway may later have preferred brandy to air and absinthe to dew. But early in his career, before drinking had done him too much harm, he was still closer to Dickinson and Williams than to McAlmon, his erstwhile companion at Pamplona and Burguete, with whom he was ultimately to share an alcoholic's fate.[36] Despite its reputation as Hemingway's celebration of drinking, *The Sun Also Rises* subtly affirms sobriety as a means to the sheer drunkenness of the writer's art.

4

The Drunkard's Holiday:
Tender Is the Night

In a 1933 letter to his editor, Maxwell Perkins, F. Scott Fitzgerald confided that he was going on the wagon: "but don't tell Ernest because he has long convinced himself that I am an incurable alcoholic due to the fact that we almost always meet on parties. I am *his* alcoholic just like Ring is mine and do not want to disillusion him, tho even *Post* stories must be done in a state of sobriety."[1] Hemingway cast Fitzgerald, as Fitzgerald in turn cast Ring Lardner, in the role of rummy's rummy—someone whose drinking problem is perversely reassuring to a fellow alcoholic for as long as it seems worse than his own. In *A Moveable Feast,* where Hemingway settled scores with friends and acquaintances from the 1920s, Fitzgerald figures prominently as "poor Scott," a pathetic example of great talent drowned in the bottle. Hemingway recalls an auto trip in 1925, during which the hypochondriacal Fitzgerald, who was drunk much of the time, convinced himself that he was dying. "He did have a point though, and I knew it very well. Most drunkards in those days died of pneumonia, a disease which has now been almost eliminated. But it was hard to accept him as a drunkard, since he was affected by such small quantities of alcohol."[2]

Fitzgerald's fabled small capacity—which links him to the godfather of American literary drunks, Edgar Allan Poe, who also supposedly got plastered on minute quantities of alcohol—is one of many legends that surround his drinking. It may even be true, as several biographers have asserted, that Fitzgerald had an unusually low tolerance for alcohol. But during the period before his crack-up, when he tried to control his intake by switching from gin to beer, "his consumption of beer was so gargantuan (estimated by a friend to have reached a high of thirty-seven bottles in one day) that it led directly to his hospitalization in September 1935."[3] It is possible that Fitzgerald cultivated the public impression that he could not hold his liquor in order to foster the private belief, in himself and others such as Hemingway, that he was not really a drunkard.[4] Fitzgerald's alcoholism was never finally in doubt, however, except to Fitzgerald himself.

Whereas the London cult and the Hemingway industry have often ignored, evaded, or flatly denied the alcoholism of these writers, scholars of Fitzgerald have faced the issue squarely, and they have already produced several excellent studies of his drinking and its effects.[5] It would be superfluous, then, to rehearse the twice-told tale of Fitzgerald's drinking career except in its barest outline. Although it cannot be determined exactly when he became an alcoholic, it was definitely no later than the mid-1920s, about the time when he was writing *The Great Gatsby* (1925), and probably earlier. From its beginning, the marriage of Scott and Zelda Fitzgerald was saturated with booze, and drinking was a major cause of its failure. By the time of Zelda's first breakdown in 1930, a collapse in which her own drunkenness was a factor, Scott could also have benefitted from treatment. But whenever the subject of Scott's drinking arose in his dealings with Zelda, who pressed him to acknowledge how *his* behavior had wrecked their marriage, he became fiercely defensive. In a letter to Oscar Forel, Zelda's Swiss psychiatrist, Fitzgerald insisted that alcohol was essential to his health and, furthermore, that he would not relinquish the inalienable right to drink:

> To stop drinking entirely for six months and see what happens, even to continue the experiment thereafter if successful—only a pig would refuse to do that. Give up strong drink permanently I will. Bind myself to forswear

wine forever I cannot. My vision of the world at its brightest is such that life without the use of its amenities is impossible. I have lived hard and ruined the essential innocene [sic] in myself that could make it that possible [sic], *and the fact that I have abused liquor* is something *to be paid for with suffering and death perhaps but not with renunciation.* For me *it would be as illogical as permanently giving up sex because I caught a disease* (which I hasten to assure you I never have)[.] I cannot consider one pint of wine at the days [sic] end as anything but one of the rights of man.[6]

As Zelda moved in and out of mental institutions, Scott exercised his rights so freely that he was obliged to enter the hospital several times for detoxification; and he came to rely on medical intervention, sometimes in the form of resident nurses, to regulate his consumption and obtain physical relief between binges. During his last four years, spent mainly in Hollywood, Fitzgerald did curtail his drinking in order to protect his screenwriting job and his relationship with Sheilah Graham. He apparently endured weeks and perhaps months of abstinence, but he never achieved sustained sobriety.[7] To the end of a life abridged by drinking, paid for in full with suffering and death, Fitzgerald clung to the hope that he still might prevail alone over alcohol.

So central to Fitzgerald's life, drinking was central to his work as well. "From the beginning it was a subject he liked to write about," Scott Donaldson notes. "There are drunks or drinking bouts in all his novels, just as there had been one in *A Regular Fix,* the first of the Elizabethan dramatic club plays he wrote and participated in as a St. Paul teen-ager."[8] From "Shadow Laurels" (1915), the first story Fitzgerald published in *The Nassau Literary Magazine* at Princeton, to the Pat Hobby stories that he was grinding out for *Esquire* at the end of his career, his short fiction also focused often on alcoholic characters.

The most significant of Fitzgerald's fictions about drinking is *Tender Is the Night* (1934), the locus classicus of American drunk narratives, in which a drunkard's tragic downfall is played out against a backdrop of Spenglerian cultural decline. Dick Diver's alcoholism reflected that of his author, whose own life was falling apart during the nine years he struggled to finish the novel, which at one point in its evolution was titled "The Drunkard's Holiday." "It is apparent," as Tom Dardis says, "that Fitzgerald, by using alcohol as both cause *and* effect in the creation of Diver's malaise, was drawing a parallel between his fictional couple and Zelda and himself." Although he does not emphasize Diver's drinking until late in the novel, he nevertheless "permits us to observe that nearly all of Dick's troubles—professional and marital—have alcohol behind them."[9]

Against such assertions Diver might have argued, as Fitzgerald himself once testily remarked, "The assumption that all my troubles are due to drink is a little too easy."[10] This point is well taken for one critic:

> If, as seems incontestable, F. Scott Fitzgerald was an alcoholic and not merely a drunk, what exactly does acceptance of this fact mean for his life, his work, and his literary reputation? We know that alcoholism made Fitzgerald's days hellish and clearly brought about his early death. Yet one mustn't push this too far. Certainly Fitzgerald's alcoholism cannot—ought not—be pressed into service to shoulder all the blame for his downfall. . . . Until some of the basic questions about alcoholism are answered, one cannot know for sure whether, in Fitzgerald's case, the disease was solely to blame or whether it was a combination of the disease and his own weakness of character that brought him down.[11]

This passage exposes an underlying confusion that also characterized Fitzgerald's understanding of his drinking. In accord with the modern paradigm that emerged in the 1930s and became predominant in the second half of the twentieth century, Julie M. Irwin assumes that alcoholism is a "disease." But she is uneasy with the disease concept to the extent that its determinism would lift all moral responsibility from the alcoholic's shoulders. In her proscription about what "ought not" to be done by critics with the disease model, and in her references to "blame" and "weakness of character," Irwin betrays a residual adherence to the Victorian paradigm of intemperance that accounts for her otherwise puzzling distinction between Fitzgerald's being "an alcoholic" and his being "merely a drunk."

Or "drunkard"? This old-fashioned term is relevant because Fitzgerald, despite what he learned about the "disease" of alcoholism from Zelda's psychiatrists, never completely cast off the Victorian influences of his youth. Like

London and Hemingway, Fitzgerald was suspended between Victorian and modern understandings in a way that produced a peculiar ambivalence about drinking. "Drunkard" and "alcoholic" were not interchangeable terms; he perceived a subtle difference between them. Fitzgerald was repelled by "intemperance" at the same time that he was strangely attracted to "alcoholism"; whereas the former was stigmatized as a vice, the latter was distinguished (in both senses) as a sign of the modern.

No writer of his generation was more finely attuned than Fitzgerald to the hum and buzz of manners; he realized that there was a new "feel" to drunkenness, especially for the young, during the Prohibition era. Although it is misleading to regard Fitzgerald as a symbol of the Roaring Twenties, a philosopher of flivvers and flappers, he did embody and express the singular relationship to alcohol of a generation that defined itself chiefly through illicit and fashionably excessive drinking. As he recalled in "My Lost City" (New York), "Many people who were not alcoholics were lit up four days out of seven, and frayed nerves were strewn everywhere; groups were held together by a generic nervousness and the hangover became a part of the day as well allowed-for as the Spanish siesta. Most of my friends drank too much—the more they were in tune to the times the more they drank."[12]

In his twenties, when he liked to shock people by introducing himself as "one of the most notorious drinkers of the younger generation" or as "F. Scott Fitzgerald, the well-known alcoholic,"[13] he once affected an air of dissipated ennui for the benefit of Maxwell Perkins: "I should like to sit down with 1/2 dozen chosen companions and drink myself to death but I am sick alike of life, liquor and literature." Seventeen years later, in 1938, having gone some distance toward drinking himself to death, a soberer Fitzgerald reported to Perkins that, aside from a single three-day binge, he had been dry for over a year. "Isn't it awful," he now complained, "that we reformed alcoholics have to preface everything by explaining exactly how we stand on that question?"[14] Being a "reformed alcoholic" was finally as much of a pose for Fitzgerald as being a "well-known alcoholic." One role was the mirror image of the other, and both were part of Fitzgerald's formation of his identity as a writer around drinking. The romantic readiness of his "vision of the world at its brightest" depended as much on intoxication as did his disillusionment at the ruination of "essential innocence." Although it *would* be reductive to use alcoholism either as a single-cause explanation for Fitzgerald's life or as a skeleton key to his work, drinking was undoubtedly the efficient cause of his decline, and it had complex literary consequences.

It is easy, for example, to read the alcohol-related fiction too literally, as if it were uncomplicated by Fitzgerald's need to excuse his drinking at the same time as he pretended to face up to it. Of the story "Family in the Wind" (1932), Kenneth E. Eble shrewdly observes, "As a piece of fiction, it is marred by the author's excessive sympathy for the alcoholic central character and by elaborations of plot which evade a simpler, more painful, examination of that character. Something of the same can be said of other short fiction in which drinking figures prominently."[15] Thomas B. Gilmore makes a similar point, arguing that after the early 1920s, Fitzgerald "apparently found it too painful to write a full and honest portrait of a heavy or alcoholic drinker; except for two or three of the shortest portraits, there are always signs of evasion, of a desire to mitigate the harsh ugliness of alcoholism." Fitzgerald's most honest depiction of alcoholism is to be found not in the seemingly explicit later stories, which are, in fact, distorted by denial, but in *The Beautiful and Damned* (1922), written when he was still "willing and able to examine drinking with something close to unflinching honesty."[16]

That alcoholic denial made a liar of Fitzgerald and compromised his writing with dishonesty may be seen clearly in his notorious *Esquire* essays, "The Crack-Up" (1935), which appeared a year after *Tender Is the Night*. Contrasting his own case to that of William Seabrook, who had published a bestselling book about his treatment for alcoholism, Fitzgerald contends that his own collapse had nothing whatsoever to do with drink, since he had "at the time not tasted so much as a glass of beer for six months."[17]

This was flatly untrue.[18] During the preceding months, Fitzgerald had been drinking beer at a prodigious rate, and the profound depression that he described so powerfully in "The Crack-Up" was inextricably intertwined with his alcoholism, if not entirely caused by it. These essays serve, as Donaldson says, to rationalize Fitzgerald's breakdown by placing blame "not within himself but elsewhere: the deficient genes he was bequeathed, the contemporary climate of materialism and insincerity, the growth of motion pictures that threatened to put fiction writers out of business."[19]

That "The Crack-Up" is more of an apologia than a confession is an opinion shared by Alfred Kazin, who questions the integrity of Fitzgerald's motives and the candor of his self-revelations. Kazin asks why "The Crack-Up," for all of its "vivid painfulness," leaves him so unmoved. In reading these essays, he argues, the reader suspects that "something is being persistently withheld, that the author is somehow offering us certain facts in exchange for the right to keep others to himself. It is as if he were playing with his own tragedy; which does not make the tragedy less deep." Fitzgerald uses his gossamer prose style to interpose "a subtly diffusing eloquence between the emotion and the fact."[20]

The gap between emotion and fact, between revelation and concealment, between self-honesty and self-deceit—this is one good way of describing "denial": the mind's magical disappearing act, in which rabbits are stuffed back into hats in plain sight of the audience. In Fitzgerald's writing, however, what is denied remains present in its absence. As Kazin remarks, "It was in the very nature of Fitzgerald's mind to sculpt the contours of experience in such a way that the light falling on them, from his own ready charm and vivid perceptions, would suggest some content they did not represent."[21] Alcoholism is the content that lies hidden at the center of Fitzgerald's work. The reader senses its contours under the concealing drapery of his revealing art.

Throughout Fitzgerald's life and work, as Marty Roth observes, a curious paradox about drinking persists: it is everywhere and yet nowhere, manifest and yet invisible. In *The Great Gatsby*, for instance, there is "a great deal of drinking and much drunken behavior," but the voluminous criticism on the novel is virtually silent about these matters. This critical silence strikes Roth as "equivalent to both the social and medical invisibility of alcoholism." Drinking "is there but nobody sees it, or, if it is there to be seen, it is not connected to anything else." Thus in the first scene of *The Great Gatsby*, "the drinks are not seen attached to anyone: the four cocktails are 'just in from the pantry' as if on their own. . . . And earlier Nick had written that '[a] tray of cocktails floated at us through the twilight.' "[22]

Tender Is the Night, even more than *The Great Gatsby*, shows how denial within a literary text may be rendered invisible by the secondary denial of literary criticism. From the time of its publication in 1934, *Tender Is the Night* has often been faulted for its treatment of Dick Diver's downfall. Matthew J. Bruccoli reports that fully a third of twenty-four original reviews criticized "the credibility of Dick Diver or the convincingness of his crack-up," and he notes that "there continues to be a strong body of opinion that he is not a credible figure and that his collapse seems unconvincing or insufficiently documented."[23] Malcolm Cowley explains, in an exemplary statement of this view:

> Dick fades like a friend who is withdrawing into a private world or sinking to another level of society and, in spite of knowing so much about him, we are never quite certain of the reasons for his decline. Perhaps, as Fitzgerald first planned, it was the standards of the leisure class that corrupted him; perhaps it was the strain of curing a psychotic wife, who gains strength as he loses it by a mysterious transfer of vitality; perhaps it was a form of emotional exhaustion, a giving of himself so generously that he went beyond his resources . . . or perhaps it was something far back in his childhood that could only be discovered by deep analysis—we can argue about the causes as we can argue about the decline of a once-intimate friend, without coming to any fixed conclusion. . . .[24]

To such speculation about the reasons for Dick's degeneration, one very reasonable response might be, as Roth succinctly puts it, "Since the book is the story of a chronic alcoholic, I wonder why alcoholism is not perceived as a more than adequate cause."[25] Once it is recognized that the inner logic of Diver's character derives from his alcoholism, interpretative difficulties seem to melt away. With rare exceptions, however, any such recognition has eluded the critics.[26] How can it be that resourceful readers have repeatedly failed to grasp something so plain?

The mystery of alcoholism in *Tender Is the Night* may be compared to that of the bathroom incident at the Villa Diana. Whatever Violet McKisco witnesses there—something to do with Nicole Diver—is so alarming and so potentially damaging that Tommy Barban fights a duel to protect Nicole's honor. But the secret is withheld until the end of Book One, when the reader becomes a material witness to Nicole's mental breakdown in a Parisian hotel. The purpose of the narrative suspense is to redouble the shock of this second bathroom incident. Along with the naive Rosemary Hoyt, we suddenly understand that chaos yawns beneath the beautifully composed surface of the Divers's world, that their marriage is as fragile as Nicole's sanity.

The secret of Dick's drinking problem is similarly withheld. Although there are a few hints of his vulnerability to alcohol, it does not cause him any obvious trouble until the end of Book Two, when he gets so drunk and disorderly in Rome that Baby Warren must bribe the police to free him from jail. Although Nicole's Parisian crack-up and Dick's Roman binge are structurally parallel scenes—the climaxes, respectively, of Book One and of Book Two—the second lacks the epiphanic power of the first because Fitzgerald does not give Dick's drinking as much thematic importance as Nicole's madness.

As in the arguments between Zelda and Scott Fitzgerald, to which various psychiatrists became active third parties after 1930, there is an underlying conflict in *Tender Is the Night* about whether the wife's schizophrenia or the husband's alcoholism is the root cause and/or explanation of their marital disasters. The novel is clearly biased in favor of the idea that the pernicious effects of Nicole's insanity—as well as her recovery into a monstrous kind of sanity—far outweigh whatever damage might be attributed to Dick's excessive drinking. For Fitzgerald, this was *not* "the story of a chronic alcoholic," but rather the story of a crazed and ruthless woman who first drives her husband to drink and then blames his drinking for her own failures.

For most critics of *Tender Is the Night*, alcoholism does not seem an adequate cause for Diver's deterioration because the novel simultaneously displays and covers up its significance. In this respect, the most perceptive early reviewer was D. W. Harding, who, like Kazin in his wary response to "The Crack-Up," sensed that there is "an emotional trick being played" on readers of *Tender Is the Night:* they are "trapped into incompatible attitudes towards the same events." The trap springs from the doubleness of Fitzgerald's characterization. Dick is presented as "the tragic fantasy hero who is so great and fine that everyone else expects to go on taking and taking from him and never give back; and so he gets tired, so tired; and he breaks under the strain with no one big enough to help him, and it's terribly pathetic and admirable." What's vital to Fitzgerald is that Diver "should remain admirable and (posthumously) win everyone's remorseful respect." But this is a "childish fantasy," one so egregiously sentimental that Fitzgerald must temper it with "a much more mature bit of knowledge: that people who disintegrate in the adult world don't at all win our respect and can hardly retain even our pity." A "harrowing," rather than "tragic," effect is achieved by Fitzgerald's "inviting our hearts to go out to the hero of the childish fantasy and then checking them with the embarrassment which everyone nearest him in the story, especially Nicole his wife, feels for the failure."[27]

Although Harding himself overlooks the pertinence of Diver's alcoholism to this incisive analysis, he nonetheless elucidates how denial in *Tender Is the Night* works through Fitzgerald's ambivalent identification with Diver—his narrative oscillation between sentimentality and tough-mindedness, self-pity and self-disgust. Fitzgerald was more distressed by the "attacks on the verisimilitude of Dick's decline" than by anything else in the reviews, Bruccoli says, because he "resented the implication that he had been clumsy and that he had lost control of his material." Bristling at what he takes to be unfair objections, Bruccoli insists that Dick's fate is rooted deeply in his character and his romantic view of life: "To say that the reader is not prepared for Dick's crackup is absurd. *Tender Is the Night* does not resemble an unmotivated operetta in which the prince suddenly dies on the eve of his elopement with the commoner."[28] As Harding perceives, however, the novel *does* resemble a soap-operatic melodrama insofar as its impact depends on our seeing Dick Diver as a prince—and thus on an unearned increment of sympathy for this character that seems ultimately to derive from Fitzgerald's alcoholic self-pity. During the prolonged gestation of the novel, Fitzgerald clearly did lose control of both his life and his fiction.

The writing of *Tender Is the Night* dragged on for years as he cadged advances from Scribner's, begged loans from his agent, and concocted potboilers for the *Saturday Evening Post* and the other slicks. It was only in 1932, after six years and as many aborted drafts, that something resembling the published text finally began to come into focus. In Fitzgerald's preliminary sketches for what he was now calling "The Drunkard's Holiday," the main character's drinking received more emphasis than it would in the finished novel. "Show a man who is a natural idealist, a spoiled priest," Fitzgerald wrote in his General Plan, "giving in for various causes to the ideas of the haute Burgeoise [sic], and in his rise to the top of the social world losing his idealism, his talent and turning to drink and dissipation." Later in the outline he added that this character has "taken to drink a little" during the war and that "it continues as secret drinking after his marriage." Secret drinking has opened into "another life of his own which his wife does not suspect, or at least he thinks she doesn't." This double life, created initially to conceal the drinking, comes to include adulterous affairs initiated under the influence of alcohol. The major theme of "The Drunkard's Holiday" was to be "the break up of a fine personality" as the result of "really tragic forces such as the inner conflicts of the idealist and the compromises forced upon him by circumstances."[29] The hero's turn to "drink and dissipation," that is, was envisioned as an *effect* of his downfall. He drinks because he is in decline; he does not decline because he drinks.

In its published form, *Tender Is the Night* is less clear on this point than was Fitzgerald's preliminary plan. On the one hand, the novel offers numerous reasons other than alcoholism for Dick's deterioration; on the other, it subtly reveals the self-destructiveness of Dick's drinking. But most readers have been distracted from the evidence that Diver declines *because* he drinks by the excuses Fitzgerald provides for the drinking—excuses that are inseparable from the Spenglerian ethos of the novel. Typical of the critical response are the remarks of Arthur Mizener, Fitzgerald's first biographer:

> This change occurs very deep in his [Dick's] nature. Fitzgerald is careful to prevent the reader from thinking it is some change controllable by the will, some drift into dissipation or the idleness of the rich. Dick does begin to drift in these ways, but that is only a symptom of his trouble, a desperate search for something to fill the time and stave off boredom after the meaning and purpose have gone out of his life. What destroys Dick is something far more obscure and difficult to grasp, some spiritual malaise that is anterior to any rational cause and is—as has become much plainer since Fitzgerald noticed it—as widespread among sensitive people in our time as was accidie in the middle ages or melancholia, the "Elizabethan malady," in Shakespeare's.[30]

This "spiritual malaise," which is allegedly epidemic among "sensitive people" most in touch with the zeitgeist—that is, elite intellectuals and artists whose outlook and values have been molded by modernism—is recognizable as the White Logic of The Modern Temper. Something like this mental and emotional posture was once described by Robert Penn Warren, in regard to *A*

Farewell to Arms (1929), as "the great romantic alibi for a generation, and for those who aped and emulated that generation." As much as Hemingway, in Warren's view, Fitzgerald shows "how cynicism or disillusionment, failure of spirit or the worship of material success, debauchery or despair, might have been grounded in heroism, simplicity, and fidelity that had met unmerited defeat."[31]

The characteristic modernist note of romantic disillusionment is struck in one of the few passages in *Tender Is the Night* that directly concerns drinking. Rosemary Hoyt wonders why Abe North gets drunk so often:

> "What did this to him?" she asked. "Why does he have to drink?"
>
> Nicole shook her head right and left, disclaiming responsibility for the matter: "So many men go to pieces nowadays."
>
> "And when haven't they?" Dick asked. "Smart men play close to the line because they have to—some of them can't stand it, so they quit."
>
> "It must lie deeper than that." Nicole clung to her conservatism; also she was irritated that Dick should contradict her before Rosemary. "Artists like—well, like Fernand don't seem to have to wallow in alcohol. Why is it just Americans who dissipate?"
>
> There were so many answers to this question that Dick decided to leave it in the air, to buzz victoriously in Nicole's ears. He had become intensely critical of her.[32]

Nicole's probing question and its many answers are left to float permanently in the air. In this passage, as throughout the novel, attention is diverted from drinking to the Divers's marriage and its psychodynamics. Even in Book Three, where Dick's alcoholism becomes too obtrusive to be ignored easily, his actual drinking is seen to be less disturbing than Nicole's symbolic drinking: her vampirish consumption of Dick's spirit(s) as he is drained to the lees by her "dry suckling at his lean chest" (p. 359).

Just as Fitzgerald leaves unanswered the question of why Americans dissipate, he leaves unchallenged the idea of alcoholism as a courageous response to the Decline of the West. Earlier, in the scene at the Paris train station, Nicole, Rosemary, and Abe's wife, Mary North, stand with him in "an uncomfortable little group weighted down by Abe's gigantic presence: he lay athwart them like the wreck of a galleon, dominating with his presence his own weakness and self-indulgence, his narrowness and bitterness" (p. 108). Like the galleon, a formidable but militarily obsolete vessel, the drunken North signifies the simpler European past that was wrecked on the western front—the "beautiful lovely safe world" that, as Dick muses on the battlefield outside Paris, "blew itself up here with a great gust of high explosive love" (p. 75). In this context, Abe's annihilation by booze resembles death in battle during the Great War. If the alcoholic is a modernist martyr, then alcoholism itself becomes nothing less than the moral equivalent of war!

No wonder, then, that the three women with Abe are so "conscious of the solemn dignity that flowed from him" and also "frightened at his survivant will, once a will to live, now become a will to die" (p. 108). Because of his communion with the White Logic, which resembles here the Freudian death instinct (Thanatos), "a man drunk" inspires a "curious respect" that, as the narrator later remarks, is "rather like the respect of simple races for the insane." Such respect, rather than the fear that might be expected as a response, arises from the "awe-inspiring" spectacle of "one who has lost all inhibitions, who will do anything." Of course, adds the narrator, in the self-pitying tone so prevalent in *Tender Is the Night*, "we make him pay afterward for his moment of superiority, his moment of impressiveness" (p. 141).

Gilmore notes the "oddity" of Fitzgerald's dividing the alcoholism between Diver and Abe North, "with most of the stereotypically crude or obnoxious traits of the alcoholic going to North." In Book One, North's flamboyant and suicidal drunkenness serves to conceal Diver's less flagrant drinking problem. Because Dick is thus exempted "from any strongly objectionable behavior," his attractiveness remains "intact partly because his alcoholism becomes clear only when the novel is nearly two-thirds finished."[33]

In fact, Dick's drinking is shown to be problematic far earlier in the novel. Although he is never noticeably drunk in Book One, and although Abe dubs him "the only sober man with repose" (p. 67), Dick has already begun his downward slide. What is "not at all apparent to Rosemary," and thus also invisible at first to the reader (who is largely confined in Book One to Rosemary's innocent point of view), is that "in reality a qualitative change had already set in" (p. 27). Although we are told in the next sentence that the Divers are drinking sherry as Rosemary talks with them on the Riviera beach, alcohol is not immediately implicated in this change—because Abe North is Fitzgerald's designated drunkard at this stage of the novel.

When the characters move on to Paris, Abe seems to have grown a "thin vinous fur over him"; his bloodshot eyes and his frequent detours into bars have become so conspicuous that even Rosemary notices (pp. 79–80). By comparison, Dick is the soul of moderation. At her birthday party, Rosemary nonetheless feels "some necessity" to drink champagne for the first time: "Dick drank, not too much, but he drank, and perhaps it would bring her closer to him, be a part of the equipment for what she had to do" (p. 80). She intuits, correctly, that alcohol is a major piece of *his* equipment—an insight that is subtly confirmed when he later calls from a bistro to confess his fascination with her. As he stares vacantly across the café, he hears her voice:

> "Rosemary."
>
> "Yes, Dick."
>
> "Look, I'm in an extraordinary condition about you. When a child can disturb a middle-aged gent—things get difficult."
>
> "You're not middle-aged, Dick—you're the youngest person in the world."
>
> "Rosemary?" Silence while he stared at a shelf that held the humbler poisons of France—bottles of Otard, Rhum St. James, Marie Brizard, Punch Orangeade, André Fernet-Branca, Cherry Rocher, and Armagnac.
>
> "Are you alone?"
>
> —*Do you mind if I pull down the curtain?*
>
> "Who do you think I'd be with?"
>
> "That's the state I'm in. I'd like to be with you now."
>
> Silence, then a sigh and an answer. "I wish you were with me now."
>
> (Pp. 122–23)

The "humbler poisons of France," which this dingy bar near the American film studio apparently stocks for its humbler patrons (or else for its tasteless American clientele), invoke what William E. Doherty calls the novel's "potion motif," in which alcohol, drugs, and poison are all "associated with the illusory adventure."[34] Dick's middle-aged infatuation with Rosemary is one such adventure; his "extraordinary condition" is a kind of emotional addiction that is closely intertwined with his enchantment by alcohol.

Rosemary's naive remark about Dick's youth discomfits rather than reassures him because he knows how young she must be to say such things: too young for a man old enough to know better. In the pain of his self-awareness, Dick unconsciously seeks an anodyne. His eyes fall, as if naturally, upon the liquor shelf. And not just liquor in general. Although his attention is ostensibly focused on his conversation with Rosemary and not on the bar, each bottle registers distinctly in his mind; instantly, he renders an authoritative judgment about the quality of the liquor that reflects a familiarity with the nobler as well as the humbler poisons of France. The amazing particularity of Dick's observation is striking evidence of alcohol's allure for him.

His thoughts then drift to another painful subject. Dick is recalling what Collis Clay has told him of Rosemary's sexual experience: "some heavy stuff" aboard a train with a Yale man, who pulled down the curtain for privacy, only to be caught by the porter and publicly upbraided. When Dick heard this gossip, he felt "a change taking place within him. Only the image of a third person, even a vanished one, entering into his relation with Rosemary was needed to throw him off his balance and send through him waves of pain, misery, desire, desperation" (pp. 115–16). The repeated line, "Do you mind if I pull down the curtain?"—which Dick attributes to his vanished Yale rival—has become the refrain of his own sexual obsession with Rosemary and, specifically, with her virginity.

During Book One, Dick's erotic adventure with Rosemary effectively displaces his drinking problem, but the future course of his alcoholism is nevertheless foreshadowed by his loss of emotional and moral control. Dick's transition from sexual to alcoholic intoxication first becomes apparent in a meeting with Elsie Speers, Rosemary's mother, to whom he confesses his romantic involvement. Again the young woman is related to the "potion motif": "In a hundred hours she had come to possess all the world's dark magic; the blinding belladonna, the caffein converting physical into nervous energy, the mandragora that imposes harmony" (p. 215). It is a different drug, however, to which Diver now turns. When he arrives back at the Villa Diana after his meeting with Mrs. Speers, he pours himself "an ounce of gin with twice as much water" (p. 217). During the long train trip south, the narrator then ominously reports, Dick consumed "a whole bottle of wine save for Nicole's single glass" (p. 218).

Diver's drinking soon picks up where North's leaves off in his collapse into drunken disarray at the end of Book One. The warning signs of Dick's alcoholism start to appear just after Abe disappears from the novel.[35] Somewhat obscured by the long flashback in Book Two is the fact that Abe and Dick are essentially the same character. Their underlying identity was recognized by Malcolm Lowry in his brilliant (but unproduced) screenplay of *Tender Is the Night*. A fellow alcoholic, Lowry grasped the deeper logic of Fitzgerald's novel—that "a man drunk" (p. 141) is the true protagonist and that the main narrative line traces and then retraces the destruction of this character, who prefigures Lowry's own alcoholic modernist hero in *Under the Volcano* (1947). As Lowry noted, somewhat oracularly, "[I]n the subterranean part of the book, Abe—the duel—Peterson—Abe's Death—Dick becomes Abe—there is a law of cause and effect going on that works out almost like a collaboration between the Buddha and Sophocles."[36]

In Lowry's screenplay, this insight underlies a stunningly effective interpolation: a long scene, set in New York City, in which Dick becomes not only Abe's double, but also an alter ego of Lowry's Consul, Geoffrey Firman[37]—the hopeless drunk as the modernist Everyman, a symbol of suffering humanity in the apocalyptic twentieth century. Lowry thought that Fitzgerald had erred artistically in having Diver redundantly follow North's downward gyre; the ending seemed "too preoccupied with absurd forces of a tragedy of disintegration" that had also governed *Under the Volcano*. Lowry wished, therefore, to devise a more positive, but still tragic, denouement: "Refusing to release Dick to the bleakness of a death-in-life, Lowry finds for him a means of spiritual realization in the end."[38] In the final scene of the screenplay, Dick courageously goes down with the ship on which he has signed aboard (as a doctor) after leaving Nicole and his old life behind on the Riviera.[39]

In the novel itself, however, Diver's downfall does not, as Lowry thought, exactly replicate Abe North's. Whereas Abe dies squalidly in a bar-room brawl, Dick merely fades away into the hinterland of upstate New York. Fitzgerald was consciously aiming for the effect of a "dying fall," and he wanted Dick Diver, despite his personal disintegration, to retain something of his charm and gentility to the bitter end. For this reason, he resisted cutting a scene from the last serial installment of *Tender Is the Night* in *Scribner's Magazine*. Although the scene in question—Dick's rescue from jail of Mary North Minghetti and Lady Caroline Sibley—seemed expendable to Maxwell Perkins, Fitzgerald insisted that it was absolutely necessary. "OTHERWISE DICKS CHARACTER WEAKENS AND NOVEL FORSHOTENS [sic] TOWARD END," he argued in an urgent telegram to Perkins, dispatched at 1:28 in the morning. "IT IS NEEDED AND WAS WRITTEN TO BOLSTER HIM UP IN INEVITABLY UNDIGNIFIED CUCKOLD SITUATION." A minute later, he sent a second wire: "FEEL DOWNRIGHT ESSENTIAL FOR READER TO GET GLIMPSE OF DICK THROUGH IMPERSONAL EYES . . . TO SUSTAIN HIM AT THE END OTHERWISE FINAL TRIAL [sic] OFF INSPIRES SCORN INSTEAD OF PATHOS."[40]

Fitzgerald's desire, as Donaldson says, "to preserve some trace of the 'dignified and responsible' protagonist he had depicted in the first part of the book" led him also to minimize the effects of alcohol in Dick's final scene on the Riviera.[41] In the draft conclusion of "The Drunkard's Holiday," Dick talks with Mary Minghetti on the terrace overlooking Gausse's Beach. As he stands up to go, he suddenly keels over, passed out from the several drinks he has consumed that morning. A helpful waiter brings him around by sloshing water in his face and then props him upright.

> On the high terrace Dick sway⟨ed⟩ing in the arms of a waiter raised his right hand and making a papal cross blessed the beach "semper terram (quote from ⟨Mass⟩ last of mass or benediction). Then under the impression that he was still talking to Mary he mumbled in a loud voice—
>
> "Final message of Sairy Gamp, the drunken nurse: Power measured in women How many women is power Women are the real gold standard.
>
> By that time two waiters had him and wer[e] helping him toward a cab still waving ⟨benedictions over the beach⟩ blessing and consecrating with his hand the ⟨earthly⟩ material paradise he had casually created for a certain group at a certain time as he explained to the waiters.[42]

In this scene as it was finally published, Dick remains not entirely sober, but he is far less sloppily drunk: "As he stood up he swayed a little; he did not feel well any more—his blood raced slow. He raised his right hand and with a papal cross he blessed the beach from the high terrace" (p. 406).

One point of this sequence is to contrast the integrity, however dishevelled, of Dick Diver to the corruption of Mary Minghetti, whose superficial concern for his welfare masks her complacent self-satisfaction:

> Mary was having a good time, though she did not know it, as she had sat down with him only out of fear. Again she refused a drink and said: "Self-indulgence is back of it. Of course, after Abe you can imagine how I feel about it—since I watched the progress of a good man toward alcoholism—"
>
> Down the steps tripped Lady Caroline Sibley-Biers with blithe theatricality.
>
> Dick felt fine—he was already well in advance of the day; arrived at where a man should be at the end of a good dinner, yet he showed only a fine, considered, restrained interest in Mary.   (P. 405)

"In advance of the day" means that Dick has already reached before noon the optimal state of intoxication one would ordinarily attain after the evening meal: a civilized dinner graced by plenty of vintage wine. Fitzgerald implies that Dick's gallantry under the influence of alcohol refutes Mary's comparison of him to Abe and her criticism of his "self-indulgence." Mary's counsel is thus shown to be as misplaced as Nicole's pity when she realizes that her marriage to Dick has failed and feels "as sorry for him as she had sometimes felt for Abe North and his ignoble destiny, sorry as for the helplessness of infants and the old" (p. 388).

Fitzgerald's desired effect was pathos, not scorn. He intended for Dick in the final scene to appear weakened but not helpless, down but not down-and-out like Abe. Most important, he did *not* imagine Dick to be an alcoholic—at least not yet. In undated notes titled "Summary of Part III," Fitzgerald wrote, "The Divers, *as a marriage* are at the end of their resources. Medically Nicole is *nearly* cured but Dick has given out & is sinking toward alcoholism and discouragement." Although Dick may eventually slide into alcoholism, that is, he has not yet reached that low a point by the end of the novel.[43]

The denial here, which extends beyond the character of Dick Diver to Fitzgerald himself, is even more explicit in the draft version of this same passage in the manuscript of "The Drunkard's Holiday":

> She was having a good time and though she had sat down with him out of duty and fear, having come in her new world to think of him as an *homme manque,* socially and professionally. She ⟨drank took⟩ refused ⟨a new⟩ another sherry and said
>
> "Drink is back of it. And of course after Abe you can imagine how I feel about drink, drink to excess. It's simply a horror to me, a horror. Just once
> ⟨"Abe thought he was not an⟩
> to watch to [sic] progress of a charming man toward alcoholism"
>
> "Abe thought he was not an alcoholic in a different way from the way I think I'm not an alcoholic."
>
> "Well, you can see how I feel." Down the steps came Lady XX, ⟨with a swell neat⟩ tripping with blithe theatricality ⟨on the heals⟩ on the heels of a neat spick Lesbian with a starched ⟨light⟩ light blue shirt and a lovely boy's face. "⟨Anything⟩ Nothing is as bad as drink, nothing, nothing."
>
> ⟨The drinks he had taken warmed him comfortably; he was where⟩ Dr. Diver felt fine—he was already well ⟨past⟩ in advance of the day ⟨already, he not drunk⟩ he was where a man could comfortably be at the end of a ⟨fine⟩ good dinner, and he showed nothing of it; only the fine considered yet restrained interest which he directed on Mary [44]

The draft is remarkably revealing of how Fitzgerald mitigates Diver's alcoholism in *Tender Is the Night.* Whatever Mary may think—and she is clearly meant to be exposed here as a self-righteous temperance crank (hence Fitzgerald's decision to have her refuse rather than accept another sherry)—Dick's drinking is not bad enough by any means to count as evidence of "alcoholism." Far from being an *homme manqué* (or an *homme raté* or an *homme epuisé,* as Fitzgerald put it in later drafts before he dropped the phrase altogether),[45] Dick is still an old-fashioned gentleman. The courtliness he learned from his father is intact, and his manners remain impeccable even in the company of a woman who does not merit such consideration.

Furthermore, as the ironic juxtaposition of Lady Caroline's entrance to

Mary Minghetti's statement suggests, there *is* something as bad as drink—something, indeed, far worse. Fitzgerald told Perkins that the purpose of Dick's midnight rescue of Mary Minghetti and Lady Caroline was to "bolster him up" in an "inevitably undignified cuckold situation." But the dignity of the betrayed husband is saved at the expense of the two women, who are held up to ridicule and moral disgust as cross-dressing lesbians who get depraved thrills by preying on supposedly innocent girls. When the drunken Dick is bailed out by Baby Warren in Book Two, Fitzgerald's emphasis falls on her cynical use of wealth and power to gain "a moral superiority over him for as long as he proved of any use" (p. 306). When the situation is reversed, however, and Dick becomes the one who buys off the police, the novel still is tilted to his advantage. "I have never seen women like this sort of women," Gausse confides to Diver, in a moment of intimacy that hinges on the shared disbelief of men at the perversity of women. "I have known many of the great courtesans of the world, and for them I have much respect often, but women like these women I have never seen before" (p. 396). Women who practice the elegant prostitution of courtesans know their proper place at least.

"Courtesans" is the key word here; for it echoes another passage, early in the novel, in which the narrator meditates on what Nicole Diver, Mary North, and Rosemary Hoyt have most in common: "Their point of resemblance to each other and their difference from so many American women, lay in the fact that they were all happy to exist in a man's world—they preserved their individuality through men and not by opposition to them. They would all three have made alternatively good courtesans or good wives not by the accident of birth but through the greater accident of finding their man or not finding him" (p. 69). The womanly ideal in this regard is exemplified by Elsie Speers, a military widow who favorably impresses Dick with her "air of seeming to wait, as if for a man to get through with something more important than herself, a battle or an operation, during which he must not be hurried or interfered with. When the man had finished she would be waiting, without fret or impatience, somewhere on a highstool, turning the pages of a newspaper" (p. 216).

In *Tender Is the Night*, as Donaldson points out, Fitzgerald "grafted onto Spengler the basic argument of D. H. Lawrence's *Fantasia of the Unconscious*: that modern men and women were engaged in a struggle for dominance, and that women were winning."[46] The Great War had ushered in the greater war between the sexes, and men like Dick Diver were fast becoming relics of another and better time, when men were men and women were wives—or possibly courtesans, for lack of good men—but certainly never lesbians. Mary North Minghetti shows what happens to the wayward woman who grows unaccountably discontented in the man's world. As long as she remains a duly submissive wife to an alcoholic husband—"a brave, hopeful woman . . . changing herself to this kind of person or that, without being able to lead him a step out of his path, and sometimes realizing with discouragement how deep in him the guarded secret of her direction lay" (p. 82)—Fitzgerald treats Mary sympathetically. But once Abe has left her, Mary is shown to lose direction. She marries again for money and title; and in trying to establish her individuality in opposition to men, she turns inevitably, it seems, *contra naturam*.

Unlike Gauss, Dick the cosmopolite has seen such women before. They are to be found in Paris, for example, at the Left Bank party to which he takes Rosemary. In a house on the rue Monsieur (the street is aptly named)—a house decorated so futuristically that it induces "a definite nervous experience, perverted as a breakfast of oatmeal and hashish" (p. 94)—they encounter a strangely artificial group of women who strike poses as if they were rehearsing on a movie set. For Fitzgerald, this is strictly a horror movie. Dick and Rosemary are said to be swallowed up by "the Frankenstein" (the monstrous house itself) and then disgorged into a room where a trio of tall and slender women in tailored dark suits, with hair slicked back like a manikin's, wave their heads gracefully about like "long-stemmed flowers and rather like cobras' hoods" (p. 96). As Rosemary overhears their hissing gossip about the Divers ("I prefer people whose lives have more corrugated surfaces") and the Divers's entourage ("Why, for example, the entirely liquid Mr. North?"), another young woman serpentinely slithers around her. "Desperately she kept sweeping things from between them, afraid that Rosemary couldn't see her, sweeping them away until presently there was not so much as a veil of brittle humor hiding the girl, and with distaste Rosemary saw her plain" (p. 96).

"Wasn't it terrible?" Dick exclaims after they escape this den of lesbian vipers (p. 97). As if to expunge her distaste, Rosemary falls weeping into his arms: "Her breasts crushed flat against him, her mouth was all new and warm, owned in common" (p. 98). By contrast to Left Bank lesbianism, the humdrum heterosexual adultery of Dick with Rosemary, despite its incestuous overtones, is meant to seem refreshingly normal and relatively innocuous—just as the liquid Mr. North shows to advantage against the cross-dressed cobras of the rue Monsieur.

During their time in Paris, Scott and Zelda Fitzgerald had mingled on occasion with the circle of lesbian artists and writers, many of them expatriated Americans, who revolved around the salon of Natalie Clifford Barney at 20 rue Jacob. At least twice during 1928 and 1929, according to Donaldson, the Fitzgeralds attended Barney's salon, and they also visited the studio of the lesbian painter Romaine Brooks. Although Scott was apparently friendly with Djuna Barnes,[47] Zelda's slightest attentions to Dolly Wilde, reputed to be as notorious a libertine as her uncle Oscar Wilde, were enough to scandalize him. Dolly Wilde appears as the wickedly lesbian Vivian Taube in a fragment deleted from *Tender Is the Night*.[48] Likewise jettisoned from an early draft was the "Wanda Brested" episode, which "forcefully conveys the disgust of Francis Melarky (and the author) at discovering that Wanda, a girl he desired, was 'a hysterical Lesbian.' 'God damn these women!' he thinks."[49]

What made lesbians so damnable for Fitzgerald was not simply homophobia but homosexual panic. He felt threatened by Zelda's charge, first made in 1929, that he himself was homosexual—along with his pal Ernest Hemingway. A rumor to this effect was spread around Paris by Robert McAlmon, whom Fitzgerald, in retaliation, pilloried as Albert McKisco in *Tender Is the Night*. The rumor also surfaced in the draft of "The Drunkard's Holiday." In Dick's final scene with Mary Minghetti, she chastises him for his drunken indiscretions:

> "Your friends still like you, Dick. But you say such awful things to people when you've been drinking. And you do such awful things. I spend most of my time defending you this summer."
>
> He laughed.
>
> "That remark is one of the world's classics," ⟨he said⟩
>
> "But it's true. Nobody cares whether you drink or not ⟨illeg.⟩ but you're so mean." She hesitated, "Even Abe when he ⟨was⟩ drank hardest never made

as many enemies as you do. Do you think those men like to be called fairies to their face?"

"But I understand now I'm a fairy."

"Oh, I have heard that but of course it's nonsense."[50]

In the draft of "The Drunkard's Holiday," the last two lines, cut before publication, were an allusion to cognate material, also deleted. There had been an earlier reference to Dick's alleged homosexuality, in which the rumor was attributed to a malicious actress; and in the yacht scene, Lady Caroline had insulted Dick "with the statement that he was seen associating with homosexuals in Lausanne."[51] In the published novel, this accusation is obfuscated: "I simply said you were observed associating with a questionable crowd in Lausanne." To which Dick retorts: "So I am actually a notorious——" (p. 351). In order to fill in this blank, the reader must recall that Lausanne is where Dick consulted with Pardo y Cuidad Real about his "degenerate" son Francisco, a homosexual alcoholic. What remains ambiguous, however, is whether Dick himself has been labeled a notorious homosexual, a notorious drunkard, or both.

Bruccoli asserts, "The entire episode with the Chileans could have been omitted without damaging the novel, for its function is merely to emphasize the corruptness of the society Dick once undertook to heal. It has no direct influence on Dick's crack-up."[52] But the scene *does* bear on Diver's degeneration insofar as it provides an important part of the alibi for his drinking. When Diver asks Francisco, who has been dubbed "the Queen of Chili," whether his unhappiness derives "from the drinking or from the abnormality," the young man replies, "I think the drinking is caused by the other" (p. 316). "Abnormality" may lead to alcoholism, in other words, but alcoholism is not nearly so abnormal as homosexuality. If the ultimate excuse for drinking in *Tender Is the Night* is the Decline of the West, then sexual "degeneration" is Fitzgerald's primary metaphor for this decline. Besides the incestuous rape of Nicole Warren by her father, says Donaldson, "other forms of sexual deviance penetrate every corner of the book's expatriate society."[53]

In such a world, the novel implies, alcoholism is not only an understandable outcome, but also a badge of courage, an honorable sign of bravery in the face of post-war conditions so nerve-shattering that it seems as if the combat never ended. Fitzgerald's answer to Rosemary's question about Abe North—"Why does he have to drink?" (p. 129)—is implicit in the scene where Abe drunkenly departs from the Gare Saint Lazare. In broad daylight, in the middle of the crowded station, a woman slightly known to the Divers cold-bloodedly assassinates a man with a small revolver. This violent act (of the sort that has since become all-too-commonplace) reverberates throughout the novel. As the Divers and their friends leave the station, the narrator broods that "the shots, the concussions that had finished God knew what dark matter" have not merely terminated their Parisian interlude. The shots have "entered into all their lives: echoes of violence followed them out onto the pavement"—where, in the comments of two railroad porters, Fitzgerald underscores the significance of the incident. One porter says (in French) that the pearl-handled gun was so small that it looked like a toy. But potent enough, sagely replies the other. Did you see his shirt? So bloody you would think you were back in the war (p. 112).

If the conditions of war define the modern condition, then combat readiness would seem to be required of anyone hoping to endure. This theme in *Tender Is the Night* links the novel to the vast literature of post-war disillusionment that constitutes the established canon of American modernism. But as feminist critics have argued, women writers have been largely excluded from this canon because the formative literary-historical narratives center on the Great War, of which women had only peripheral experience. Shari Benstock observes that such influential critics as Malcolm Cowley and Frederick J. Hoffman "base the expatriate Modernist experience on a form of male bonding produced by the actual experiences of World War I," while Hugh Kenner and Susan Stanford Friedman "see the war as an apocalyptic revelation announcing the end of Western civilization in its pre-1914 form."[54]

The canonical modernist hero, then, is a certain type of manly man; and in Fitzgerald, as in London and Hemingway, wartime male bonding is perpetuated by the culture of drinking, in which alcoholism becomes, in effect, a key sign of "manliness." But the culture of drinking is also linked, as we have seen, to male gender anxiety, misogyny, and homophobia. What "penetrates" every corner of *Tender Is the Night*, as well as *John Barleycorn* and *The Sun Also Rises*, is an ideology of sexual difference that militates against "deviance" from male heterosexual norms, such that homosexuality and lesbianism are understood as the ultimate symptoms of cultural decline—worse, after all, than incest.

In the Lausanne chapter, there is a telling juxtaposition of the haplessness of Francisco, who wallows pathetically in his "degeneracy," to the miraculous rise from his death bed of Nicole's alcoholic father. Said to be dying from cirrhosis of the liver, Devereux Warren somehow manages, as in the Biblical story that Dick invokes, to take up his bed and walk. "It was instinct," Dick later explains to Nicole. "He was really dying, but he tried to get a resumption of rhythm—he's not the first person that ever walked off his death-bed—like an old clock—you know, you shake it and somehow from sheer habit it gets going again" (p. 324). Although Devereux Warren is the despoiler of his daughter's virginity and thus the root cause of her insanity, his apparent triumph over alcohol seems to elicit a respect and even admiration from Diver that the novel never accords to the same-sexually "abnormal" characters.

This episode is so bizarre and implausible, in fact, that the reader must wonder how and why it was spared by Fitzgerald's editorial hand. The reason may be that Devereux Warren's rise from the dead—in which the miracle of Lazarus is implicitly set against the fatal bullet of the Gare Lazare—embodied Fitzgerald's deepest and fondest fantasy about his own drinking: that whatever the warnings of his physicians, whatever the swelling of his own liver might portend, he was finally invincible.

5

The Infernal Grove:
Appointment in Samarra

In the late nineteenth century, when the phrase "Irish drunkard" was considered redundant, John O'Hara's immigrant grandfather, a two-fisted boozer in his youth, bootstrapped himself up the ladder of success by taking the temperance pledge.[1] Unfortunately, Michael O'Hara could not dissuade his son Martin from experimenting with alcohol; and the boy was crushed one evening when he fell drunkenly beneath the wheels of a train. Martin's brother Patrick, who became a prominent physician in Pottsville, Pennsylvania, earned a reputation for rectitude, especially when it came to drinking. Citing Martin's tragic example, Doctor O'Hara exhorted his children to tread the straight and narrow path of teetotalism. But John O'Hara, the doctor's oldest child, was tippling communion wine as an altar boy before he reached the age of ten; by the advent of Prohibition, when he was fifteen, he was getting drunk with some regularity. Doctor O'Hara thundered that his prodigal son would be dead before he turned thirty, and then nearly fulfilled his own prophecy by braining John with a chair when he found him still drunk one morning from the night before.

Quarrels and occasional beatings continued, but without effect on young O'Hara's defiant devotion to drinking. As a member in good standing of "The Purity League," a parodically named gang of Pottsville hellions, O'Hara abetted various drunken pranks. He was ousted from the Schuylkill Country Club several times for brawling, and he passed at least one night in jail for public intoxication. Expelled from two private academies for his poor attitude and poorer grades, O'Hara finally hit his stride at Niagara University Prep School, where he was named both valedictorian and class poet. But the night before commencement in June 1924, he went out on a celebratory spree and crawled home at dawn in a drunken stupor. Awakened by a school official in the company of an enraged and mortified Dr. O'Hara, who had arrived to witness his wayward son's moment of glory, the young scholar was stripped of his honors, banished from the ceremonies, and drummed out of his class. O'Hara arrived home slightly later than his parents, since they refused even to share the same train with so ignominious an offspring; and although he had hoped to enter Yale in the fall, he was put to work instead at odd jobs and eventually as a cub reporter for the Pottsville newspaper.

O'Hara never did go to college—Hemingway sneeringly proposed years later that a fund be established to send him to New Haven—but he still envisioned joining a fraternity. In April 1923, when he was eighteen, O'Hara told an older friend, now a student at Dartmouth, of his plans for a hometown drinking club:

> As to the drinking part, I'm going to continue to get drunk just as much as I can, club or clubless. The beauty of a drinking club is the identical spirit that actuated the first cave-dweller in opening up a bar. What I mean is that since drinking is patently a "social vice" (a man who drinks much alone is dangerous) there is always a feeling of comfort in knowing that there is at least one good frater in urbe who will respond to the call of one of his fellows and go out on a bat. I daresay I have boozed a little more than anyone else in the gang . . . and I know that I don't get as much kick out of deciding to get boiled and *then* going to a saloon and making up with a bare acquaintance or even absolute stranger and getting fried as I did on our last summer's parties when someone would suggest something and we were off.[2]

Like young Jack London, O'Hara took pride in his alcoholic capacity, and he looked to drinking for the male companionship that would in turn protect him from a solitary "social vice."

O'Hara came closer than London to fitting the nineteenth-century pattern of the "chemical" dipsomaniac—a drinker whose affinity for alcohol seemed hereditary, whose craving was uncontrollable, and whose excessive consumption produced symptoms of physical and/or mental degeneration—but he conformed more obviously to the modern category of the "alcoholic" as a habitual drinker, an alcohol addict. Although none of O'Hara's biographers has explicitly pinned this label on him, it seems obvious that he showed signs of alcoholism from early in his drinking career, perhaps from the beginning.

Drinking certainly altered the course of O'Hara's life. It cost him not only a college education, but also several jobs, including a position on the *Herald Tribune* after he had moved to New York to cast his lot as a journalist. "It was the general opinion," says Matthew J. Bruccoli, "that he had a promising future—if drink didn't get him."[3] Frank MacShane, who dates O'Hara's compulsive drinking from the death of his father in 1925, adds that alcohol "could quickly change his disposition and threatened to ruin his career and happiness."[4] O'Hara was often an ugly drunk: he became violent and abusive, especially toward women. Drinking destroyed his chances to marry Margaretta Archbald, his childhood sweetheart; it undermined his first marriage to Helen ("Pet") Petit, who later died of her own alcoholism; and it shadowed his second marriage to Belle Wylie, who endured public humiliations by O'Hara as well as the private ordeals of his binges.[5]

Alcohol fueled paranoid delusions and maniacal rages in O'Hara that sometimes triggered dangerous bar fights. His suicidal depressions seem also to have been induced or exacerbated by alcohol. On the eve of the Fourth of July in 1933, O'Hara started to walk out a twelfth-story window in a Pittsburgh hotel. Although he drew back from the edge on this occasion, he still seemed destined to follow the example of a young man, notorious in the speakeasies of New York, who proposed to drink himself to death and then did so within a few months. At the center of his first two novels, *Appointment in Samarra* (1934) and *Butterfield 8* (1935), O'Hara placed a main character who is "a guilt-ridden alcoholic suicide."[6]

In time, the whiskey did come close to killing him. O'Hara had developed ulcers by 1939, but he ignored medical advice and continued to drink. Only when the ulcers hemorrhaged and he nearly died in August 1953 did he finally heed his physician's warning that he must either quit drinking or face the consequences. "My chief trouble," he told a close friend, "is that the belly resists booze, and if I take too much of it I'm liable to fall over dead. As simple as that. A hell of a way for booze to treat me after I've been so kind to it."[7]

Faced with his own mortality, O'Hara then suffered the shock of Belle's sudden death from heart failure. Feeling intense guilt about his treatment of Belle, wondering if his drinking had shortened her life, he poured the last of his whiskey down the drain on the night of her death, 9 January 1954, and thereafter remained completely sober until his own death in April 1970.

The abstinent O'Hara burrowed into himself and the secure domesticity of his third marriage to Katharine Barnes ("Sister") O'Hara. He became extremely prolific as a writer, producing eight novels, six collections of stories, four novellas, two volumes of essays, and one of plays during the sixteen remaining years of his life. (This average of a book a year or better doesn't count additional volumes that were published posthumously.) Off the sauce, O'Hara was "like a tamed lion, polite and courteous, dull and withdrawn."[8] Far less gregarious than in his pub-crawling days, he came to shun the company of active drinkers, some of them old cronies who would privately aver that they had liked him better in his cups, that "he was a better writer before he stopped drinking."[9]

For Wolcott Gibbs, a *New Yorker* friend and fellow alcoholic, the real O'Hara was inseparable from the era of Prohibition, when drinkers had basked in the complacent glow of supposing they were engaged not merely in frivolity but in serious social protest. It was a "queer time," Gibbs recalled: "the fact that everybody was part of the same general conspiracy against a silly law broke down many barriers so that it was hard to tell what might happen before any night was over—and the things I remember about it are queer."[10] Yet another *New Yorker* rummy, James Thurber, excused O'Hara's drunken truculence by allowing that anyone with so sensitive an ear and mind would naturally be given to bouts of hypersensitivity. If O'Hara sometimes seemed "to exhibit the stormy emotions of a little boy, so do all great artists, for unless they can remember what it was like to be a little boy, they are only half complete as artist and as man."[11] Implicit in such statements is the modernist conception of drinking as a means of liberation from bourgeois conventionality and a vehicle to new frontiers of personal and artistic experience.

From the example before him of American expatriates in Europe and of hard-boiled journalists at home, O'Hara could only suppose that spirits were inseparable from inspiration, that drinking was natural to the real writer's life. He tried to live accordingly. During his stint as a Hollywood screen writer during the 1930s, O'Hara once informed his publishers, with a mixture of remorse and bravado, that he had been "living at the bottom of a bottle";[12] and he fostered the impression that he could glide effortlessly from the bar to the typewriter, that drinking feats gave forth literary prodigies. Alfred M. Wright, a member of O'Hara's California circle, detailed a typical day that sounds like something out of *The Sun Also Rises*. O'Hara would get up for lunch at one or another Hollywood hangout and then drink with his bar friends all afternoon. Belle joined him for a late dinner, followed by more drinking at nightclubs until two o'clock closing time, or perhaps earlier if O'Hara became immobilized. "If he was still upright when he reached the Westwood apartment, Belle would give him a bowl of cereal, and he would work until dawn." With his trusty portable propped on the coffee table, O'Hara could bang out a perfectly finished story. Sometimes, Wright recalled, "it did not go so well if he was too smashed to type decently, but I have seen one of his stories after a night of drinking without a single typographical error or an x-ing, and he would mail it off to the *New Yorker* without a correction."[13]

Bruccoli doubts the veracity of such tales, noting that O'Hara "claimed that he never wrote when he had been drinking, and there is no question about the fact that he went on the wagon for his novels."[14] But even if O'Hara was not technically drunk during the act of composition, he was never very far from the bottle. For thirty years, from his teens into his late forties, his writing was bonded to his drinking in a cycle of literary and alcoholic binges.

During a 1946 interview, reported by Earl Wilson in his syndicated gossip column, O'Hara confided that "If I write any extended work . . . I gotta god damn well get offa the booze." Eager to scotch the rumor that he had written *Pal Joey* while he was drunk, he explained that the idea had come to him, in fact, on the morning *after* a terrible two days of "getting stiff and passing out" in his room at the Hotel Pierre. Having drunk himself sober, he felt so remorseful that he tried to imagine someone, anyone, who was worse than he. But who? "Al Capone, maybe. Then I got it—maybe some night club masters of ceremonies I know." He promptly sat down and wrote the first in the series of *New Yorker* stories—stories he knocked off rapidly, like so many shots—that became *Pal Joey:*

> "That was the only good thing I ever got out of booze, but mind you, Wilson, I wasn't on a bender at the time I wrote it. I was perfectly sober! Have you got that down in your notebook?
> "Orange blossom," he said to the barman. "Double."[15]

The archness of this ending coyly suggests that O'Hara was no more sober during the interview than he had likely been when he wrote *Pal Joey*. Wilson begins the column by asserting that "Edgar Allan Poe, the Lush of Literature, wrote while all canned up, but up till press time today, nobody's been able to do it since." He then introduces O'Hara, "a pretty good boy with the juice," exclaiming incredulously that he "practically came out for prohibition for writers while they're working." So although Wilson is ostensibly debunking a myth about the drunken origins of *Pal Joey*, he actually reaffirms and, in effect, glamorizes the legend of O'Hara as an alcoholic writer: a Lush of Literature worthy to bend elbows with Poe. Or, as O'Hara himself might have suggested, with F. Scott Fitzgerald.

O'Hara revered Fitzgerald as a literary older brother who, despite a half-generation's difference in age, was spiritually at one with the younger set. Late in the 1920s, O'Hara began writing adulatory letters to Fitzgerald, and the two men eventually met, early in 1934, after Fitzgerald had read the unfinished draft of *Appointment in Samarra* and O'Hara had offered to return the favor by reading proof for *Tender Is the Night*. Fitzgerald's "first judgment" of O'Hara's first novel was decidedly mixed—"yes-yes-but-also-no,"[16]—but favorable enough on balance to encourage him to finish the book. "The little we talked when you were in New York did it," O'Hara wrote in thanks. "I reasoned that the best parts of my novel will be said to derive from Fitzgerald, and I think I have muffed my story, but I became reconciled to having done that after talking to you and reading Tender Is the Night in proof." That novel, O'Hara assured him, was "in the early stages of being my favorite book, even more than This Side of Paradise." He could think of nothing to compare with it: "and I guess in its way that is the most important thing I've ever said about any book."[17]

It is not known what specific advice Fitzgerald dispensed about *Appointment in Samarra;* but he shared enough of O'Hara's background to recognize, as he shrewdly observed in a later notebook entry, that the young writer was "in a perpetual state of having discovered it's a lousy world."[18] O'Hara, for his part, must have felt the shock (and aftershock) of recognition as he read and reread the proofs of Fitzgerald's novel; for there were striking similarities between Julian English and Dick Diver. This resemblance is not unexpected, considering O'Hara's self-conscious indebtedness to Fitzgerald, but it is not, after all, purely a matter of literary influence. What these writers had most in common was an intimate acquaintance with John Barleycorn during the "real dark night of the soul" in which, as Fitzgerald famously remarked, "it is always three o'clock in the morning, day after day."[19] *Tender Is the Night* impressed O'Hara so profoundly because he understood, as he later said, that it was "a dangerous book to encounter during some of the moods that come over you after you're thirty. You don't like to think of yourself, lone, wandering and lost, like Richard Diver, going from town to town in bleak upstate New York, with All That behind you."[20]

For O'Hara, when he began writing *Appointment in Samarra* late in 1933, All That included the wreckage of his marriage to Helen Petit, mainly as a result of drinking. Binges and chronic hangovers had made O'Hara so often late for work and so generally unreliable that he was unable to hold a job. His unpromising prospects exacerbated the ill will between him and Helen's domineering mother, who insisted that Helen get an abortion when she became pregnant in February 1933, since John would be, in her opinion, even less competent as a father than as a husband. The abortion, to which O'Hara reluctantly consented but about which he later felt guilty, exhausted whatever stock of hope remained in a marriage already demoralized by alcohol. As Bruccoli reports, "Pet was beginning to drink heavily too; and O'Hara's violent behavior when drunk became a familiar topic among their friends, who talked about his physical abuse of Pet. It was said that he threw her out of a moving cab. He developed suspicions—apparently groundless—about her interest in other men. There were violent scenes followed by spells of remorse."[21]

Together just over two years, John and Helen separated during the spring of 1933. At the end of June, O'Hara recounted his woes to Fitzgerald: "My pretty little wife is rolling out to Reno next week [for a divorce to be decreed in August], and the girl I loved from the time I was 17 [i.e., Margaretta Archbald] got married in Haiti last month, to a Byronic lad whom she'd known about two months. And she was the shadow on the wall that broke up my marriage. Oh, my."[22] Rejected by the only two women he had ever really loved, O'Hara was feeling doubly lost and alone as he wandered from New York to a short-lived job in Pittsburgh and then, after his suicide attempt, back to New York.

In February 1934, when he had made some progress on *Appointment in Samarra*, O'Hara told his brother Tom that "the story is essentially the story of a young married couple and their breakdown in the first year of the depression."[23] The novel drew deeply, that is, upon its author's recent marital disasters. O'Hara's emotional devastation was reflected in his working title, "The Infernal Grove," taken from an untitled poem of William Blake:

> Let us agree to give up love
> And root up the infernal grove,
> Then shall we return and see
> The worlds of happy Eternity.
>
> And throughout all Eternity
> I forgive you, you forgive me.
> As our dear Redeemer said:
> This the wine and this the bread.[24]

The love of man and woman, which for O'Hara always involved the primal force of sex, had turned Eden into Hell; and in his postlapsarian gloom, he could find no hope of paradise regained except in a dream of recaptured innocence and mutual forgiveness.

When O'Hara had finished about half of the novel, he was electrified by a passage from Somerset Maugham's *Sheppey* in which Death expresses her surprise at encountering a certain young man in Baghdad: "for I had an appointment with him tonight in Samarra."[25] The novel was immediately retitled, despite the publisher's objections, because, writes Bruccoli, "the author insisted that the Samarra legend conveyed 'the inevitability of Julian English's death.'"[26] The idea of inevitability was so vital for O'Hara because in Julian English's self-destruction he imagined a fate that might easily have been his own, had he carried his drinking to its deadly limit. In the writing of *Appointment in Samarra*, O'Hara worked through the grief and bewilderment common in the aftermath of a failed marriage, but he also painfully explored the linkage of his marital and other failures to his drinking. Although Julian English was not in any simple way an autobiographical character, he was O'Hara's oblique self-portrait, by way of Fitzgerald, of the modernist artist as an alcoholic.[27]

Like Fitzgerald, O'Hara denied his alcoholism even as he attempted to manage it. Immediately after his suicide attempt on 3 July 1933, but before he started work on *Appointment in Samarra*, O'Hara became what he called a "sober citizen." "[T]he most I have had in any one day since then has been a cocktail and a glass of wine at dinner," he bragged to his brother in October. "At no other time I have taken so much as a single cocktail."[28] O'Hara cut his drinking quite severely, given his accustomed intake of a quart or more of whiskey a day, and he apparently did remain relatively sober for two years. But he was never entirely free of alcohol, and he fell off the wagon completely for the night of Christmas Eve 1933, when Robert Benchley enticed him to join in the holiday spirit(s)—in the form of a few Black Velvets. For O'Hara, as for many alcoholics, swearing off booze temporarily was a subtle form of denial: a means of extending his lease on the drinking life by showing that he could curb his consumption if he wished. Once he had proven his "control" to his own satisfaction, he then felt entitled to suspend the demonstration. Precisely two years after he had become a "sober citizen," O'Hara resumed unrestricted drinking on the Fourth of July, 1935, just as he was finishing the draft of *Butterfield 8*, another novel about alcoholic self-destruction.

In the criticism on *Appointment in Samarra*, an impenetrable mystery has sometimes been seen to envelop Julian English because his death seems inadequately motivated. Edmund Wilson, for instance, complains that although Julian is "apparently the victim of a bad heredity worked upon by demoralizing influences," still the "emotions that drive him to suicide are never really shown." The novel offers an elaborate explanation of why Julian throws a drink at Harry Reilly; "yet the explanation doesn't convince us that the inevitable end for Julian would be the suicide to which his creator brings him."[29] James W. Tuttleton agrees that the "central question of *Appointment in Samarra* is why Julian English committed suicide," but, unlike Wilson, he believes that "it is possible to adduce half a dozen good reasons to explain the mystery." None of these "presumed reasons" is finally "quite relevant," however, for "it was simply *time* for Julian to die and nothing could avert the fate awaiting him."[30]

Along similar lines, Robert Emmet Long argues that uncertainty about Julian's "deepest motivation" need not be regarded as "a flaw of characterization" because it is "consistent with the pattern of the novel that the sufferer should not himself know why he suffers, that he should lose everything without knowing why."[31] Matthew J. Bruccoli also appeals to the design of the novel in rebutting the charge that O'Hara "fails to make the reader understand Julian" or the reasons for his actions: "That is what O'Hara intended. The novel is not superficial: Julian is a superficial human being. He is not a tragic character and was not intended as one."[32]

Some critics have assumed, on the contrary, that Julian *was* meant to be tragic: a representation, as Arthur Mizener says, of "the true American gentleman, refined, aware, instinctively gallant, whose bad behavior is a result of his sensitive nature's being driven beyond restraint by the crudeness of the people around him."[33] Such a reading may seem too sympathetic toward Julian's character, but it does capture, as less partial views do not, his resemblance to the spoiled priest, Dick Diver, as well as to Jay Gatsby, whose grandeur transcends his meretriciousness and criminality.[34] Sheldon Grebstein finds "an undefinable winningness" in Julian's nature: "One might almost say that he has an aura of beauty about him, or of the potentially beautiful: a zest, a joy in living, a sense of the comic, a spontaneity." Like Dick Diver, Julian has "the gift of stimulating others by his very presence, of bringing them an illusion of happiness," but he also lacks "moral stamina to sustain the surface beauty."[35]

The idea of Julian as a romantic hero tallies with O'Hara's own view in a

1960 letter to the prospective producer of a film version of *Appointment in Samarra*. O'Hara asserted that the "universality of the character Julian English is largely responsible for the wide and enduring acceptance of the novel," and he insisted that there could be no Hollywood ending. "This man has got to die by motor car, by Cadillac motor car," he explained, because no other fate is imaginable for this particular character at the particular historical moment at which he lived and died. A later version of Julian would be more of a survivor, however:

> He would be Alfred Eaton as I wrote him in FROM THE TERRACE. A present-day Julian does not commit suicide; he just drifts. It is nobler to commit suicide if you have to. But we are at the stage of the development of the welfare state when we are not even allowed despair. The decline of love is another example of what is happening to us, but Julian English lived and died too soon to be affected by the decline of love. We are having honest fear and despair and love processed out of us, and the big imminent tragedy now is that we don't know it.[36]

Although these (somewhat cranky) opinions were expressed more than a quarter century after the publication of *Appointment in Samarra*, they seem to be consistent with O'Hara's original aims insofar as the novel itself ascribes nobility to Julian's "honest fear and despair."

By making his suicide the focus of interpretation, and by reading it either as an overdetermined act with a complex of causes or as an inexplicable act for which no cause ultimately matters, critics have missed a plain and simple fact: that drinking is the main reason, if not the only one, for Julian's death.[37] Much depends, moreover, on whether Julian's drinking is seen to represent a Fitzgeraldian romantic readiness or the reckless abandon of alcoholism. For Caroline English, as she struggles to grasp some meaning in her husband's self-destruction, Julian's drinking defines him completely only to those who are blind to his undefinable superiority: "They would say he was drunk, but he wasn't drunk. Yes he was. He was drunk, but he was Julian, drunk or not, and that was more than anyone else was. That was what everyone else was not." Thus whatever makes Julian seem "more than anyone else was" exists apart from his drunkenness. In her thoughts Caroline goes on to compare Julian to a dashing hero in uniform, "someone who had died in the war"—except that his gallantry "had nothing to do with fighting but was attitude and manner."[38]

Caroline's views may reflect the bias of her love and grief, but her sense of Julian is affirmed by the novel as a whole. Like *Tender Is the Night*, however, *Appointment in Samarra* suggests that the romantic hero's superiority does not consist merely in his attitude and manner, but rather in his heightened sense of life's futility: an admirably unillusioned vision that signifies his initiation into the White Logic of John Barleycorn. Julian's character and actions make no more sense than Dick Diver's, unless he too is recognized as an alcoholic exponent of The Modern Temper.

The modernist ethos of O'Hara's fiction has been best articulated by Lionel Trilling in his insight that O'Hara's attention to detail may sometimes be excessive but is never gratuitous, because it is always at the service of his "sense of the startling anomaly of man's life in society, his consciousness of social life as an absurd and inescapable fate, as the degrading condition to which the human spirit submits if it is to exist at all." For Trilling, O'Hara comes unexpectedly close to Kafka in the "terrible imagination of society" as if it were "some strange sentient organism which acts by laws of its own being which are not to be understood." In *Appointment in Samarra*, no less than in *The Trial*, "one does not know what will set into motion its dull implacable hostility, some small thing, not very wrong, not wrong at all; once it begins to move, no one can stand against it."[39]

Julian English certainly appears to be the victim of such a monstrous organism: a man destroyed by hostility awesomely incommensurate with the degree of his social transgression.[40] Several critics, in accord with Bruccoli that "*Appointment in Samarra* is a sociological novel, not a psychological novel," [41] have argued effectively that Julian's fate is inexorably determined by hereditary and environmental forces. But the sociological cannot be distinguished so easily from the psychological. The best example of their juncture in the novel is Julian's alcoholism, which is embedded within both a cultural context and his individual character.

Set in 1930, the first year of the Great Depression and one of the last years of Prohibition, *Appointment in Samarra* was meant, as O'Hara later wrote, to capture a particular mood: "Remember that in 1930 there was not yet an FDR to revive hope; the nation was stunned by the first blows of the depression, with other blows yet to come. In [Westbrook] Pegler's great phrase, the Era of Wonderful Nonsense was at an end, but the only hope people had was that the Era was not over; the hope was not for a bright future; the hope was for the resumption of the immediate past."[42] As Americans backed into a depressingly uncertain future, they lifted their spirits with bathtub gin and other liquid concoctions peculiar to the "experiment noble in purpose" (as Herbert Hoover called it) that had ignobly and obviously failed by 1930.

In 1960, the same year he wrote the letter just quoted, O'Hara published a triptych of brooding novellas about Gibbsville in the 1930s. In "Imagine Kissing Pete," James Malloy bitterly assesses the corrosive effect of Prohibition on his generation. By breeding routine contempt for the law, Prohibition fostered a climate of pervasive dishonesty that "made liars of a hundred million men and cheats of their children." As cynicism strangled the spirit of idealism, it also induced emotional rigor mortis:

> We knew so much, and since what we knew seemed to be all there was to know, we were shockproof. We had come to our maturity and our knowledgeability during the long decade of cynicism that was usually dismissed as "a cynical disregard of the law of the land," but that was something else, something deeper. The law had been passed with a "noble" but nevertheless cynical disregard of men's right to drink. . . . And when the law was an instant failure, it was not admitted to be a failure by those who had imposed it. . . . They gained no recruits to their own way; they had only deserters, who were not brave deserters but furtive ones; there was no honest mutiny but only grumbling and small disobediences. And we grew up listening to the grumbling, watching the small disobediences; laughing along when the grumbling was intentionally funny, imitating the small disobediences in other ways besides the customs of drinking.[43]

In his drinking as well as his anxiety about the future, Julian is representative of his time and place. During his final two days—the interval from three o'clock on Christmas morning to nearly midnight on December 26, feast of the first Christian martyr, St. Stephen—Julian drinks continually, except for the few hours he spends in bed, more unconscious than asleep. Although he is drunker at some times than others—and drunkest in the hour of his death—he is never truly sober. For all of its determinism, however, the novel does not treat Julian's drinking as something beyond his control. There is no hint in *Appointment in Samarra* that O'Hara had any familiarity with the emergent model of alcoholism as a disease. On the contrary, he depicts drinking, within the Victorian paradigm, as a matter of individual choice. Julian is not a pathetic drunkard trapped in a bottle; rather he appears to seize willfully upon alcohol for the escape he seeks from the dis-ease of his existence.

Just as Julian's life revolves around alcohol, so does the life of every other character, alcoholic or not; for the whole of Gibbsville society, from the upper crust to the underworld, has been informed by Prohibition. The plot of the novel, like the social order itself, is shaped by the economy and culture of drinking: how illicit alcohol is supplied by the gangster Ed Charney through his minion Al Grecco; how it is then consumed by the country club set, whose heavy drinking is the envy of the socially ambitious middle class (although it is a scandal to the stolid bourgeoisie). Two characters are clearly marked as drunkards: Bobby Herrmann, "persona grata at the inner sanctum" (p. 11) of the Lantenengo Country Club by virtue of his booze-inspired hi-jinks; and Helene Holman, Charney's sluttish mistress, who drinks supposedly out of bitterness at his neglect. Nearly everyone else in Gibbsville drinks at least a little, and tolerance is apparently high for drunken misdemeanors, especially if committed by members of the upper class. When Julian worries about the consequences of his throwing a drink in Harry Reilly's face, he takes comfort in remembering greater offenses that have been forgiven. Lute Fliegler believes that even Julian's coming on to Helene may be overlooked because it was lechery under the influence: "You were cockeyed, and that's one consolation. Maybe Charney will take that into consideration" (p. 213).

Julian receives no such latitude from his wife, however. Long before she fell in love with him, Caroline Walker knew of Julian's reputation. When one of her boyfriends accused him of cheating at cards and taking dope, Caroline retorted, "He doesn't do any such thing. He *drinks* too much, maybe" (p. 143). Caroline must have realized soon after the wedding that there was no "maybe" about it; for as the novel opens, conflict has long since developed in the marriage over Julian's drinking. The psychodynamics of the relationship, in fact, are largely controlled by this conflict.

On Christmas morning Julian arises with a dreadful hangover from the country club party at which he had drunkenly assaulted Reilly, with whom he (erroneously) suspects Caroline has been having an affair. She is still distressed by her husband's behavior the night before: his verbal abuse on the ride home, when he called her "whore and bitch and a lot worse" (p. 34); the public humiliation of the Reilly incident; the folly of his attacking a man she believes capable of doing "anything short of murder" to get even (p. 32). Since Julian owes Harry a lot of money, Reilly is free to choose a bloodlessly economic, but no less terminal, means of homicide.

Later in the day, at the home of Julian's parents, Dr. English offers Caroline a martini, noting snidely that his son, whom he has long considered a wastrel, will "drink anything, and you know it" (p. 71). The novel suggests that Julian's rebellion against paternal authority and expectation is one key to his self-destruction. Dr. English, afraid that his son had reincarnated the evil of his own larcenous father, branded Julian as a thief when he was caught shoplifting as a child. The burden of moral disapproval and emotional rejection has weighed so heavily on Julian that he has found relief and revenge in outraging the doctor's genteel righteousness. As early as his college days, Julian learned that drunkenness effectively punished others as well as himself.

Caroline is more aware than Julian of the retaliatory motives behind his drinking because she too has become a target of his alcoholic excesses; and she takes umbrage when he comments—after a cross-link breaks on the tire chains as they are driving to the country club dance—"I might as well fix it now while I'm sober" (p. 88). This offhand but pregnant remark signals Julian's intention to get drunk at the club, and it sparks the escalating marital warfare that leads directly to his suicide the following night. Telling Julian that he can drink as long as he does not "get crazy" (p. 89), Caroline extracts his promise of good behavior in exchange for her agreement not only to keep a sexual rendezvous in the car during intermission, but also to forego any contraception. (Caroline's insistence on postponing motherhood, which Julian sardonically calls her "Five Year Plan" [p. 86], has so far prevailed over his own desire for a child.)

Just before this crucial scene, it has been established that Julian expects complete submission, sexual and otherwise, from his wife and that Caroline understands the bargaining power of her compliance. As an inducement for Julia to apologize to Harry Reilly, she agrees to wait at home for him in bed. Julian knows that once Caroline has made a sexual date with him, she always sets her mind on "the ultimate thing" and begins "to submit." He also knows "that with Caroline that was the only part of their love that was submission" (p. 75). After he joins her in bed, she begins to undress him and then waits, lying "with her face down in the pillow, shutting out everything else until he was with her." So passive a position, with its hint of *coitus a tergo,* is unusual for Caroline and thus unusually erotic for Julian. Their intercourse is nothing less than "the greatest single act of their married life. He knew it, and she knew it. It was the time she did not fail him" (pp. 79–80).

O'Hara's emphatic use of "the" in this sentence underscores the desperate state of the Englishes' marriage, which has become a cycle of mutual disappointment that always ends in Julian's getting drunk. The only proof he will accept of Caroline's love and fidelity is her willingness to immolate herself on the altar of unquestioning wifely devotion. Because Caroline can only fail to meet his demand for her self-abnegation, his expectation of her failure becomes self-fulfilling. Except for *the* time, Julian always suffers a rejection that he unconsciously conspires to ensure—and thus provides himself with a grievance to justify his drinking.

This destructive pattern is evident in the way Julian and Caroline interact after they arrive at the club. She issues a pointed reminder to him of his promise to stay sober, and he cooperates at first. But unwonted self-restraint makes Julian feel jumpy: "Whenever he was on a party and did not drink too much he needed a secret game to play or a mental task to perform the while he apparently was observing the amenities" (p. 102). He is trying to distract himself, in other words, from his craving for a drink: a need he does not fully recognize in himself but that he must nonetheless meet, if necessary by self-deception.

Alcoholic compulsion leads Julian to make a serious "error in judgment." Instead of crossing the room to join his wife when she descends from the powder room—"He saw she was too far away to have it worth making a point of going to her" (p. 103)—he gravitates instead to the locker room for a belt of whiskey from the bottle he keeps there. Julian tells himself that he *had* to go into the locker room in order to talk privately with Father Creedon about the Harry Reilly imbroglio. Time passes (an hour in all), and one drink leads to another (five in all), and Julian finally emerges in a state of intoxication that is obvious enough to aggravate his wife. From long experience, she knows how to cut through Julian's excuses to the truth he prefers not to face: "You were getting drunk and you just happened to give him [Father Creedon] one drink so you could truthfully say you'd been with him" (pp. 117–18). Denying this charge, Julian continues to antagonize his wife—"If you don't mind my saying so, you give me a pain in the ass"—at the same time he is trying to ingratiate himself with her—"I'm sorry. Please forgive me. . . . Have we still got a date for midnight?" (p. 119). Since Julian has broken his promise, Caroline feels released from hers. Besides, as she later reflects, Julian is far less "irresistible" than he thinks when he has had a few drinks (p. 221).

By laying bare his ulterior motives, Caroline refuses to be manipulated by Julian: "You make me very angry about something and then you refuse to go on with the discussion, but instead you blithely talk about love and going to bed. It's a dirty trick, because if I refuse to talk about loving you, you become the injured party and so on. It's a lousy trick and you do it all the time" (pp. 119–20). The rendezvous in the parking lot devolves into a volley of recriminations. He cannot fathom her understandable lack of sexual desire except as evidence of either adultery or the unexpected onset of menstruation![44] The quarrel leaves Caroline feeling frustrated by Julian's insensitivity to her emotional needs and Julian feeling justified in returning to the locker room, "where there was enough liquor for anyone in the world to get drunk" (p. 124).

For Julian, as an alcoholic, this has been the real objective all along. But denial requires him to cover his tracks by shifting blame onto Caroline and transforming his own self-pity into resentment against her. Armed with an ironclad excuse to get extremely drunk, Julian then uses intoxication as an excuse for viciously humiliating Caroline at the Stage Coach Inn. Although Julian later swears that he "didn't lay that girl," what really matters, as Lute tells him, is that "everybody thought you did and that amounts to the same thing" (p. 212). Julian knows very well that fooling around with Ed Charney's girl would be "suicide," as Lute says, for anyone in the gangster's own crowd

(p. 211). But Julian enjoys a perverse high from his misdeed with Helene: "the tremendous excitement, the great thrilling lump in the chest and abdomen that comes before the administering of an unknown, well-deserved punishment. He knew he was in for it" (p. 182).

Punishments now converge on Julian from all directions. He awakens with another crushing hangover, downs a morning bracer, and picks a fight with the cook, Mrs. Grady, simply because she has observed, "I seen you was taking a drink of liquor so I didn't know if you wanted the eggs" (p. 197). In his private thoughts, Julian's petulance extends to the entire class of "servants, cops, waiters in restaurants, ushers in theatres—he could hate them more than persons who threatened him with real harm" (p. 198). But Julian knows the cure for these petty irritations: "He had to laugh, and pour himself a drink" (p. 199). At the office, he must endure a tongue-lashing by Lute Fliegler and, worse, the disapproving silence of his secretary, Mary Klein, a gorgan of Lutheran respectability: "For weeks, and probably months, she had behaved like someone, a school teacher, who was meaning to speak to him about his lessons or conduct. She was Right, and he was Wrong. She could make him feel like a thief, a lecher (although God knows he never had made a pass at her), a drunkard, a no-good bum" (p. 218).

Julian now contemplates suicide as he takes a pistol from his desk drawer. But even before he gingerly puts the barrel into his mouth, he knows that "he was not going to do it that way" (p. 231). Remembering a bottle of whiskey in another drawer, he takes a self-consolatory drink instead; as he weeps with his head on his arms, he mutters to himself, "You poor guy . . . I feel so sorry for you" (p. 232). It's off to the club for lunch, only to be assailed by the self-righteous fury of Froggy Ogden, supposedly a bosom friend, who spits at Julian, "I always hated your guts when you were a kid, and I hate you now. You were never any damn good" (p. 235). Then a brawl that pits Julian against "the Polack war veterans and whoremasters" (p. 238), as he insultingly dubs some guests who have, in his view, defiled the club's ethnic purity.

Finally, Julian must confront his wife, who in the wake of the Stage Coach incident has been brooding and grieving and pondering divorce all day. In their final conversation, just after Julian's fight at the club, Caroline "fails" him once more:

"This is a pretty good time for you to stick by me."

"I can't stick by you if you don't tell me what for."

"Blind, without knowing, you could stick by me. That's what you'd do if you were a real wife, but, what the hell."

"Where are you going? To get drunk I suppose."

"Very likely. Very likely."

"Julian, if you leave now it's for good. Forever. I won't ever come back to you, no matter what happens. I won't ever sleep with you again or see you, not even see you."   (P. 256)

Having lost his wife, his friends, and likely his business, all that remains for Julian is to get drunk and then abandon life itself; within a few hours, he does exactly that.

Although Julian's death, according to the coroner, is "an open-and-shut case of suicide by carbon monoxide gas poisoning, the first of its kind in the history of the county" (p. 282)[45]—the real cause of death is alcohol. During his last hours, Julian's drinking becomes purposefully crazed. After killing one bottle of whiskey (with a little help from Miss Cartwright, the reporter from the *Standard*), he opens a fresh bottle and makes a gigantic highball in a vase. He drinks from the vase when he is sitting down and from a glass when he is staggering around. As he moves to the garage, Julian takes the bottle along. He has three more drinks in the car while he waits for oblivion from the exhaust fumes, and he is working on a fourth when he passes out and slumps down in the seat. A few minutes later, futilely, he tries to get up; in another twenty minutes, he is gone.

In claiming that alcohol kills Julian, I do not mean simply that he is too drunk to save himself when he tries to retreat from death or that drinking alone has caused all the troubles that culminate in his suicide. The point is that Julian's despairing sense of himself as the victim of a cruelly indifferent universe may itself be seen as a symptom of his alcoholic deterioration. Julian has been communing so long with John Barleycorn that he finally answers the annihilating call of the White Logic. Although he is locked on a self-destructive course from the beginning, he seems to rush willingly toward his fate at the end, embracing death with a gleeful grimace.

In *Appointment at Samarra,* as in Tolstoy's *Anna Karenina,* the romantic tragedy of suicide is framed, and thus diminished, by the perspective of mundane reality. The first sentence of the novel, which opens the story within the ordinary "mind of Luther L. (L for LeRoy) Fliegler" (p. 3), is echoed by the opening sentence of the final chapter: "Our story never ends" (p. 281). In this flat declaration of the continuity of life, there is an implication, which the last chapter develops, that Julian's death may have been pointless—because things could have been patched up at the club, because Harry Reilly was never all that upset, because even Caroline would have come around, as she always had before. If there was no need for Julian to kill himself, then whatever fatally impelled him had less basis in reality than he thought. He might be said to have died for a delusion—seduced into suicide by alcoholic depression and paranoia.

This conclusion has never been drawn about *Appointment in Samarra,* either by critics who regard Julian unsympathetically as a weak character from whom O'Hara naturalistically detaches himself or by those who read the novel romantically and admire Julian as a Fitzgeraldian hero with whom O'Hara identifies himself. In either case, the novel seems finally not to question the validity of Julian's "honest fear and despair"; implicitly, it rationalizes his suicidal drinking as a natural, even a noble, response to a meaningless universe. If O'Hara the honest writer and meticulous observer depicted the psychology of an alcoholic with remarkable authenticity, O'Hara the alcoholic followed Fitzgerald's lead in *Tender Is the Night* and used the waste land as an alibi.

Despite O'Hara's complex characterization of Caroline English, the novel also lends support to Julian's self-serving belief that he has been doomed not by his drunkenness but by his wife's prim intolerance.[46] "If Julian can be considered the victim of one particular thing," Bruccoli asserts, "he is the victim of Caroline's bitchiness."[47] The Blake poem from which O'Hara derived his original working title contains a pertinent stanza:

> Till I turn from Female Love
> And root up the Infernal Grove
> I shall never worthy be
> To Step into Eternity.[48]

At the end, before he steps into eternity, Julian English does turn completely away from female love. He has already uprooted the infernal grove of his marriage; next, as he attempts to seduce Miss Cartwright, his desire turns suddenly to repulsion.

> "Just kiss me," she said, but she put her hand under his coat and opened his vest and shirt. "No," she said. "Just kiss me." She was terribly strong. Suddenly she jerked away from him. "Whew! Come up for air," she said. He hated her more than anyone ever had hated anyone.
> "Drink?" he said.
> "No, I don't think so. I must go."
> "Don't go," he said. He wanted to call her all kinds of bitches. (P. 275)

What accounts here for the depth of Julian's disgust? How can he feel such intense hatred for a woman he hardly knows? When Miss Cartwright begins to unfasten Julian's vest, she repeats what Caroline did—but knew enough to *stop* doing—*the* time "she did not fail him." For Julian, Miss Cartwright's bitchery exceeds even Caroline's: she is far too sexually aggressive for his comfort; she seems to take cynical pleasure in gaining control over men through prick-teasing.

There is no question for Julian that men must rule over the site and symbol of potency. Sexual domination, in the form of delayed ejaculation, has long been the hallmark of his adult male identity. He recalls the momentous significance of his discovery that "he, Julian English, whom he had gone on thinking of as a child with a child's renewable integrity and curiosity and fears and all, suddenly had the power of his own passion; that he could control himself and use this control to give pleasure and a joyous hiatus of weakness to a woman" (p. 264). Women are, no doubt, grateful to men like Julian for his gift; they are evidently incapable of achieving the "joyous hiatus of weakness" for themselves.

Caroline, whose initiation into sex was an assault upon her private parts by a grimy child at the Gibbsville Mission, seems to be typical in having learned to keep passion tightly under rein. Caroline has generalized from this "first completely unpleasant encounter with the male sex" to the idea "that that was what you could expect of men, what she had been brought up to expect of men." Like the Mission boy, some men had already "run over her with their hands"; she had permitted a few of them to do so. Until the Mission incident, however, she had mistakenly thought she "had sex pretty well under control":

> After the attack she reorganized, or entirely disorganized, her ideas about men and the whole of sex; and the one permanent effect of "that afternoon at the Mission," as she referred to it in her frequent introspection, was that her ignorance of sex was pointed up. She knew herself for a completely inexperienced girl, and for the first time she began to remember the case histories in Havelock Ellis and Krafft-Ebing and the lesser psychologists as more than merely pornography. (Pp. 128–29)

Since what the sexologists label as perversion exists in the real world of men, Caroline must take control of herself and also of men. When in early adolescence her desire for a British cousin leads her to become completely vulnerable to his will (fortunately, the cousin is a gentleman), the moment of surrender passes quickly: "She was ashamed and grateful, because she never before had let herself go that way" (p. 131). And she never does again: "She was in demand, and she kissed a good many men with as much abandon as she had kissed Jerome Walker, except that now she knew how and when to stop" (p. 132).[49]

Except for *the* time, it seems, Caroline has vied with Julian for sexual mastery within their marriage. Even as she unlocks herself sexually to Julian, she steadfastly refuses his demands for her complete passivity. The "worst fear he had ever known" arises from his groundless suspicions of her infidelity: the horrible thought that "sometime she would open herself to another man and close herself around him. Oh, if she did that it would be forever" (p. 231).

Even the loss of his wife to another man would hurt Julian less, however, than the blow his self-esteem suffers from Froggy Ogden. The "thing that in its way was more important than anything between him and Caroline" is "the never-to-be-buried discovery" that one of his closest friends from boyhood has been his mortal enemy all along: "That was worse than anything he could do to Caroline, because it was something that did something to him. It made a change in himself, and we must not change ourselves much" (p. 263). This reflection immediately precedes Julian's meditation, quoted above, about the "last time there had been a change in himself"—namely, when the discovery of his sexual power made him a man. It is significant that Julian's most tormented thoughts involve his relationship to another man; homosocial male bonding is an important, but largely buried, subtext in *Appointment in Samarra*.

In O'Hara's novel, as in the other texts we have considered, an underlying misogyny is linked to an affirmation of drinking as man's best means for escaping woman's domination. Crucial in this regard are the thoughts that cross Al Grecco's mind as he stands watch over Helene Holman at the Stage Coach Inn. Al has been assigned this onerous duty by his boss, Ed Charney, who feels obliged to spend Christmas with his family and fears that his mistress will likely avenge his absence by getting drunk and making up to another man. As Al thinks about how women "nearly always got the dirty end of the stick," he does not use the word "women," but, rather, "another name which he used for all female persons except nuns" (p. 159). Since "bitches" appears elsewhere in the novel, the word in question must be even cruder. "Cunts"? After a few minutes, in any case, such thoughts begin to irritate Al; he wants to get women completely off his mind:

> But that was not possible here, at the Stage Coach. It was a woman's place. All dance places, night clubs, road houses, stores, churches, and even whore-houses—all were women's places. And probably the worst kind of woman's place was a place like this, where men put on monkey suits and cut their necks with stiff collars and got drunk without the simple fun of getting drunk but with the presence of women to louse things up.   (P. 159–60).

Al's longing for the saloon world of male camaraderie, where the pleasure of drinking is not spoiled by women, is drunkenly echoed by Julian when he lurches over to Al's table and asks him if he knows "anybody that could let me have some Scotch" (p. 174). As Julian disjointedly explains, he is not interested merely in buying himself a drink; rather, he seeks the intimacy that only comes from treating: "Well, it's like love, Al. . . . You buy a drink, and that's all it is, just a bought drink. Whereas, on the other hand, au contraire, au contraire, Al, uh, you uh, uh, somebody gives you a drink and that's like love. Why, say, who is this?" (p. 175). That Julian, distracted at this point by Helene, now ignores Al is yet another instance of how the presence of women/"cunts" louses things up.

A serious point is disguised by Julian's drunken babble, which resembles the self-conscious and hysterical banter of Bill Gorton when he tries to express his affection for Jake Barnes. Like Hemingway, O'Hara veers from the very idea of love between men except as an object of humor or contempt. Al is taunted by Loving Cup, the campily homosexual waiter at the Apollo Restaurant: "Don't try and bluff me. . . . I know you're queer" (p. 60). Later, Helene vents her anger with Ed Charney by mocking Al: "Was he nothing but a yes-man? Was he a unique? Did he know what a unique was? A unique, she told him, was a morphadite" (p. 160). Al's job of guarding Helene may make him a eunuch, at least figuratively; but in his own thoughts he has nothing in common with the decorator whom Ed once hired to remodel the Stage Coach Inn—a "pansy" who was "driven once back to New York by the practical jokes of the boys" before he could finish the job under an order of protection from Charney (p. 82).[50]

It is nevertheless true that Al gets an emotional "chill" from his intense and filial loyalty to Charney, toward whom he feels "the way you feel about your mother" (p. 21). And Al takes a fondly protective interest as well in Julian English, whose dangerously weaving car he follows just to be sure he arrives home safely. To Al, who relates more easily to machines than to humans, Julian English is an artist behind the wheel of his car. Julian is simply "all right": "One of those guys that can drive when they're drunk or sober, the only difference being that when they're drunk they have no consideration for what they might be doing to the car" (p. 25).

In the naive deference of Al's admiration, in fact, there is the purity of submission that Julian never finds in his wife or any other woman. The idea of turning away from female love appealed to O'Hara no less than to London or Hemingway or Fitzgerald, but only if it was detached from the corollary idea of turning *toward* male love. As we have seen, the culture of drinking, as figured by these manly modernists, served both to assuage and to arouse anxiety by simultaneously reinforcing and dissolving gender boundaries. It remained for Djuna Barnes to erase the boundaries altogether by inverting the male culture of drinking.

6

Transcendence Downward:
Nightwood

"There's no doubt that all of us, of the 'Lost Generation,' had, when thinking it over, a most extraordinary and unusual time of it," wrote Djuna Barnes, then in her seventy-fourth year, to Natalie Clifford Barney, then in her ninetieth; "not all of it was 'wasted'!"[1] Barney and Barnes, who had briefly been lovers in the 1920s, were among the last survivors of the colony of expatriate women artists who once had assembled in Paris. Although Barnes was well known at Barney's salon, she reputedly spent many a "wasted" afternoon or evening hanging around the Left Bank cafés on the Boulevard du Montparnasse with a drinking crowd that included Robert McAlmon and other former denizens of Greenwich Village. From the memoirs of male expatriates arose a legendary Djuna Barnes, renowned for her beauty and notorious for her eccentricity and slashing wit. But while her patronym, combined with the address of Barney's salon at 20 rue Jacob, provided the protagonist's name in *The Sun Also Rises*, neither Barnes nor her writing would become as familiar to the reading public as Hemingway's fictional character. She was to receive high praise from her literary peers and to attract a cult following, but as her biographer notes, she "would manage to enjoy simultaneous fame and obscurity, boasting in the 1960s that she had become the world's most famous unknown writer."[2]

Nightwood (1936), perhaps the world's most famous unknown novel, is a book dipped into more often than read through, more admired than comprehended. Although its reputation as one of the most forbiddingly difficult and allusive of high modernist texts is certainly deserved, *Nightwood* does reward close and patient reading with its poetic majesty and tragic force. To some extent, the novel has been held hostage to the stories that circulate about its author. "Like the myth of the expatriate experience itself," says Shari Benstock, "the myth of Djuna Barnes 'expatriate woman writer' has been the creation of a male culture"—by which she is sometimes cast as "a tough, vulgar, butch lesbian whose masculine wit struck its mark" or else as "a pathetic victim of the Parisian nightworld, her 'basic heterosexuality' undermined by the evils of a lesbian community, her beauty lost in drunken brawls, her wit turned acid." Feminists such as Benstock have argued that Barnes is best understood in the context of "a community of serious women writers in Paris" and suggested that "the informing despair of *Nightwood* might be interpreted beyond the biographical details of her own life."[3]

While some of these details may have figured too easily and often in readings of the novel, others have never been properly assessed. That is, while critics continue to dispute whether *Nightwood* is a roman à clef in which Nora stands for Barnes, or whether Barnes herself was lesbian or bisexual or "basically heterosexual,"[4] the bearing of Barnes's alcoholism on *Nightwood* (and the rest of her career) remains largely unexplored.[5] Those committed to elevating her literary reputation, including those who embrace Barnes as a "lesbian culture hero,"[6] have been oblivious to her drinking, as if it were an inconvenient or inconsiderable matter. In this respect, Barnes's advocates are no different from champions of the canonical male modernists whose alcoholism has been similarly ignored or denied. But Barnes was one of the first female American writers to develop a drinking problem, and *Nightwood* plays off the conventions of male-authored drunk narratives in order to subvert the gendering of "alcoholism" itself.

On the roster of one hundred alcoholic American writers (see Chapter Two, table 2), only fifteen are women, and none appears before such female members of the Lost Generation as Katherine Anne Porter (b. 1890), Djuna Barnes (b. 1892), Edna St. Vincent Millay (b. 1892), and Dorothy Parker (b. 1893). These facts are hardly surprising. During the nineteenth century, the cult of "True Womanhood" made female abstemiousness a sign of gentility.[7] The ideology of the temperance movement, moreover, deemed drunkenness to be almost exclusively a male problem. Especially after the founding in 1874 of the W.C.T.U.—an extremely powerful organization that arose when female activists literally took to the streets to shut down the saloons—women were defined as the innocent, but far from helpless, victims of intemperance. The female drunkard became nearly unimaginable except in the stereotype of the drunken harlot, who was almost invariably represented in temperance literature as an immigrant and/or working-class woman whose inebriation signified her defective racial stock and overall moral degeneracy.[8]

In the decade before World War I, however, the use of alcohol emerged as "a prominent element in the feminist revolt" of middle-class American women, especially those, in increasing numbers, who went to college. The practice of men and women drinking together "became a firmly established part of the dominant culture in America," writes historian Andrew Sinclair, "and drinking occasions from which women were excluded became increasingly rare."[9] One side effect of Prohibition was to stimulate even heavier consumption among women, particularly the younger generation. In resistance to the law and the oppression it symbolized, mixed company liberally consumed mixed drinks at the cocktail party (an invention of the 1920s). "Public drinking became so fashionable that both decent and indecent women went to the speak-easy, even though the old-time saloon had been a male preserve, only spotted by the occasional prostitute. For women, too, liquor became a flag of their new freedom."[10]

Inevitably, some otherwise respectable women became alcoholics. But insofar as it perpetuated the idea of a "male preserve," the drinking culture of modernism provided no place for such a woman except as she conformed, like Brett Ashley, to an updated version of the drunken harlot: the alcoholic nymphomaniac. As in this denigrating formulation, "alcoholic" in its adjectival form (as a synonym for "drunken") might be applied to women, but as a noun it still referred only to men. Within the ideology of modernism, that is, there might be such a thing as an "alcoholic female," but a "female alcoholic" was something of a contradiction in terms because the "alcoholic" was implicitly or explicitly gendered male. A woman might drink out of sheer wantonness, but no woman was privy to the manly secrets of the White Logic—except, perhaps, one so "manly" that she wasn't "really" a woman. If the alcoholic female was oversexed (a slut), then the female alcoholic was unsexed (a dyke).[11]

Djuna Barnes, observer and participant in the expatriate drinking culture of the 1920s, refused to accept this choice of identities. Instead she explored how the "alcoholic" was defined within a larger system of gender. "All of Djuna Barnes's writing can be read," Benstock asserts, "as a critique of woman's place in Western society."[12] And although *Nightwood* has been interpreted by Constance M. Perry as "a story of women and alcohol, in which lovers see their relationship destroyed by addiction and the Paris café culture that supports it,"[13] the novel does not, in fact, deal simply with either alcoholic relationships or the evils of addiction. Barnes not only satirizes the temperance genre of the cautionary tale; she also subverts the modernist drunk narrative.

Scholars of Barnes's work agree that its profound engagement with woman's place in a patriarchal order derived from her upbringing in a bizarre extended family in which her father "made what amounted to a religious cult out of sex."[14] Wald Barnes (born Henry Budington) kept numerous mistresses and sired several illegitimate children, sometimes insisting that they cohabit with his wife and legitimate children. He also apparently violated his adolescent daughter: possibly by ritually raping her himself, or by giving her for sexual initiation (and marriage) to a middle-aged man.[15] The exact nature of Barnes's childhood sexual trauma, which was incessantly but obliquely reworked in her writing, remains in question; but it seems to have been incestuous, and the psychological wounds were primal and unhealing.[16]

The most positive force within Barnes's domestic environment was her paternal grandmother, Zadel Barnes Gustafson, a feminist and writer who was responsible for whatever education young Djuna received (almost none of it formal). Zadel too led a sexually unconventional life. Her divorce from Wald Barnes's father and subsequent remarriage to a younger man (who was a foreigner) was highly unusual for a woman of her generation. As Mary Lynn Broe asserts, she also had an "erotic involvement with Djuna."[17] Both Zadel and her son Wald molded their lives, says Andrew Field, in "violent rebellion against the prohibitions of strict Methodism," as personified by the displaced patriarch of the clan: Zadel's first husband, Henry Aaron Budington.[18]

Among the strictest prohibitions of Henry Aaron Budington, as mandated in his tract, *Man Makes His Body; or, The Ascent of the Ego Through Matter* (1899), was the one against alcohol and all other drugs:

> If anyone indulges in abnormal physical habits: the use of tobacco, alcohol, chloral, opium, hasheesh, gluttony, sex excess—all these habits force the spirit to deposit in that part of the brain, protoplasm to enlarge the special organ which is needed to intensify that habit. The balance of the faculties is upset, the desire for the abnormal experience is increased, the brain organ for that special passion is enlarged, and the spirit, thrown out of nature's proper channel, rushes on, building up the structure which will gratify that desire, until the habit becomes so overpowering that the spirit can no longer supply the organ, and collapse of the special organ occurs, and the spirit leaves the body in an abnormal manner.[19]

From the time she came of age and emancipated herself by becoming a successful freelance journalist in New York, Djuna Barnes showed signs of a "special passion" for alcohol. Living in Greenwich Village, she was drawn to the bars where avant garde artists and writers congregated, and she established a pattern of attachment to alcoholics, including Marsden Hartley, Else Baroness von Freytag-Loringhoven, Eugene O'Neill, and Courtnay Lemon (to whom she may have been married briefly). When Barnes moved to Paris in 1920, she immediately joined the drinking crowd, and she probably dabbled in other drugs as well. She crossed the line into alcoholism during the most passionate and wrenching relationship of her life.

Soon after her arrival in Paris, Barnes met Thelma Wood, another expatriated American artist, who had already established a reputation for excessive drinking. After they began to live together, in an apartment that Barnes bought and elaborately furnished, Wood took to bar-hopping and drunken couplings with men and women alike. Some nights, as if she were playing the role of the long-suffering wife in a temperance melodrama, Djuna (whose secret identity to Thelma was "Irene") kept vigil at home, fretting with worry, anger, and jealousy until Thelma ("Simon") staggered in. Other nights, however, Barnes trailed Wood from dive to dive, drowning her own sorrows along the way and often getting so drunk that she needed more help than Wood to get home. "Djuna spent a great deal of energy trying to get Thelma to stop drinking," her biographer reports. "In the end, drinking became a very serious problem for Barnes herself. She did not drink to unwind but to take refuge. For long stretches of time Thelma would come home merely to sleep off a hangover."[20] By 1927, when Wood abandoned Barnes for another woman, their ménage had become hellish; despite later reconciliations, the relationship was tattered beyond repair, and Barnes ended it for good in 1931.

Drinking had undoubtedly been the most destructive element in Barnes's life with Wood. During their separation in 1927, swearing that "he" would "be a man" and take his medicine, "Simon" abjectly pledged sobriety and begged "Irene" for one more chance:

> I feel so shy at saying any thing for fear it sounds like excusing which God knows I don't—but I've thought over it all and I think if I didn't drink maybe things wouldn't have happened—as that is usely [sic] when I get involved—
>
> Now Simon will not touch one drop till you come to America and I'll have my exhibition done—and I'll try and be financially independent—and then maybe if you still care—and look him over—and he again looks sweet to you. Perhaps we could try it a new way—perhaps that too would make things better—and if you will I will never again as long as you love me take one small drop of anything stronger than tea.
>
> If this sounds like bunk to you precious—drop me a little note and say no use. But if there is any slight chance for Simon if he bucks up let him know that too—I tell you angel darling the only reason your Simon doesn't drop off that boat is because I've made you sufficiently unhappy as it is—[21]

"Simon's" promises and protestations proved to be bunk, after all, and each woman would descend alone into deeper alcoholic anguish before she eventually sobered up. Thelma Wood kept drinking for decades, but the year before her death in 1970, she wrote to Barnes that she had not had a drink in "about ten years."[22] Barnes suffered several booze-related breakdowns that required hospital treatment. When she went pub-crawling in London in the late 1930s, she experienced delirium tremens; and in 1940, after she had returned to New York as a refugee from occupied Paris, her family was so appalled by her condition that they conspired to confine her to an institution. Instead Barnes moved into a cell-like apartment on Patchin Place in Greenwich Village, where she lived as a virtual hermit until her death in 1982. Barnes may have tried to control her drinking now and then. During a visit to Arizona in the early 1940s, she was notably irritable, apparently as a result of unaccustomed (and temporary) abstinence. She finally stopped drinking completely by about 1950, at the age of fifty-eight.[23]

Unlike John O'Hara, however, Barnes gained no significant benefits from sobriety in terms of either literary productivity or personal serenity. On the contrary, she became increasingly agitated and querulous. Hank O'Neal, who spent more hours with her than anyone else at the end of her life, found her sometimes charming but often depressing company: "Barnes was pessimistic in her writing, and most of her general beliefs were gloomy. She felt most people were vile, insufferable charlatans, or stupid. Some manifested only a few of these characteristics; she thought most had all of them."[24] Drinking or not, she accomplished very little after finishing *Nightwood*: a few poems and an abstruse closet drama, *The Antiphon* (1958). O'Neal reports that her writing methods almost seemed designed to prevent her from completing anything:

> Barnes's work habits were very sloppy when I knew her, and the thousands of pages around her apartment indicated it had been the case for years. She could not begin work on a poem, stop, and begin the next day where she had stopped. She began again and again, each page noted again with her name, address, and date. The result was hundreds of versions of the same poems, all retained and mixed up, a draft from 1965 next to one from 1975 and many others mixed in seeming chaos. As years went by the papers piled higher and higher.[25]

This picture is very different from Benstock's portrayal of Barnes as an exemplary feminist ascetic. Benstock asserts that gossip about Barnes—"She was rumored to have been an alcoholic and drug-addicted lesbian in her early life and known to be an eccentric and surly recluse in her later years"—has fostered a gross misunderstanding of her work and of her later "retreat from the world." The truth, Benstock believes, is that Barnes abjured her bad habits for the higher cause of her art. She "stopped the self-destructive pattern of the Paris years and ceased to drink, smoke, and involve herself in wearying love affairs in order to write." Benstock claims that age was actually a boon for Barnes because it liberated her from the distractions of sex. Once her body, which had been "the object of sexual desire by both men and women, was no longer on display and no longer vulnerable to sexual involvement, Barnes began to care for it. She stopped smoking and drinking, put herself on a high protein diet, and took vitamins."[26] Having adopted this chastely salubrious regime, Barnes supposedly dedicated her last thirty years to an ambitious long poem, later found among her papers.

Benstock, who rightly complains about biographical myths perpetrated by others, indulges here in some mythmaking of her own. Clearly, Barnes's discipline as a writer never took the forms of a health kick. She continued to drink heavily until she was nearly sixty and to smoke heavily until chronic emphysema make it impossible for her to continue.[27] And during the years she was no longer drinking, she remained addicted to pain killers, especially Darvon, "even though it produced no particular relief" from her arthritis of the spine.[28] If she took vitamins, it was probably to supplement her meager fare: she ate next to nothing because her badly fitted dental plate severely restricted her dietary options. The long poem, which existed only in those endless drafts described by O'Neal, was left in a state of hopeless confusion and incompletion. As for being "vulnerable to sexual involvement," perhaps Barnes had something to learn from Natalie Barney, who wrote to her when she was ninety-two and Barnes was seventy-five: "Have you no 'mate' to torment and exalt you? Love is a better drug than drink. So I lift this glass of hope to you."[29]

At the time she was writing *Nightwood*—between 1932 and 1934, mainly at Peggy Guggenheim's baronial English estate and artists' colony, Hayford Hall—Barnes had lost both her mate and her hope. She was also drinking. How heavily is not certain, but likely on a regular basis, since alcohol was deemed essential to the communal spirit and social life of Hayford Hall, where everyone "drank far too much"; and "when the drinking was well along in the middle of the evening," says Field, "games were played."[30] The novel came out of the hell of Barnes's relationship with Thelma Wood, which was made over into fiction and placed within an imaginative landscape so nightmarish that it seems to have been inspired by delirium tremens. As an early English reviewer put it, with wry understatement:

No, *Night Wood* is not a comforting book to read. Imagine the worst of hangovers, complicated by acute remorse and extreme retrospective jealousy—all thickened into a view of modern civilisation and contemporary social life that, for bitterness and crazy violence, leaves the darkest chapter of *Ulysses* far behind. There is not a single "sane" character in the entire story; and a narrative peopled by one uncommonly neurasthenic Jew, three unusually dotty Lesbians and a drunken, melancholic Irish doctor who, in his spare time, retires to his squalid attic bedroom and there lies in misery and solitude, wearing a thick mask of paint and powder, a feminine nightgown and a curly Mary Pickford wig, is bound to make heavy demands on the reader's tolerance.[31]

The dreariness of *Nightwood* is comparable, in fact, to the worst visitations of the White Logic in *John Barleycorn*.[32] As Matthew O'Connor insists at one point, imploring Nora Flood to cease grieving the loss of her beloved Robin Vote, "Can't you be done now, can't you give up? Now be still, now that you know what the world is about, knowing it's about nothing?"[33]

Although the world of *Nightwood* may be about nothing, and although the novel itself resists the critical redaction it seems devised to evoke, it has nevertheless been taken to be about everything under the moon. Broe remarks, "As the great art novel of the twentieth century—a kind of epistemological romp on the figural plane—*Nightwood* invites theory construction as it has encouraged critics over the past five decades to ransack the literary canon for analogies; at various times, *Nightwood* has been called surrealistic, Eliotic, Dantesque, elegiac, fugal, Elizabethan, baroque, even Gothic."[34] And that doesn't count what *Nightwood* has been called by baffled readers who might agree with Marianne Moore's quip: "Reading Djuna Barnes is like reading a foreign language, which you understand."[35] It helps, in Field's opinion, to realize that, for the purpose of disguising Barnes's deepest preoccupations, "always a portion of her work means nothing, is meant to mean nothing." Diversionary tactics, including the strategic deployment of subplots and minor characters, are used in *Nightwood* to draw attention away from the "too painful centre," which is "the drama of the tragic love of Nora and Robin."[36]

Other critics agree that indirection and concealment are among Barnes's most important devices for questioning literary and social assumptions. For Annette Kolodny, Barnes's technique seems to place readers "in precisely that situation in which the main characters of more recent women's fiction find themselves: that is, embroiled in the hopeless task of trying to decode or decipher a strange and incomprehensible reality."[37] Barnes's fiction, in other words, is metafictional in its concern with how meaning itself is created and reality is construed; it recognizes that the formation of prevailing common sense is part of the play of gender difference.

Feminist critics and theorists have likened Barnes's text "to a woman's body whose envelope (style or code) must be broken in order for the substance to be recovered and explained. Reading is rape, a submission of the text (woman) to patriarchal (critical) priorities."[38] Logically, submission of the text even to *anti*-patriarchal priorities would also be implicated in such critical rapine. In this respect, perhaps, Barnes herself is more consistent and rigorous than some of her feminist admirers in accepting the darkest implications of her work. As Judith Lee says, Barnes "shows that the dichotomy between masculine and feminine does not define the most profound experience of difference, but she denies the signifying value of her own deconstruction. She exposes the failure of values embedded in the masculine, and yet she does not counter that failure, for she denies that her 'feminine' text has meaning beyond itself." *Nightwood* may thus be considered a "virtuoso performance that denies, in the end, the possibility of giving voice to (feminine) silence."[39]

Although it may be folly to suggest that *Nightwood* is finally "about" anything (except nothing), there has been no shortage of meaningful interpretations, some as recondite as the novel itself. *Nightwood* has also been ingeniously (re)connected to its historical context of pre-war European dis-ease during the 1930s.[40] No detailed reading will be attempted here, however. For my purposes, it will be sufficient to explicate the relationship of "transcendence downward" in *Nightwood* and the drinking of its main characters.

In an early study, Kenneth Burke pointed out that the novel turns on a series of "turnings," which are signified by words derived from the Latin root -*vert*. As a tale about unrequited love, *Nightwood* attempts "to make lamentation a source of pleasure for the reader"; its plot gravitates "about a conversion to perversion, or inversion." By contravening conventional expectations, the novel ultimately "aims at another mode of transcendence, a kind of 'transcendence downward,'" which consists in "a perverse 'ascent' in terms of decay whereby corruption and distinction become interchangeable terms."[41] Burke's insight has been widely echoed in the criticism—as, for example, in Louis F. Kannenstine's reference to "*Nightwood*'s scheme of inversion, whereby the degraded becomes the exalted."[42] Recent feminist approaches, however, show a disinclination to follow Burke insofar as he may be taken to imply, homophobically, that *in*version = *per*version. Preferring to credit Barnes with *sub*version, such critics nevertheless accept the idea that reversal is central to her technique.[43]

Of the major reversals in *Nightwood*, one is common to the modernist drunk narrative: the inversion of the "Puritan" *mores* of Prohibition America in regard to drinking. Drunkenness is not merely tolerated; it is celebrated in the cynically reckless spirit of Baudelaire:

> One should always be drunk. That's the great thing; the only question. Not to feel the horrible burden of Time weighing on your shoulders and bowing you to the earth, you should be drunk without respite.
>
> Drunk with what? With wine, with poetry, or with virtue, as you please. But get drunk.[44]

In *Nightwood*, this will to drunkenness is flamboyantly displayed by "Dr. Matthew-Mighty-grain-of-salt-Dante-O'Connor" (p. 80), the homosexual bar-fly and part-time abortionist, whose swirling verbal arias give voice to the funereal tones of the novel. Drunk without respite, the torrentially loquacious O'Connor is linked by his alcoholism to the preverbally inarticulate Robin Vote (based on Thelma Wood), who sullenly cruises the bars of Paris, moving "from table to table, from drink to drink, from person to person" (p. 59). Both Felix Volkbein and Jenny Petherbridge also fall into drunkenness as part of their futile attempt to possess Robin, who is for them, as for their rival Nora Flood, the elusive object of desire. Jenny, detestably incapable of other than "second-hand dealings with life" (p. 66), drinks in clumsy and uncomprehending imitation of Robin: "Taken to drink and appropriating Robin's mind with vulgar inaccuracy, like those eighty-two plaster virgins she bought because Robin had one good one" (p. 124).

Felix, who is deserted by Robin after he marries her and she bears him a child, tells O'Connor early in the novel that "I never drink spirits." "You will," predicts the doctor (p. 23); and by the end, he does:

> Felix ordered a *fine*. The doctor smiled. "I said you would come to it," he said, and emptied his own glass at a gulp.
>
> "I know," Felix answered, "but I did not understand. I thought you meant something else."
>
> "What?"
>
> Felix paused, turning the small glass around in his trembling hand. "I thought," he said, "that you meant that I would give up."
>
> The doctor lowered his eyes. "Perhaps that is what I meant—but sometimes I am mistaken." He looked at Felix from under his heavy brows. "Man was born damned and innocent from the start, and wretchedly—as he must—on those two themes—whistles his tune."   (Pp. 120–21)

Having given up Robin, his dreams of social status, and even his hopes for his "[m]entally deficient and emotionally excessive" son, Guido (p. 107), Felix ultimately joins the drunken Frau Mann, decamps with her for Vienna, and frequents the cafés. "Perfectly correct and drunk" (p. 122), he tries there to preserve a facade of pseudo-aristocratic dignity in his alcoholic stupor: "Felix drank heavily now, and to hide the red that flushed his cheeks he had grown a beard ending in two forked points on his chin" (p. 122).

There are no such pretenses for Matthew O'Connor, who preaches to Felix "the acceptance of depravity." "Man is born as he dies, rebuking cleanliness," proclaims the doctor; "cleanliness is a form of apprehension; our faulty racial memory is fathered by fear. Destiny and history are untidy; we fear memory of that disorder" (p. 118). By invoking the doctrine of original sin—"Man was born damned and innocent from the start"—O'Connor hints at the underlying reason for his drinking. Drunkenness is not, he implies, a matter of "giving up"; it is a matter of bearding despair, of coming face to skull with the fundamental misery and inescapable emptiness of the human condition. As the doctor tells Felix early in the novel, when Felix is not yet drinking, "No man needs curing of his individual sickness; his universal malady is what he should look to" (p. 32). Alcohol is the only "cure," however ineffective, for the universal malady.

This truth escapes many of O'Connor's fellow American expatriates, who have been formed by the culture of Prohibition and who regard drinking as dirty and degrading. "The French are dishevelled and wise," the doctor explains to Nora; "the American tries to approximate it with drink. It is his only clue to himself. He takes it when his soap has washed him too clean for identification. The Anglo-Saxon has made the literal error; using water, he has washed away his page" (p. 90). Nora herself represents the type of "Anglo-Saxon" in *Nightwood*: the side of Barnes herself that was rooted in prim, well-scrubbed, Calvinist New England. "The French have made a detour of filthiness," the doctor exhorts Nora. "Whereas you are of a clean race, of a too eagerly washing people, and this leaves no road for you. The brawl of the Beast leaves a path for the Beast. You wash your brawl with every thought, with every gesture, with every conceivable emollient and *savon,* and expect to find your way again" (p. 84). But Nora will remain lost because, as James B. Scott says, "Americans, with their cult of cleanliness, have washed away their own instinctual tracks."[45] Such Americans, even when they try to use drink to approximate what they have washed away, continue to regard drunkenness with deadly Puritanical disgust.

Although Nora's deep suffering over Robin forces her to confront the seamier realities of life, she understands too late what Robin tries to tell her one drunken night. Nora later tells the story to O'Connor. Someone had called her from a bar to say that Robin was too sick to get home, and she had gone out to rescue her. Nora herself had long since desisted from accompanying Robin "because I couldn't bear to see the 'evidence of my eyes.'" When Nora found Robin that night, she was far from grateful. For blocks she ran behind Nora, angrily hurling insults. "You are a devil! You make everything dirty! . . . You make me feel dirty and tired and old!" Robin barked (p. 143). Then she humiliated Nora by wantonly embracing a policeman on the street; while he fondled her, she continued spitting abuse at Nora. When Nora walked away, Robin grabbed her shoulder, grinningly stumbled against her with mock desire, and then demanded money to give a wretched whore she had spied in the gutter:

> "'Give her some money, all of it!' She threw the francs into the street and bent down over the filthy baggage and began stroking her hair, gray with the dust of years, saying, 'They are all God-forsaken, and you most of all, because they don't want you to have your happiness. They don't want you to drink. Well, here, drink! I give you money and permission! These women— they are all like her,' she said with fury. 'They are all good—they want to save us!' She sat down beside her." (P. 144)

Robin rebukes Nora because of her attitude toward drinking. It might be argued that Robin, like many an alcoholic in the throes of self-righteous self-destruction, blames the victim of her drinking for driving her to drink by wishing to save her. But such a reading would miss Barnes's point, which is precisely to critique the conventional assumptions that privilege Nora's "civilized" values. In Robin's eyes, Nora is not a victim but a victimizer: the prohibitory and oppressive voice of sexual restraint and moral decency; "'a good woman,' and so a bitch on a high plane," as the Doctor puts it, "the only one able to kill yourself and Robin!" (p. 146).[46] As Nora herself comes to realize, "It was *me* made her hair stand on end because I loved her. . . . She wanted darkness in her mind—to throw a shadow over what she was powerless to alter—her dissolute life, her life at night; and I, I dashed it down" (p. 156).

In her desperation, Nora once tried to follow Robin's downward path: trying to do what she had done, to love what she had loved, and ultimately "to become 'debauched'": "I haunted the cafés where Robin had lived her night-life; I drank with the men, I danced with the women, but all I knew was that others had slept with my lover and my child" (p. 156). As O'Connor tells her, Nora is too "clean" to be capable of true debauchery, and so her experiment necessarily fails. Nora does not understand, in short, the real nature of drinking, which is not degrading but uplifting, not dirty but holy. Although Nora may not be a complete abstainer,[47] she exhibits the merciless sobriety of an American teetotaler.

Nightwood suggests that Nora's aversion to alcoholic spirits threatens the preternatural spirits that inhabit Robin. Nora remembers how Robin passed out in their bed after she had staggered home that dreadful night. Nora then prayed over her:

> "'Die now, so you will be quiet, so you will not be touched again by dirty hands, so you will not take my heart and your body and let them be nosed by dogs—die now, then you will be mine forever.' (What right has anyone to that?)" She stopped. "She was mine only when she was drunk, Matthew, and had passed out. That's the terrible thing, that finally she was mine only when she was dead drunk. . . . I tried to come between and save her, but I was like a shadow in her dream that could never reach her in time. . . ." (P. 145)

Nora echoes what the narrator has earlier remarked: that her love for Robin takes the form of a desire to save Robin, and thus to possess her, whereas there is something too primordial about Robin (what attracted Nora in the first place) to be tamed by human possession. "To keep her (in Robin there was this tragic longing to be kept, knowing herself astray) Nora knew now that there was no way but death. In death Robin would belong to her" (p. 58). Ironically, when Robin does return to Nora in the end, she *is* in a state of dead drunkenness; and she is literally being nosed by a dog that is itself deranged by this human's animal antics.[48]

"Nora thinks her tragedy lies in loving a woman who is faithless and drunken, a liar and a cheat," Benstock remarks; "she does not realize that she herself is an instrument of Robin's tragedy: Nora's 'crime' is her effort to make Robin conform to a moral code based on patriarchal self-interest and misogyny."[49] What goes unnoticed here is how Barnes's treatment of drinking bears on her critique of the patriarchal order. As "a woman who is faithless and drunken," Robin both reinforces and subverts the stereotype of the drunken harlot/alcoholic nymphomaniac. By perceiving Robin in this misogynistic way, Nora aligns herself with London, Hemingway, and other male writers who propagated the modernist culture of drinking. However, Robin's bisexuality calls the stereotype and its underlying heterosexist assumptions into question; for although Hemingway might have imagined a Robin Vote getting drunk with a Brett Ashley in the Left Bank bars of the 1920s, he would have found it unimaginable for them to go upstairs together. There was a difference, after all, between Djuna Barnes and Jake Barnes!

Despite critics who read *Nightwood* as a confessional roman à clef, Barnes was also different from Nora Flood. Although the tragedy of Nora's love for Robin was undoubtedly inspired by the tribulations of "Simon" and "Irene," the novel significantly altered some of the circumstances. Most important, it displaced Barnes's own drinking from Nora to Matthew O'Connor. That the character of O'Connor was so obviously based on a real person—Dan Mahoney, an alcoholic and homosexual expatriate from San Francisco, who performed secret abortions (including one on Barnes) and who was celebrated throughout Paris for his transvestitism and drunken magniloquence—made him the perfect cover. Through O'Connor, Barnes could explore her own drinking without fear of detection by readers holding a biographical key to *Nightwood*.

Matthew O'Connor had made a brief appearance in Barnes's earlier novel, *Ryder* (1928), but the O'Connor of *Nightwood* is a far more complex and commanding figure, one endowed with such erudition and philosophical gravity that he attains, as Field says, a "Shakespearean stature." This O'Connor is "certainly one of the most memorable literary characters of our century."[50] In fact, the doctor bore only a superficial resemblance to his supposed model. Those who knew the real Dan Mahoney recall him as a ribald and entertaining fellow who actively cultivated his own legend as an outrageous drag queen in order to sponge drinks, but who never reached the level of soaring verbal brilliance manifested in O'Connor's monologues. Thus although Mahoney "positively revelled" in what he claimed was the perfect likeness of Barnes's portrayal and "dined off the depiction in Paris for years after," there is reason to believe, from a less self-interested point of view, that the fictional doctor was a composite character, based generally on Mahoney but enhanced by Barnes's lending him many of her own gifts. As Field suggests, "the *words* and *tone* and *substance* of what O'Connor says belong solely to Barnes"; the "seeds of his discourse" may be found in stories and plays she wrote long before she ever knew Mahoney.[51]

As we have seen, the modernist culture of drinking gendered the alcoholic "male" and figured the "female alcoholic," insofar as she could be imagined to exist at all, as a "manly" woman, a dyke. This was the role accepted by Thelma Wood, who as "Simon" apologized for "his" drinking problem to "Irene."[52] But Barnes deconstructed this role in *Nightwood,* where she represented the female alcoholic through a clever and ironic double displacement by imaginatively cross-dressing herself as a man who cross-dresses himself as a woman. With self-parodic self-pity, O'Connor bewails his fate to Nora: although he desires to fulfill a domestic fantasy "for children and knitting," and although he "never asked better than to boil some good man's potatoes and toss up a child for him every nine months by the calendar" (p. 91), he is hopelessly trapped inside his uselessly male body. He has no choice, it seems, but to drown his sorrows.

Because O'Connor is a man, he qualifies as a true "alcoholic"; but because he is a "womanly" man, he seems also to stand for the "female alcoholic." However, since O'Connor's notion of the womanly role is of a conventional and housewifely sort, he also represents what the manly modernists dreaded: the infiltration and violation of a male preserve by hated feminine influences. Barnes thus appropriates the modernist idea of the alcoholic as part of her overall scheme of inversion. O'Connor's "degenerate" status as a homosexual transvestite undercuts the modernist ideology of gender that constructed the alcoholic as a rugged man among men. In fact, none of the drunken characters in *Nightwood,* especially Robin Vote, fits this type. The novel thus undermines the security of the culture of drinking; male bonding itself becomes irrevocably problematic because, in *Nightwood,* same-sexuality and alcoholism have become interchangeable rather than antithetical.

Nightwood is dominated by the two long sections (titled "Watchman, What of the Night?" and "Go Down, Matthew") in which Nora turns for solace to O'Connor, whose drunken monologues help Nora to face painful truths about herself and Robin but also plunge the doctor himself into despair. Because her quiet voice is overwhelmed by O'Connor's drunken ranting, critics have sometimes overlooked Nora's presence in these scenes. But they are not merely occasions for the doctor's eloquence; they are duets of lamentation that dramatize Barnes's inner dialogue between contradictory identifications: Nora Flood/Matthew O'Connor, female/male, rational/irrational, conventional/Bohemian, restrained/excessive, sober/drunken. Robin is the absent third party to this dialogue: a representation of something before and beyond the binaries of discourse itself.

The question under debate between Matthew and Nora is what to do about Robin. The worst horror of this nightmarish novel may be that nothing finally matters; but however hopeless their search for an answer may be, Nora and Matthew ponder whether drunkenness offers any advantage either in understanding Robin or in overcoming the pain of losing her. Under the influence of alcohol, it seems, O'Connor achieves a wisdom and compassion for human suffering that is otherwise unobtainable. But the doctor's generosity of spirit, evoked by Nora's lament, leads only to his own deeper anguish. He rails drunkenly:

> "Talking to me—all of them—sitting on me as heavy as a truck horse—talking! Love falling buttered side down, fate falling arse up! . . . Now that you have all heard what you wanted to hear, can't you let me loose now, let me go? I've not only lived my life for nothing, but I've told it for nothing—abominable among the filthy people—I know, it's all over, everything's over, and nobody knows it but me—drunk as a fiddler's bitch—lasted too long—"
> He tried to get to his feet, gave it up. "Now," he said, "the end—mark my words—now *nothing, but wrath and weeping!*" (Pp. 165–66)

Alcohol does not provide escape from travail. On the contrary, by the end of his long night's journey into the spectral light of the White Logic, O'Connor has been stripped of his defenses and left twitching in agony. Precisely because it opens into the depths of squalor and meaninglessness, drunkenness becomes O'Connor's means to the paradoxically redemptive damnation of nihilism: the inverted "transcendence downward" of "fate falling arse up!"

In her presentation of the alcoholic as modernist culture hero, Barnes participates after all in the alibi of The Modern Temper. In this respect, *Nightwood* recalls *Tender Is the Night* and its Spenglerian ethos. *Nightwood* has even closer affinities to *Under the Volcano,* a novel also obsessed with "transcendence downward" amid the decadence of the 1930s; it is not surprising that Barnes's novel, like Fitzgerald's, fascinated Malcolm Lowry. In a 1952 letter to the prospective translators of *Nightwood* into German, Lowry reported:

> (I have met Djuna Barnes in New York. . . . She was painting some sort of semi-female male demon on the wall, reproved me roundly for the success of the *Volcano,* generously gave me six quart bottles of beer, and expressed herself frightened by *Nightwood.* . . . I myself cannot make out whether *Nightwood* is a work of genius or a disorder of the kinaesthesia: probably both. . . . but despite the great formal and linguistic merits of *Nightwood* I find the sources of its inspiration so impure and non-universal that I have been reluctant mentally really to visit them and so properly and in detail apprehend that work, if indeed it deserves to be apprehended other than in some unique category of the monstrous, though on another plane it possesses admirable technical virtues. . . . I should be the last to deny the relative heroism, and even significance, of that book, even if finally one hates it.)[53]

Lowry's evident discomfort with the "impure" sources of *Nightwood* produced a highly ambivalent response. Because he must have recognized the similarities between the workings of his own imagination and that of Barnes, he could not but acknowledge the technical genius of her novel and the "heroism" of its bleakly modernist vision. But *Nightwood* was rendered "monstrous" for Lowry by its hatefully "deviant" characters, and he implicitly judged it a failure for its supposed lack of "universality." *Volcano,* with its conventionally heterosexual love triangle, was, he supposed, superior in that regard.

In *Nightwood,* Barnes both parodied and appropriated the modernist culture of drinking and the genre of the drunk narrative, of which *Under the Volcano* is the sublime example. In the character of Matthew O'Connor, alcoholism is affirmed, as it is in the work of male modernists from London to Lowry, as the source of the highest philosophical enlightenment; that is, drunkenness leads to recognition of cosmic chaos and the annihilating influence on the White Logic. The alcoholic doctor earns an honored place at the bar beside such unillusioned modernist he-men as Lowry's Consul, who achieves his apotheosis by drinking himself to death. But because of the "abominable" O'Connor's place "among the filthy people," his presence there becomes anomalous and subversive. As much a clown as a philosopher, O'Connor carries the pessimism of the White Logic to the limit where the sublime tips over into the ridiculous and solemnity becomes too lugubrious to be endured without a belly laugh. While the tragic high seriousness of *Nightwood* has advanced Barnes's claim for inclusion in the high modernist canon, the carnivalesque nature of that tragedy works to expose the pretentiousness of The Modern Temper.

7

After the Lost Generation:
The Lost Weekend

When *The Lost Weekend* appeared in January 1944, Malcolm Lowry had been toiling for nearly a decade over successive drafts of *Under the Volcano* (1947), the magnum opus on which he had pinned his hopes of literary immortality. For Lowry, the true originality of this work consisted in his use of an alcoholic as a representative man, a symbol of the tragic modern condition. He was understandably devastated by the pre-emptive publication of Charles Jackson's novel, with its unprecedented account of a binge from the drinker's point of view, and envious of its clamorous reception: critical praise, bestseller popularity, a lucrative Hollywood contract. An outstanding film adaptation of *The Lost Weekend* was subsequently honored at the first Cannes Film Festival and awarded Oscars for best picture, best screenplay, best director (Billy Wilder), and best actor (Ray Milland).

Lowry's work was always inseparable from his life, and he inevitably transformed into fiction his resentment of Jackson as a fortunate rival who had stolen his thunder and blighted his dreams of success. Sigbjørn Wilderness in *Dark as the Grave Wherein My Friend Is Laid* is shocked to hear about a hit movie based on a novel called *Drunkard's Rigadoon*. His wife, who has been shielding him from the bad news, attempts to offer consolation: "It's purely a clinical study; it's only a small part of yours. . . . It could be anything else, not drinking. . . . Let him have his little triumph. When there's so much *more* in your book." But Wilderness recognizes that his novel cannot now escape seeming derivative, no matter how much "*more*" it may contain.

> It had meant everything to him, the writing of *The Valley of the Shadow of Death*, the feeling of turning his greatest weakness—he loathed the phrase—into his greatest strength . . . the feeling that he, who up to that time had been haunted by the suspicion that he would never write anything original, that he was destined to copy all his life, had sunk his teeth into that appalling theme, that he was breaking not merely new ground, but building a terra nova, achieving something that was unique, in a sort of ultima thule of the spirit. And now . . . he would merely be told, as he had already been as much as told by his agent and the two American publishers who had so far rejected it, that—and had they stopped to think they must have known it could not have been so—it was merely a copy of *Drunkard's Rigadoon!*[1]

In a letter to Jonathan Cape, one of the rejecting publishers, Lowry confessed that he regarded *The Lost Weekend* "as a form of punishment," as retribution for sins against his own artistic talent and integrity: "Youth plus booze plus hysterical identifications plus vanity plus self-deception plus no work plus more booze."[2]

Booze eventually destroyed Malcolm Lowry, but in the long run of literary history, *Under the Volcano* has fared much better than *The Lost Weekend*. In retrospect, it seems that Lowry worked himself up over nothing. The very popularity of Jackson's novel should have assured him that it could not pose any threat to the ultimate triumph of his own with readers of discriminating taste—taste molded by the prevailing climate of modernism to favor dense and esoterically symbolic novels like *Under the Volcano* over readable and unpretentiously realistic ones like *The Lost Weekend*. Whereas the former has inspired adulation befitting a literary "terra nova" or an "ultima thule of the spirit," the latter has slipped from view except by association with the classic film. Virtually nothing has been written on Jackson's work since the initial reviews of his four novels and two collections of stories. No biography exists, and little personal information is available.[3]

Born 6 April 1903, in Summit, New Jersey, Charles Reginald Jackson grew up in Newark, New York, a village east of Rochester. His closest companion from childhood onward was his younger brother, Frederick, who was a model for Wick, the alcoholic Don Birnam's brother in *The Lost Weekend*. Another brother and sister were killed in an auto accident when Charles was thirteen; his father left home when he was twelve. After graduating from high school in 1921, Jackson worked as a reporter for the *Newark Courier* and, later, as a bookstore clerk in Chicago and New York. He also attended Syracuse University for two semesters. After the onset of tuberculosis in 1927, he was medically confined for several years. Along with his brother, who too was infected, he sought treatment at the sanatorium in Davos, Switzerland, that had provided Thomas Mann with the setting for *The Magic Mountain* (1924). While a patient there from 1929 to 1931, Jackson developed a drinking problem through the use of alcohol as a painkiller.

Living in New York City during the Depression, Jackson could not find steady work, and his drinking grew unremittingly worse until November 1936, when he checked into Bellevue Hospital. There in the alcoholic ward, where street drunks deposited by the police often served as experimental subjects as they dried out, Jackson's physician was Norman Jolliffe, a physiologist who had undertaken a long-term study of "the etiology of chronic inebriety."[4] After Jackson sobered up, he found a job with the Columbia Broadcasting System, where he wrote radio plays, both originals and adaptations, as well as the daytime serial, "Sweet River." In 1938, he married Rhoda Booth, a staff writer at *Fortune* who, like Helen in *The Lost Weekend*, had been steadfast during the worst of the drinking. The next year he went freelance, continuing to produce successful scripts while teaching radio writing at New York University.

Always a voracious reader, Jackson had conducted his own literary education during his prolonged convalescence, and he had also begun writing fiction—all of which remained unpublished until two of his stories were accepted by the *Partisan Review* in 1939. The same year, he began an autobiographical novel about an alcoholic binge, and he finished the first draft in fourteen months. Four years later, the overnight success of *The Lost Weekend* put Jackson in the limelight. Critics raved; sales boomed; Hollywood beckoned. In April 1944, he began a sixteen-week contract as a screenwriter for Metro Goldwyn Mayer, and his earnings of $1,000 a week allowed him to buy a splendid colonial farmhouse in Orford, New Hampshire, where he lived with his wife and two daughters for the next decade. Jackson's success as a writer carried him through the 1940s. His second novel, *The Fall of Valor* (1946), a frank exploration of homosexuality, was respectfully reviewed and widely circulated by the book clubs; his short stories were selling briskly to mass-market magazines.

Jackson's third novel, *The Outer Edges* (1948), was less favorably received, however, and by 1950, he was running heavily into debt. Although Jackson had quit drinking in 1936, he remained dependent on sedatives (mainly Secanol) to break through writer's block and to keep his inspiration flowing. The strain of revising *The Fall of Valor* led to a spell of mental exhaustion in 1945, and to a jag on drugs early the following year. In July 1947, during another such binge, Jackson started drinking beer as well as taking drugs. Early in 1951, his relapses became more serious and more chronic, as he resumed periodic heavy drinking after fifteen years of nearly complete abstinence. He quickly spiraled downward, and after a suicide attempt in 1952, he was readmitted to Bellevue. Jackson did not recover his stability until he entered a clinic for alcoholism in the summer of 1953 and joined Alcoholics Anonymous upon his release.

Sober again but frozen in a writer's block, Jackson saw his productivity drop off and his celebrity fade. Having ceased to publish much fiction, he sold used cars to make a living. The Jacksons were forced to sell their Orford farm in 1954, and they moved to a rented house in Sandy Hook, Connecticut. In his later years, Jackson again worked for the broadcasting industry—as a television script editor—and he remained very active in A.A. After a long absence from the literary scene, he attempted a come-back in 1967 with *A Second-Hand Life,* a novel he had started in the early 1950s. The book enjoyed good sales, but it fizzled critically. The following year, his health deteriorating, Jackson ended his own life with an overdose of sleeping pills. At the time of his death, he was writing a sequel to *The Lost Weekend.*

Despite Jackson's present obscurity, *The Lost Weekend* remains a compelling novel fifty years after its first publication. Its title has passed into the American vernacular, and its portrait of the alcoholic has lost none of its psychological acuity. In addition to literary merit, *The Lost Weekend* has historical importance for marking a major shift in the representation of alcoholism in American literature. Although the novel owes an obvious debt to *Tender Is the Night*— which Don Birnam considers, despite its failures, to be "the most brilliant and heart-breaking performance . . . in recent fiction"[5]—it neither denies the alcoholism of its protagonist nor elevates him into a culture hero. "We are far from the romantic drinkers of Hemingway and Scott Fitzgerald," as Edmund Wilson says of Birnam. "The man himself is dreary in the extreme."[6]

The man's existence during a five-day bender—the novel was originally titled "The Long Weekend"—is also extremely dreary. As Birnam drinks his way through bottle after bottle, worrying constantly about his supply and borrowing booze money at every turn (but always losing track of it), he inflicts awful damage on himself and those who care about him. An intelligent, charming, and decent man when sober, Don is transmogrified by alcohol into a scheming liar who ruthlessly exploits his well-meaning brother and long-suffering girl friend, a petty thief who cleverly (he thinks) steals a purse but humiliatingly gets caught, and a sodden bar-fly who laments his non-existent wife's "frigidity" as he angles for a date with the hostess and then forgets about it in a blackout. Having finished off the whiskey on Friday night, he is desperate for a Saturday morning eye-opener, and he rushes out to raise a stake by pawning his typewriter—only to discover, after walking block after block for miles, that he is the butt of a joke "beyond laughter" (p. 109): every pawn shop in New York is closed for Yom Kippur! When Birnam reaches the stumble-drunk stage, he topples down the stairs and wakes up in the hospital with a fractured skull. The next day, as his binge is finally winding down, he must endure the torments of delirium tremens: a horrific hallucination of a bat devouring a mouse.

At the end, Don feels ready nonetheless for another "spell of riot" (p. 3). As he hides pint bottles about the apartment, making careful allowance for the loss of those his brother will likely find and confiscate, Don reassures himself that his lost weekend couldn't have been so bad as all that; he has survived it, after all. "God knows why or how but he had come through one more. No telling what might happen the next time but why worry about that? This one was over and nothing had happened at all. Why did they make such a fuss?" (p. 244). Don is trapped by such denial in an alcoholic's vicious circle; his prospects are bleak, his situation seems hopeless.

In its stark realism about what Lowry called "the calamitous suffering drink [can] cause to the drinker,"[7] *The Lost Weekend* resembles *Under the Volcano;* but Jackson does not partake, as Lowry does, of the modernist spirit(s) of the White Logic. It is Jackson's refusal to amplify his material—to extrapolate from one drunkard's downfall to a symbolic utterance about the Tragedy of Life or the Decline of the West—that distinguishes *The Lost Weekend* from such grandiose modernist masterpieces as *Under the Volcano.* The force of Lowry's novel is centrifugal; it spins outward from its center (the Consul), traversing the cosmos as it accumulates layer upon layer of Higher Meaning. The force of *The Lost Weekend,* on the contrary, is centripetal; it turns in on itself toward a purposefully reductive focus on drinking, unadorned by any larger significance. Why, Birnam wonders at one point, are there so many kind and faithful women who get themselves mixed up with hopeless drunks?

> But from there you went on to: Why were drunks, almost always, persons of talent, personality, lovable qualities, gifts, brains, assets of all kinds (else why would anyone care?); why were so many brilliant men alcoholic?—And from there, the next one was: Why did you drink?
>
> Like the others, the question was rhetorical, abstract, anything but pragmatic; as vain to ask as his own clever question had been vain. It was far too late to pose such a problem with any reasonable hope for an answer—or, an answer forthcoming, any reasonable hope that it would be worth listening to or prove anything at all. It had long since ceased to matter Why. You were a drunk; that's all there was to it. You drank; period.   (Pp. 221–22)

With tough-minded pragmatism, *The Lost Weekend* renounces the abstract and rhetorical inflation of drunkenness common to the modernist texts we have so far considered. Jackson, in fact, lampoons this sort of thing in a passage where Birnam the frustrated writer ("the books begun and dropped, the unfinished short stories; the drinking the drinking the drinking" [p. 17]) is inspired with an idea for a modernist masterpiece as he leans on the bar, gazing at himself in the mirror and recalling the literary idols of his childhood ("Poe and Keats, Byron, Dowson, Chatterton—all the gifted miserable and reckless men who had burned themselves out in tragic brilliance early and with finality" [pp. 15–16]). The story of his own miserably drunken life, he suddenly realizes, could be "a classic of form and content" on the artistic order of *Death in Venice* (p. 16).[8] First the perfect title ("In a Glass") leaps to mind, and then the entire book marvelously unfolds before him:

> At this moment, if he were able to write fast enough, he could set it down in all its final perfection, right down without a change or correction needed later, from the brilliant opening to the last beautiful note of wise and grave irony. . . . Whole sentences sprang to his mind in dazzling succession, perfectly formed, ready to be put down. Where was a pencil, paper? He downed his drink. . . .
>
> But caution, slow. Good thing there was no paper handy, no chance to begin impulsively what later must be composed—when, tonight maybe, certainly tomorrow—with all the calm and wise control needed for such an undertaking. (Pp. 16–17)

Needless to say, Don will be too drunk either tonight or tomorrow for any literary work, if he should even happen to remember what came to him so effortlessly on a bar stool. But the fantasy spins itself out. Already, he can see the pyramidal stacks of copies in the bookshop window; he can hear a puzzled girl in the subway paying him inadvertent but profound tribute by confessing to a friend, "I can't make head or tail of this"; he can savor the bewilderment of his hopelessly ignorant mother, who will regret "the fact that he hadn't published a book she could show the neighbors and why didn't he write something that had 'human interest'" (p. 18). But then a wave of self-disgust crashes over Birnam, and he dismisses "In a Glass" as "so much eyewash": "How could he have been seduced, fooled, into dreaming up such a ridiculous piece; in perpetrating, even in his imagination, anything so pat, so contrived, so cheap, so phoney, so adolescent, so (crowning offense) sentimental!" (p. 18).

But caution, slow! Now the final page appears in Birnam's mind's eye as "clear and true as if he had seen it in print." Yes! Something in the vein of

Thomas Mann, but with an ending straight out of Hemingway: with a wise and gravely ironic tag-line worthy of "Isn't it pretty to think so?":

> The hero, after the long procession of motley scenes from his past life (would the line stretch out to th' crack of doom?)[9]—the hero decides to walk out of the bar and somewhere, somehow, that very day—not for himself, of course: for Helen—commit suicide. The tag: "It would give her a lifelong romance." Perfect; but not—oh more perfect still—was the line that came next, the *new* ending: the little simple line set in a paragraph all by itself beneath the other, on the last page:
> "But he knew he wouldn't." (P. 18)

Of course, "In a Glass" parodies *The Lost Weekend* itself insofar as it recalls *The Sun Also Rises, Tender Is the Night,* and other modernist drunk narratives. Jackson pointedly calls this genre into question by mocking its bombast and complacency. Later in the novel, once again standing at a bar, Birnam drunkenly wallows in his immense affinity for the White Logic:

> Was there a limit to what he could endure? It seemed not. He was more vulnerable to suffering—and at the same time, paradoxically, he had a greater capacity for it—than anyone he knew; and this was no idle or egotistic boast, something he merely fancied to be true and was proud of because it set him apart, spoke of a superior sensitivity or sensibility. An occasion or period of suffering in his past which, reckoned now in perspective, was a mere incident, one out of many in a long chain, would have stood out in the average life as a major crisis, perhaps indeed the only one, a moment where the victim had reached a peak or depth from which recovery was a lifelong process. But such moments, such peaks and depths, were his very pattern—natural, it seemed, perhaps even necessary, to his development. Why had he not been destroyed by all that happened to him? How is it he could take it over and over again and yet again? What capacity, vitality, or resilience did he have that others did not? Was it that his imagination laid hold of that suffering and transmuted it to experience, an experience he did not profit from, true, but experience all the same: a realization of who and what he was,

a fulfillment of self? Was he trying to find out, in this roundabout descent to destruction, what it was all about; and would he, at the final and ultimate moment, know? (Pp. 201–2)

In a review of *The Lost Weekend*, Edmund Wilson singled out this interior monologue as the novel's "most revealing passage," characterizing it as a "curious perverse meditation in which the hero justifies his drinking to himself as a purposive way of life with a special kind of moral dignity."[10] A special kind of moral dignity? Or a typically alcoholic kind of bloated self-pity? Wilson fails to note that a sober Don Birnam later castigates himself for what he regards as a shameful indulgence in egoism. "Some minor incident of suffering in his past would have stood out in the average life as a major crisis—he had actually thought and said to himself some such thing as that. How true could it be?" (p. 219).

Jackson suggests that truth for Birnam is relative to his sobriety. When he is drunk, Don's imagination heightens minor incidents into calamities, making them "greater in retrospect than they ever were at the time"; and he easily forgets that "what happened to him was no greater or no worse than what happened to everybody else." Other people suffered, "but did their self-centeredness, their self-absorption and preoccupation with self, magnify their troubles or experiences out of all proportion to the actuality and blind them to the fact that trouble was the lot of all?" (p. 219). When Don is sober, however, remorse drives him to the other extreme of self-contempt. Even as he berates himself, he knows that "this chastisement and searching of self" is "all merely part of his present low and depleted state, symptomatic of his physical condition only, and that tomorrow or next week he would bounce right back, all ego again" (pp. 219–20).

Built on a series of such interior monologues, *The Lost Weekend* is, as Roger Forseth remarks, "psychologically exact in remaining largely in the mind of the alcoholic, for that is always where the alcoholic is." In this and other ways, the novel gives "the alcoholic stripped to the essentials" and captures "in amber the clinically defined disease of alcoholism."[11] The oscillation so evident in Birnam between self-absorption and self-contempt, between inflation and deflation of the ego, might be taken as a psychological characteristic of alcoholics.

Thus although the novel is not, as Lowry suggested, "purely a clinical study," it does have a didactic dimension that links it to temperance fiction of the nineteenth century. Whether intended by Jackson or not, one effect of *The Lost Weekend*, both as fiction and as film, was to inform the public about "alcoholism" by disclosing the inside story from the perspective of the "alcoholic" himself.

These terms were becoming more and more common in ordinary usage by the time *The Lost Weekend* appeared, mainly through the success of what historians have called the "Alcoholism Movement" in recasting American attitudes toward habitual drunkenness.[12] Between the 1930s and the 1960s, as Bruce H. Johnson observes, a new consensus took shape as "the traditional moralistic interpretations of this form of deviant behavior were abandoned in favor of a 'scientific' or medical point of view according to which the chronic drunkard is the victim of a physiological or psychological aberration."[13] This transformation of public opinion was accomplished, with remarkable efficiency, by a relatively small band of dedicated campaigners associated with a trio of allied institutions with overlapping memberships and interlocking purposes: Alcoholics Anonymous, the National Committee for Education on Alcoholism (later renamed the National Council on Alcoholism), and the Yale Center for Studies of Alcohol (later renamed the Yale Center of Alcohol Studies).

During its first decade (1935 to 1945), Alcoholics Anonymous branched out from its two original groups in New York and Akron, Ohio, to several other cities; and membership rose exponentially from its founding partners (William Griffith Wilson, a.k.a. "Bill W." and Robert Holbrook Smith, a.k.a. "Dr. Bob") to include a few dozen and then about 15,000 persons, nearly all of them white, middle-class men.[14] Thanks in large part to extensive and favorable press coverage, the A.A. fellowship mushroomed to over 100,000 members by 1951.[15] Much of this coverage was generated and orchestrated by Marty Mann, founder of the N.C.E.A., who combined a genius for public relations with an ambition to proselytize for the "disease" concept of alcoholism she had encountered in A.A. (Having first joined in 1939, she became the first female member to remain sober.) Although Mann officially dissociated herself and the N.C.E.A. from A.A., her mission was to develop the grass-roots organization needed to spread the fellowship's message. The academic wing of the Alcoholism Movement, which revolved around the research center created at Yale by Howard W. Haggard and Elvin Morton Jellinek, maintained a dispassionately scientific distance from the more fervent elements of the coalition. But the goal was much the same: to detach the study and perception of habitual drunkenness from the moral frame of reference associated with temperance and Prohibition.

The planks of the Alcoholism Movement's platform, already nailed down by the late 1930s, were that alcoholism is an illness rather than a failure of character and, therefore, a medical rather than a moral issue; that treatment of alcoholism is a public health imperative; and that, fortunately, complete rehabilitation is possible if the alcoholic is placed in competent hands. In one 1938 magazine article, "an eminent physician" was deferentially quoted (in italics, no less) as he put the weight of his medical authority behind the new common sense:

> "*Alcoholism*," he insists, "*is not a vice but a disease. The alcoholic is not a moral weakling. He is tragically ill with a mental malady. If taken in time he can often be cured. The spread of the disease can be stemmed and turned back, but only with the aid of the doctors and the psychologists who have made it their field of research and experiment. To try to do so by sumptuary laws* [i.e. Prohibition] *is like trying to cure and prevent tuberculosis with a cough-drop.*"[16]

The visibility and respectability gained by the allied organizations of the Alcoholism Movement reflected one of its major goals: not only to promote a medicalized understanding of alcoholism, but also to create an improved image for the alcoholic—one commensurate with the perception of a post-Prohibition increase of problem drinking within the American middle class. By the 1940s, as ever more such families were affected by habitual drunkenness, the public became receptive to the idea, as Johnson says, that if "well educated, industrious members of the upwardly-mobile middle class could succumb to [the] ravages of habitual drunkenness," then perhaps "problem drinking was not merely a matter of weak willpower and moral degeneracy." Not surprisingly, the temperance stereotype of the drunkard as a skid-row derelict gradually gave way to a far more sympathetic view as the N.C.E.A. disseminated "the image of the alcoholic as a hard-working business executive who was the unfortunate victim of a disease" that strikes indiscriminately at every social level.[17]

As articulated by E. M. Jellinek, the acknowledged spokesman for the Yale Center, the new paradigm of alcoholism posited a sharp distinction between "normal" drinkers and "alcoholics," whose addiction was evinced by an intense craving for drink and a complete loss of control over drinking. Alcohol, that is, was seen to be addictive only for a certain group: those who developed an increased tolerance, who experienced withdrawal symptoms if they tried to quit drinking, and who exhibited bodily deterioration as a result of heavy and habitual consumption. The "disease" of alcoholism was thought to be progressive (it moved from psychological to physiological dependence) and irreversible (the alcoholic could never safely return to normal drinking). The only effective treatment, according to the Alcoholism Movement, was lifelong abstinence.

Except for its absolute distinction between alcoholics and normal drinkers— a distinction that won the praise and support of the liquor industry for locating addiction in the person rather than the substance—the modern disease model offered little that was new. Its major ideas were derived from the Victorian concept of inebriety and a wealth of scientific investigations dating from the late nineteenth century (see Chapter Two). Jellinek himself first came into prominence through his work of digesting and summarizing all of the old published research on drinking and drunkenness. The new paradigm was, in essence, a triumph of publicity and conceptual packaging. "What was scientific about the disease concept of alcoholism besides its articulation by scientists is . . . not apparent," one historian drily observes. "Neither of its key terms— *alcoholism* and *disease*—was clearly or consistently defined. . . . Nor were any of its key propositions supported by controlled empirical research."[18] Jellinek himself later retreated from his own theories.[19] And by the 1950s, several of the scientists associated with the Alcoholism Movement were troubled by a continuing lack of validation: "In spite of all the propaganda that had been distributed, the scientific evidence supporting the disease concept was extremely tenuous."[20]

Written when the disease concept was still rapidly gaining adherents, Jackson's novel had a symbiotic relationship with the Alcoholism Movement. Early in 1944, according to Ernest Kurtz, a Hollywood producer sought the help of

Alcoholics Anonymous in making a feature "that would dramatize A.A.'s understanding of alcoholism." This project became superfluous in view of the 1945 Paramount film of *The Lost Weekend,* for which director Billy Wilder requested A.A. literature "to assist in the movie production." At about the same time, Jackson's publisher, Stanley M. Rinehart, wrote to Bill Wilson, co-founder of Alcoholics Anonymous, to announce the imminent publication of *The Lost Weekend* and to request "A.A.'s help in promoting the book."[21] That Rinehart sought such an endorsement (which was not granted) shows that the novel's success was perceived to depend in part on the favor of A.A. But successful propagation of the disease concept was likewise perceived by the Alcoholism Movement to depend in part on the public's reaction to a story that had potential to transform the common understanding of alcoholism.

After the movie version was released late in November 1945,[22] it was anxiously reviewed in the Yale Center's journal by Selden D. Bacon, a prominent researcher. Because Americans were, in Bacon's judgment, "poorly informed and at the same time easily excited about excessive drinking as a moral problem," the impact of *The Lost Weekend* could be extremely damaging insofar as the film (which was seen to follow the book "quite closely") misled audiences into believing that all alcoholics are like Don Birnam, that anyone who drinks might become like him, that the alcoholic's prognosis is hopeless, and that "hospitals and doctors are not only useless for this condition, but are, in addition, heartless, inefficient and horrendous." What was sorely needed, Bacon insisted, was a "rational solution of the problems of alcohol," a solution based on a sound "medical viewpoint" that had not yet fully crystallized, despite the best efforts of scientific authorities. Unfortunately, the public "does not regard the Don Birnams as ill men engulfed in their habit because of their illness, and needing good medical care, not moral suasion or moral damnation. The serious student of alcoholism has tried earnestly to get public recognition of the fact that the alcoholic is an ill man; *The Lost Weekend* will not further, but will obstruct, this recognition."[23]

In a later issue of the same journal, however, a psychology instructor at New York University reported that the film did *not,* as Bacon had feared, leave audiences with the impression that alcoholism was "hopeless and incurable." On the contrary, in a poll of 116 undergraduate students, a large majority (78%)

answered "yes" to the question: "Do you think that 'The Lost Weekend' portrayed the alcoholic as an individual who is ill and requires specialized treatment?" That is, student perceptions of the movie were in accord with the Alcoholism Movement's view that "the alcoholic is ill and needs therapy."[24]

Jackson came by his own knowledge of the disease concept directly. *The Lost Weekend* was based largely on his own textbook case, including his experiences at Bellevue and with private psychiatrists. Although Jackson did not join A.A. until ten years after the novel appeared, he was acquainted with the fellowship while writing it in the early 1940s.[25] *The Lost Weekend* subtly incorporates A.A. ideas, sometimes in echoes or paraphrases of program sayings—as in the scene in which Birnam appears to have "hit bottom" (A.A. lingo for the moment when the alcoholic becomes fully and honestly aware of his powerlessness over alcohol). Don seems at last to be breaking through his denial as he casts aside his excuses for drinking:

> To hell with the causes—absent father, fraternity shock, too much mother, too much money, or the dozen other reasons you fell back on to justify yourself. They counted for nothing in the face of the one fact: you drank and it was killing you. Why? Because alcohol was something you couldn't handle, it had you licked. Why? Because you had reached the point where one drink was too many and a hundred not enough.   (P. 222)

The last sentence is a familiar A.A. slogan,[26] and the entire passage expresses the pragmatic spirit of the Alcoholism Movement; its bias toward effects rather than causes, its concern with remedies rather than etiologies.

As an intellectual, Don Birnam can't help being fascinated, however, by psychological theories about drinking—particularly by the psychoanalytic notion that alcoholism and homosexuality are closely related. Birnam recurs several times to his bad experience with "the foolish psychiatrist" who dwelt on Don's homosexual experiences in childhood. He soon discovered that "he knew more about the subject, more about pathology, certainly more about himself and what made him tick, than the doctor" (p. 53). But although Birnam rejects psychoanalytic theory as mumbo jumbo, he has nevertheless been influenced by the doctor's point of view, if only as something to resist.

The Lost Weekend was written when psychoanalysis had its greatest sway in the field of alcoholism studies and treatment. A linkage between "alcoholism" and "homosexuality," both of which terms came into clinical use at the end of the nineteenth century under the aegis of psychiatry, was hypothesized in Karl Abraham's pioneering study of 1908. Abraham claimed that alcohol "stimulates the 'complex' of masculinity" because "respect for prowess in drinking is closely bound up with respect for sexual prowess." The man who does not drink "is accounted a weakling." But alcohol also loosens the mental inhibition of same-sexual libido: "When drinking, men fall on each other's necks and kiss one another: they feel that they are united by peculiarly intimate ties and this moves them to tears and to intimate modes of address." Therefore, he reasoned, "every drinking bout is tinged with homosexuality. The homosexual component-instincts, which education has taught us to repress and sublimate, reappear in no veiled form under the influence of alcohol."[27]

Abraham's standing as Freud's loyal lieutenant gave added weight to his theories; the idea that alcoholics are "latent homosexuals" gained immediate acceptance in psychoanalytic circles and reechoed in the broader medical literature throughout the 1930s. Consider, for example, an important paper by Robert P. Knight, an American psychiatrist of the Freudian persuasion, delivered at the 1936 Congress of the International Psychoanalytic Association. Knight agreed with Abraham that excessive drinking signifies "the regressive acting out of unconscious libidinal and sadistic drives"; that alcoholics exhibit a "strong homosexual conflict," which often results in "a conscious or almost conscious fear of being regarded effeminate"; that alcoholics mask their "spurious masculinity" with alcoholic fellowship, finding that "it is regarded as not grown up, as 'sissyfied', *not* to drink, and that to drink heavily and 'hell around' with the boys is regarded as proof of manliness and potency." From his analysis of ten cases, Knight offered the additional (and tentative) generalization that alcoholics commonly have a family background in which "an over-indulgent, over-protective" mother is combined with a "cold and unaffectionate" father who is alternately severe and indulgent.[28] This parental constellation was often identified by psychoanalysts in the 1930s as characteristic as well of homosexuals.

Two years after Knight's paper, in a book aimed at the general reader, two non-analytic experts acknowledged that "unquestionably, repressed homosexuality may be found at the roots of alcoholic addiction." They also asserted, however, that "our experience does not justify any sweeping statement concerning a basic homosexual trend as the cause of alcoholism."[29] And by the 1940s, even some psychoanalysts were beginning to question the orthodox view. In a clinical study published the same year as *The Lost Weekend* (a study that cited the novel as an informed source), Edmund Bergler reiterated the conventional Freudian wisdom on the regressive nature of excessive drinking: the alcoholic as a fixated "oral" type who acts out sado-masochistic fantasies through the substitution of the bottle for the breast, etc. But in referring to the opinion that "the disease reveals unconscious homosexual tendencies," Bergler saw no necessary linkage.[30] Also in 1944, at the summer seminar on alcoholism sponsored by the Yale Center, Carney Landis drew similar conclusions about the claim that "the psychic reason for alcohol addiction is the incomplete repressed homosexuality which the individual cannot sublimate." Noting recent findings that "the occurrence of overt homosexuality is much more prevalent than was hitherto believed," Landis asserted that "homosexuality is an independent personality factor which is not necessarily associated with other forms of personality disorder, neurosis, psychosis or addiction."[31]

Set in 1936, the year Jackson himself sought treatment for his drinking, *The Lost Weekend* follows the Freudian line on alcoholism he had encountered through his reading and in psychoanalysis. One of Jackson's sources, as the manuscript of the novel reveals, was Karl Menninger's influential book on the modes of human self-destructiveness, *Man Against Himself* (1938), which contains a chapter on "alcohol addiction" as a form of "chronic suicide." Like Robert P. Knight, who was also associated with the Menninger Clinic, Menninger regarded excessive drinking as symptomatic of an underlying neurosis involving psychosexual fixation and latent homosexuality: "It is almost axiomatic that alcoholics in spite of a great show of heterosexual activity, have secretly a great fear of women and of heterosexuality in general, apparently regarding it as fraught with much danger."[32]

Throughout *The Lost Weekend*, Don Birnam is shown to be both wary of heterosexuality and terrified of homosexuality. He recalls a lover once demanding to know, " "Why do you only come to bed with me when you are drunk?"

She had not been mollified by his glib reply: "Because I'm *always* drunk!" (p. 186). As "the foolish psychiatrist" would have insisted, Don's problem lies deeper than that: in his childhood abandonment by his father; in his adolescent fantasies, during masturbation, of his friend's father rather than of Gertrude Hort, a voluptuous girl his own age; in his traumatic experience as a college fraternity pledge, when he developed a "passionate hero-worship" for an upperclassman that "led, like a fatal infatuation, to scandal and public disgrace, because no one had understood or got the story straight" (pp. 48–49). Kicked out of the Kappa U house, Don crept home to nurse psychic wounds that have never completely healed. Years later, when he happens to encounter the man who had filled his abandoned slot in Kappa U, Don is still paralyzed by dread.

This encounter itself, which revives all of Birnam's sexual fear and ambivalence, reads as if Jackson had tailored it to fit the theories of his analysts. Birnam recalls the scene—a Greenwich Village bar—in one of his drunken reveries. A handsome young man had been standing silently beside him; just as Don was about to leave, the man offered to buy him a drink. Don immediately sensed (but did not acknowledge to himself) homoerotic overtones: the hint of a homosexual overture, simultaneously enhanced and veiled by the presence of alcohol and the bar-room practice of treating:

> He looked a little worried; also faintly belligerent; the frown challenged Don not to misunderstand the impulse which prompted the invitation. Don got it at once; and as he recognized, like a veteran before a neophyte, the stage of drinking the other had reached—the confidential, the confiding stage—he began to feel superior, amused, tolerant, generous, and warmly friendly himself. "Why, thank you very much," he said with a smile. "And then perhaps you'll have one with me." . . .
>
> "You probably wonder why I did that," Brad said.
>
> "No I don't, at all." Don smiled to reassure him.
>
> "I'm staying up late tonight and I feel like talking to somebody."
>
> "I understand." Oh, he understood. How many times indeed, under just such circumstances, in just such places, had he been in on conversations of just this sort. That familiar opening line: it was the prelude to who knew

what confidences—boring, very likely; nothing to confide about; intimate but unrevealing and finally elusive or even resentful.   (Pp. 84–85)

Unlike his erstwhile fraternity brothers, Don understands that man-to-man intimacy, especially the kind inspired by alcohol, need not imply anything unmanly. Brad's familiar opening line is taken as a prelude not to sex, but to talk—and boring talk at that. Don has no more patience for boozy confidences than for homosexuals, such as the pianist at Jack's place—a "fattish baby-faced young man: Dannie or Billy or Jimmie or Hughie somebody," who sings leeringly suggestive lyrics to songs like "The 23rd Street Ferry" and "Peter and the Dyke" in which *"camping, queen, faggot, meat* were words frequently played upon" (p. 28). Birnam's homophobic disdain extends even to his taste in book-binding! He shudders to recall the Elbert Hubbard volumes in his father's library: "the sickeningly limp limp-leather Roycroft books that almost gave you the creeps to hold" (p. 148).

Don's heterosexual identity depends on his conscious revulsion from homo-sexuality. But he also conforms to the psychoanalytic profile of the alcoholic; unconsciously attracted to other men, he is "latently homosexual." This hidden truth becomes all-too-painfully clear when Birnam is accosted in the hospital by Bim, the insolently coquettish nurse, who contemptuously struts around the ward, purrs like Marlene Dietrich (p. 129), and makes Don—whom he flirt-ingly addresses as "Baby"—feel like Pola Negri being mentally undressed by "a lecherous Prussian officer in some ancient film" (p. 134):

Here was the daydream turned inside-out; a projection, in reverse, of the wishful and yearning fancy; the back of the picture, the part always turned to the wall. The flower of the ingrown seed he had in him was here shown in unhealthy bloom, *ad terrorem* and *ad nauseam.* It was aspiration in its raw and naked state, aspiration un-ennobled, a lapse of nature as bizarre and unde-niable as the figures of his imagined life were deniable, bizarre, beyond reach. All that he wanted to become and, in his fanciful world, became, was here represented in throwback. He himself stood midway between the ideal and this—as far from the one as from the other. But oh, too—oh, too!—as far from the other as from the one. If he was uncomfortable in Bim's stifling presence, did he not also have reason to be comforted? Or was midway, nothing—nothing at all?[33]   (P. 135)

In accordance with psychoanalytic theory, Don understands his own alcoholism to be akin to Bim's homosexuality in the sense that both are atavistic slippages from an evolutionary (Social Darwinian) ideal: outcroppings of a "bizarre" and disgustingly animal nature that falls far short of the spiritual heights; in short, a nightmarish "inversion" of the artist's imaginative daydream. Don takes comfort—comfort that seems also to be a form of denial—in thinking that whatever his kinship to Bim may be, he still holds a higher place on the evolutionary ladder, and he is far more secure in his manliness.

This idea is developed a few pages later, as Don belatedly formulates a response to what Bim whispered to him as he was leaving the hospital: "Listen, baby. . . . I know you" (p. 139):

> He was aware, as Bim was, of the downward path he was on; he knew himself well enough to know and admit that Bim had every reason to say what he said—but only insofar as Bim saw, in him, the potential confederate that was every alcoholic: the fellow bogged down in adolescence; the guy off his track, off his trolley; the man still unable to take, at thirty-three or -six or -nine, the forward step he had missed in his 'teens; the poor devil demoralized and thrown off balance by the very stuff intended to restore his frightened or baffled ego; the gent jarred loose into unsavory bypaths that gave him the shudders to think of but which were his natural habitat and inevitable home so long as drink remained the *modus operandi* of his life. . . .
>
> (P. 144)

Yes, Birnam allows, the alcoholic and the homosexual are both cases of arrested development; stuck in adolescence, neither can be fully a man. But "the trouble with homos," Don thinks, is that in their eagerness to embrace their own kind, in their knowing glances of recognition, they smugly assume too much: "They were always so damned anxious to suspect every guy they couldn't make of merely playing hard-to-get; so damned anxious to believe that their own taint was shared by everybody else" (p. 145). Bim, with "the bright eye of his kind," keenly observes the potential "homo" in Don. But what he fails to see is "that the alcoholic was not himself, able to choose his own path, and therefore the kinship he seemed to reveal was incidental, accidental, transitory at best. If the drunk had been himself he would not be a drunk and potential brother in the first place" (p. 144).

Such passages raise interpretive difficulties, some of which are inherent to Jackson's narrative technique—in which the narrator hovers near Don Birnam, the Jamesian center of consciousness, reporting both his words and his private thoughts (in free indirect discourse), while also keeping some ironic distance from him. But how much distance? How credible or reliable are Don Birnam's opinions meant to be? On the question of psychoanalytic theory, for instance, does *The Lost Weekend* finally affirm or dispute the idea that alcoholics are "latent homosexuals"? How closely may Jackson be identified with a character who is evidently based on himself?

Although Don Birnam's drunken experiences were largely derived from Jackson's,[34] the character lacks his author's sober perspective. Birnam is undercut as a self-deluded alcoholic in the grip of denial.[35] It would seem, then, that the passages quoted above are best read as evidence not of Jackson's sexual insecurities, but rather of Birnam's. Don's thinking is exposed here as a rationalization of his "latent homosexuality," to which he is no more capable of facing up than to his alcoholism. Since Birnam is poised at the novel's end to go off on yet another binge, the reader may reasonably infer that his self-deception will continue. In order for him to stop drinking, the novel implies, Don must accept that the alcoholic *is* himself and that Bim *does* "know" him—because the alcoholic is not only a "potential confederate," but also, as psychoanalysis would insist, a brother to the homosexual.

The Lost Weekend, like *Nightwood*, thus inverts the gender assumptions of those novels in which alcohol is represented as the preservative of manliness and the alcoholic as the polar opposite of the homosexual. Jackson's subversion of the drinking culture of modernism results from the assimilation into his fiction of the concept of "alcoholism" itself, along with its freight of psychoanalytic theory.

During the early decades of the twentieth century, modernism revolutionized the arts in America while Prohibition revolutionized drinking practices.

The avant garde reacted against the Victorian idea of inebriation by producing a literature that idealized intoxication as iconoclasm and lionized the drunk as an anti-Puritan rebel. A major element in such texts as *John Barleycorn, The Sun Also Rises, Tender Is the Night, Appointment in Samarra,* and *Nightwood* is the representation of excessive drinking as an inevitable response of the sensitive consciousness to the nightmarish human condition.

The Lost Weekend began to close the book on these drunk narratives by exposing the literariness of their alcoholic despair. "In A Glass," Birnam's hypothetical *Drunkard's Rigadoon,* exists only within the claustral confines of a mind soaked in modernist fiction. As Don recognizes, "His very nightmare [the bat hallucination] was synthetic: a dream by Thomas Mann" (p. 215). In his sober moments, he realizes that his existence does not live up to the high romantic tragedy of the sort he admires in *Tender Is the Night,* in which the alcoholic culture hero learns the bitter wisdom of the ages from John Barleycorn. The drunken life is "merely ludicrous—ludicrous but not worth laughing at, something merely to put up with and bear with because there was nothing else to do about it" (p. 216). In its demystification of the White Logic, *The Lost Weekend* inaugurated a new mode of American fiction in which habitual drunkenness was figured less as a sign of The Modern Temper than as the symptom of a disease.

Charles Jackson announced publicly in 1944 that his next book would be "about the regeneration of an alcoholic, a subject which he says he has found more fascinating than that of *The Lost Weekend.*"[36] "Farther and Wilder," in which Don Birnam was to reappear, still remained unfinished when Jackson died in 1968; but the "more fascinating" subject of recovery from alcoholism has nevertheless become a flourishing genre.

Once the Alcoholism Movement had reconstructed the framework within which Americans understood excessive drinking, once habitual drunkenness had been medicalized as well as psychologized, then "alcoholic" writers began to become self-conscious of their "alcoholism," and fiction about drinking changed accordingly. Since the 1940s, what might be called the recovery narrative has largely superseded the modernist drunk narrative. American novelists have continued to produce some powerful stories of alcoholic degeneration, such as Natalie Anderson Scott's *The Story of Mrs. Murphy* (1947) or Richard Yates's *Disturbing the Peace* (1975). More common, however, have been fictions about relief from alcohol (and other drugs) that reflect the influence of the Alcoholism Movement in general and of A.A. in particular. Significant examples of this type are Thomas Randall's *The Twelfth Step* (1957),[37] Roger Treat's *The Endless Road* (1960), John Berryman's *Recovery* (1972), Donald Newlove's *The Drunks* (1974), John Cheever's *Falconer* (1977), Ivan Gold's *Sams in a Dry Season* (1990), and David Gates's *Jernigan* (1991).[38]

Numerous Hollywood films, some derived from popular plays or bestselling books, have also dealt explicitly with alcoholism. In several of these, too, A.A. is offered explicitly as the means to "recovery": *Come Fill the Cup* (1950), *Come Back, Little Sheba* (1952), *Something to Live For* (1952), *I'll Cry Tomorrow* (1955), *The Voice in the Mirror* (1958), and *Days of Wine and Roses* (1962).[39]

The proliferation of such works in the immediate post-war period had much to do with the cumulative success of A.A., in which recovery narratives have always played an important part. In A.A. meetings, as in all three editions of the "Big Book," members routinely tell of their personal adventures before and after joining the fellowship and retrace their progress from drunkenness to sobriety.[40] These stories, which constitute a type of spiritual autobiography, have not only been adapted to fiction; they have also created a discourse for the rapidly expanding "recovery" movement of the late twentieth century.

A.A. itself was another creation of the Lost Generation of middle-class Americans who came of age during the early 1920s and who made excessive drinking a hallmark of their youthful rebellion. When this cohort reached middle age at mid-century, it was faced with the resultant drinking problems. (A common pattern in male drinkers is for alcoholism to develop gradually for twenty years or so and then to become acute when they reach their forties.) "The founding of Alcoholics Anonymous in 1935, and its emergence as a national movement around 1940," says Robin Room, "must be seen as the reaction of the initial 'wet generations' to the predicament in which they found themselves." Both the approach and the rhetoric of A.A., moreover, "were carefully attuned to the mind-set of members of the initial 'wet generation' and, in particular, to the men of the generation." The anti-drink discourse of A.A. provided an alternative to the now "discredited invective of the temperance movement."[41]

The blunt and deflationary pragmatism of A.A. also provided an alternative to the seductive grandiosity of The Modern Temper. Donald Newlove recalls how in his drinking days he sought "the just, pure expression of a kind of holy blackness I admired as the richest resource for dark language." Life's gruesome side, which he had often experienced on the job as an ambulance driver, had initiated him, he believed, into the darkest secrets of the White Logic. The deadliest ordeal was having to wrestle with a corpse wedged upside down between a bathtub and toilet:

> [A]s I got down and pried I told myself that if I lived through this, that then I had gone through my Guadalcanal, my Iwo Jima, my Saipan, my Tarawa, my King Lear tree-splitting storm, my Godot, my *No Exit*, my holocaust, my pie-slice of the universal horror and tragedy and that I was now an accredited Twentieth-Century Writer and fully empowered to seek and state the definitive negative statement for my times and to hold a mirror up to the power of blackness, the night within the night, my Dachau, Berlin, Hiroshima, a spiritual desolation that granted me the clear right to drink. I deserved to drink to keep my good cheer and avoid suicide.

Newlove later came to realize that, like Don Birnam, he had been aggrandizing his capacity for suffering: "I still, of course, didn't know I was a drunk or that my bottom was far, far off, and that I was now only groping about in my graveyard period, a merely literary agony."[42]

In contrast to the truly horrific suffering endured at Guadalcanal or Dachau or Hiroshima, the agony of the alcoholic "Twentieth-Century Writer"—agony that was largely self-inflicted through drinking and that served in turn to justify drinking—*was* "merely literary" more often than these writers wished to recognize. When F. Scott Fitzgerald gravely opined, "There are no second acts in American lives,"[43] he neglected to mention that he and many other modernists stuck in their "graveyard period" had gotten drunk during the first act and passed out during intermission.

Notes

1: From Intemperance to Alcoholism in the Fiction of W. D. Howells

1. Harry Gene Levine remarks that the colonists *did* consider drinking to be a problem among the Amerindians they had conquered and displaced, in part through the devastating effects of demon rum. Alcohol was seen to have a drastic effect on the "savages," transforming them into dangerously wild and violent beasts. "Only at the end of the 18th century," says Levine, "do European-Americans begin to talk seriously about alcohol as a cause of their own criminal and violent behavior. And not until the 19th century did large numbers of whites believe that alcohol affected their behavior in the same way as it did Indians." That is, only when whites "came to recognize and fear the 'Indian' in themselves—the uncontrolled savage within—did alcohol as a substance become problematic." "The Good Creature of God and the Demon Rum: Colonial American and 19th Century Ideas About Alcohol, Crime, and Accidents," in *Alcohol and Disinhibition: Nature and Meaning of the Link,* ed. Robin Room and Gary Collins, Research Monograph No. 12, U.S. Department of Health and Human Services (Washington, DC: U.S. Government Printing Office, 1983), pp. 124, 126.

2. Ian R. Tyrrell, *Sobering Up: From Temperance to Prohibition in Antebellum America, 1800–1860* (Westport, CT: Greenwood Press, 1979), p. 25. Mark Edward Lender and James Kirby Martin agree that a "general lack of anxiety over alcohol problems was one of the most

significant features of drinking in the colonial era." There were no "prerevolutionary equiv-
alents of the temperance or prohibition movements" because few thought that intemperance
"constituted a serious threat to social stability or individual rights." *Drinking in America: A
History* (New York: Free Press, 1982), p. 14.

3. Jack S. Blocker, Jr., *American Temperance Movements: Cycles of Reform* (Boston:
Twayne, 1989), p. 4.

4. Levine, "The Good Creature of God and the Demon Rum," p. 116.

5. W. J. Rorabaugh, *The Alcoholic Republic: An American Tradition* (New York: Oxford
University Press, 1979), pp. 20–21.

6. Tyrrell, *Sobering Up,* p. 125.

7. Levine, "The Good Creature of God and the Demon Rum," pp. 132, 140.

8. Noah Webster, *An American Dictionary of the English Language,* revised edition (New
York: Harper, 1846), pp. 459, 448. The definitions of "intemperance" and "inebriation" in
this later printing of the 1841 revised edition ultimately derive from the 1829 edition of
Webster's *Dictionary.* Stuart Berg Flexner, who notes that "drunk" has "more synonyms than
any other word," traces "inebriated" to a fifteenth-century English term: "from Latin *ebrius,*
drunk, from *e,* out + *bria,* wine jar, literally 'having emptied out the wine jar.'" "Temperance," Flexner says, had meant moderation and self-restraint since the fourteenth century;
"but by 1830 the American Temperance Society defined *temperance* as 'the moderate . . . use
of things beneficial and abstinence from things harmful,' going on to call hard liquor
'poison.' Thus, in regard to liquor, the American Temperance Society changed the meaning
of *temperance* to *abstinence.*" *I Hear America Talking: An Illustrated Treasury of American
Words and Phrases* (New York: Van Nostrand Reinhold, 1976), pp. 125, 355.

9. See Jean-Charles Sournia, *A History of Alcoholism,* trans. Nick Hindley and Gareth
Stanton (London: Blackwell, 1990), pp. 20–50.

10. According to Bruce Holley Johnson, the first use of "alcoholic" (*Alkoholiker*) and
"alcoholism" (*Alkoholismus*) in their modern senses—"to refer not to the physiological effects
of excessive drinking but to immoderate drinking itself"—may well have been in a paper by
Karl Abraham originally published in 1908 in *Zeitschrift für Sexualwissenschaft* and later
translated as "The Psychological Relations between Sexuality and Alcoholism," *International Journal of Psycho-Analysis,* 7 (January 1926), 2–10. See Johnson, "The Alcoholism
Movement in America: A Study in Cultural Innovation," Diss. University of Illinois 1973,
p. 474.

11. Ibid., pp. 478–79. Johnson asserts that instances of "alcoholic" as a noun are "extremely rare," even within psychiatric discourse, during the early twentieth century. He
adds: "There appear to have been no cases in which it was used as a substantive in magazines, novels, or other popular writing in England or the United States prior to the late
1930s" (pp. 477–78). In light of Jack London's modern use of "alcoholic" in the bestselling
John Barleycorn (1913), the latter claim must be discounted. It may be argued, in fact, that
London deserves major credit for the dissemination of the term. (Flexner notes that "alco-

holist" was "the fairly common word in America in the 1880s and 90s" [*I Hear America Talking*, p. 127].)

London did *not*, however, adopt the term "alcoholism," which according to Johnson "does not appear to have been used as a synonym for habitual drunkenness in popular or technical writing prior to World War I" (p. 475). Here again, contrary evidence may be cited, such as Thorstein Veblen's reference in 1899 to the "all-dominating habit of alcoholism" in *The Theory of the Leisure Class* (1899; rpt. New York: Penguin, 1979), p. 108. In general, however, it is safe to say that Victorian terminology was gradually and unsystematically superseded during the early years of the twentieth century.

12. Harry Gene Levine, "The Discovery of Addiction: Changing Conceptions of Habitual Drunkenness in America," *Journal of Studies on Alcohol*, 39 (January 1978), 149, 158.

13. Levine argues that whereas nineteenth-century temperance ideology located addiction in the substance rather than the person—hence the logic of Prohibition—the twentieth-century "disease concept" of alcoholism, as developed by E. M. Jellinek and others, abandoned the idea that alcohol was inherently addictive. "For the first time, the source of addiction lay in the individual body, and not in the drug per se. The result has been a somewhat 'purer' medical model—that is, there is less of a tendency to view addiction as self-inflicted disease." "The Discovery of Addiction," p. 162.

Blocker takes issue, however, with Levine's distinction between the Victorian and modern paradigms. Not all temperance advocates, Blocker argues, embraced the idea that alcohol was inherently addictive: "Although reformers believed that alcohol was a poison and drinking was a sin, they did not also believe that this substance was addictive for everyone. Instead, the danger in drinking arose from the combination of a hazardous substance and a weakness that human beings shared in varying degrees." *American Temperance Movements*, p. 28.

14. Virginia Berridge and Griffith Edwards, *Opium and the People: Opiate Use in Nineteenth-Century England* (New Haven: Yale University Press, 1987), p. 155.

15. Herbert Asbury, *The Great Illusion: An Informal History of Prohibition* (Garden City, NY: Doubleday, 1950), pp. 35, 46–47.

16. Although Howells imbibed socially, he was not by any means a drinking man: "For one thing, alcohol made him sleepy. He tended therefore to avoid it when he wished to be alert and to use it pretty regularly for many years as a soporific—a favorite being hot Scotch at bedtime." Edwin H. Cady, *The Realist at War: The Mature Years 1885–1920 of William Dean Howells* (Syracuse, NY: Syracuse University Press, 1958), p. 90. On Howells's attitudes toward drinking and Prohibition, see also Edward Wagenknecht, *William Dean Howells: The Friendly Eye* (New York: Oxford University Press, 1969), pp. 224–27.

17. W. D. Howells, *The Lady of the Aroostook* (Boston: Houghton, Osgood, 1879), p. 87. Subsequent quotations are identified in the text.

18. Berridge and Edwards point out that addiction was clearly defined along class lines in Victorian England. The "disease" theory itself was "applicable only to the middle-class

patient"; working-class addicts rarely figured in medical case histories. As the gaze of physicians and reformers descended the social scale, an increasing admixture of moral judgment and punitive treatment entered into the idea of addiction. *Opium and the People*, p. 158.

19. Similar to Hicks is Ralph Putney in *Annie Kilburn* (New York: Harper, 1889) and *The Quality of Mercy* (New York: Harper, 1892), who is characterized as an intelligent and sensitive man who has visited tragedy upon himself and his family through his uncontrollable drinking. On a binge Putney once crippled his own son, but not even the resulting guilt can keep him entirely sober. Howells also drew a sympathetic portrait of an opium addict in Lorenzo Hawberk, the dreamy inventor in *The Son of Royal Langbrith* (New York: Harper, 1904).

20. The chapter in which Bartley staggers home to his wife impressed Mark Twain as "the best drunk scene—because the truest—that I ever read." He told Howells: "There are touches in it which I never saw any writer take note of before. And they are set before the reader with amazing accuracy. How very drunk, & how recently drunk, & how altogether admirably drunk you must have been to enable you to contrive that masterpiece!" *Mark Twain–Howells Letters: The Correspondence of Samuel L. Clemens and William D. Howells 1872–1910*, ed. Henry Nash Smith and William M. Gibson (Cambridge: Harvard University Press, 1960), pp. 407–8.

21. W. D. Howells, *A Modern Instance*, ed. George N. Bennett (Bloomington: Indiana University Press, 1977), p. 288. Subsequent quotations are identified in the text.

22. Like Ben Halleck, Silas Lapham is certainly no drunkard, but his weaknesses of character are similarly revealed through drunkenness. The overweening Paint King's inexperience with wine leads to a salutary humiliation when he drinks too much at the Coreys's dinner party and then launches into an embarrassingly drunken monologue. Like Hicks, Lapham is stabbed by remorse for actions he cannot fully remember, and he throws himself on the mercy of Tom Corey the next morning.

23. The "Keeley Cure," popularized during the 1890s by its inventor, Dr. Leslie E. Keeley, was (supposedly) a form of aversion therapy. Removed from his normal surroundings to a sanitorium, the alcoholic patient was then injected with Keeley's secret formula: "a solution of double chloride of gold, which purportedly caused a lasting repugnance to spirits in any form." Tom Dardis, *The Thirsty Muse: Alcohol and the American Writer* (New York: Ticknor and Fields, 1989), p. 34. As Dardis suggests, the Keeley Cure was probably worthless except for the incidental opportunity it afforded for drunks to dry out.

24. W. D. Howells, *The Landlord at Lion's Head* (New York: Harper, 1897), pp. 232–33. Subsequent quotations are taken from this (first) edition and documented in the text. The novel is currently available in a facsimile edition (New York: Dover, 1983).

25. Whereas before the temperance movement the drinking habits of American men and women were more or less alike, drinking among women diminished sharply during the early nineteenth century: "As the ideology of separate public and private spheres for men and

women spread among urban women it set forth new norms for the behavior of those who aspired to 'true womanhood.' The refinement and delicacy, piety and purity, prescribed by the cult of domesticity may well have reduced both the number of women who drank and the amounts consumed by those who continued to drink, thereby widening existing differences between the drinking patterns of men and women." Blocker, *American Temperance Movements*, pp. 10–11. During the nineteenth century, according to Harry Gene Levine, "the restrictions against women's getting drunk were so strong among Protestant middle class supporters of the temperance cause that the *topic* of women's intemperance was itself almost taboo." "Temperance and Women in 19th-Century United States," in *Alcohol and Drug Problems in Women*, ed. Oriana Josseau Kalant, *Research Advances in Alcohol and Drug Problems*, 5 (New York: Plenum Press, 1980), 33.

26. Quoted in Levine, "The Discovery of Addiction," p. 155.

27. George Frederick Drinka, *The Birth of Neurosis: Myth, Malady, and the Victorians* (New York: Simon and Schuster, 1984), pp. 191, 193. On the cultural pervasiveness of "neurasthenia," see also Tom Lutz, *American Nervousness, 1903: An Anecdotal History* (Ithaca, NY: Cornell University Press, 1991).

28. See my essay, "Giving a Character: Howellsian Realism in *The Landlord at Lion's Head*," forthcoming in *Harvard Library Bulletin*.

29. Following Jonathan Miller's line of analysis in *The Body in Question* (New York: Random House, 1979), Levine observes that the idea of alcohol as a disinhibiting agent— something that supposedly "weakens the recently evolved higher brain controls, releasing the primitive impulses"—is derived from a hierarchical Darwinian topology of the mind and nervous system that became the unexamined common sense of the Victorian era. As Levine asserts, "[T]he idea that there is a higher portion of the brain which when weakened by disease or alcohol releases lower animal impulses and behavior is just plain wrong. It is false biology and neurophysiology. . . . It also derives from the Nineteenth Century upper class fears of revolution by the 'animalistic' lower classes, and from broader bourgeois beliefs about the importance of self-control and the conscience in the maintenance of social order." "The Good Creature of God and the Demon Rum," pp. 167, 171.

30. T. J. Jackson Lears, "From Salvation to Self-Realization: Advertising and the Therapeutic Roots of the Consumer Culture, 1880–1930," in *The Culture of Consumption: Critical Essays in American History, 1880–1980*, ed. Richard Wightman Fox and T. J. Jackson Lears (New York: Pantheon, 1983), pp. 8–9. See also Lears, *No Place of Grace: Antimodernism and the Transformation of American Culture, 1880–1920* (New York: Pantheon, 1981).

31. In his review of William James's *Principles of Psychology* (1890), Howells endorsed James's belief that good character results from the discipline of good habits: "In fact the will of the weak man is *not* free; but the will of the strong man, the man who has *got the habit* of preferring sense to nonsense and 'virtue' to 'vice,' is a *freed* will, which one might very well spend all one's energies in achieving." *Editor's Study by William Dean Howells*, ed. James W. Simpson (Troy, NY: Whitston, 1983), p. 324.

32. Theodore Dreiser, *Sister Carrie*, ed. Donald Pizer (New York: Norton, 1970), pp. 56–57.

33. Walter Benn Michaels, *The Gold Standard and the Logic of Naturalism: American Literature at the Turn of the Century* (Berkeley: University of California Press, 1987), p. 224 n. 11. Michaels's argument recalls Gregory Bateson's brilliant analysis of alcoholic thinking. See "The Cybernetics of 'Self': A Theory of Alcoholism," in *Steps To an Ecology of Mind* (New York: Ballantine, 1972), pp. 309–37.

34. Michaels, *The Gold Standard*, p. 35.

35. Levine, "The Discovery of Addiction," p. 165.

36. Blocker, *American Temperance Movements*, p. 110.

37. See Veblen, *The Theory of the Leisure Class*. In an enthusiastic review, Howells suggested that the fictional rendering of Veblen's social analysis offered "the supreme opportunity of the American novelist." *W. D. Howells as Critic*, ed. Edwin H. Cady (London and Boston: Routledge and Kegan Paul, 1973), p. 290.

2: Memoirs of an Alcoholic: *John Barleycorn*

1. Clarice Stasz describes *John Barleycorn* as "a curious amalgam of confession, sociological commentary, and philosophy." She also notes that although London insisted more than once that the book was "'bare, bald, absolute fact,' its facts are shaped by his strong fictional craft and his sociological bent." Introduction to *John Barleycorn; or, Alcoholic Memoirs* (New York: Signet, 1990), pp. 5, 7. *John Barleycorn* (without a subtitle) was originally published as a serial in the *Saturday Evening Post*, and then issued in book form (New York: Century, 1913). All quotations from the novel are taken from this (first) edition and documented in the text.

2. Andrew Sinclair, *Jack: A Biography of Jack London* (New York: Harper and Row, 1977), p. 188.

3. Clarice Stasz, *American Dreamers: Charmian and Jack London* (New York: St. Martin's Press, 1988), pp. 345, 228.

4. Dwight Anderson, *The Other Side of the Bottle* (New York: A.A. Wyn, 1950), p. 50.

5. Linda Schierse Leonard, *Witness to the Fire: Creativity and the Veil of Addiction* (Boston: Shambala, 1990), p. 108. The concept of denial (or "disavowal") derives from psychoanalysis; it is a term (*Verleugnung*) used by Sigmund Freud "in the specific sense of a mode of defence which consists in the subject's refusing to recognise the reality of a traumatic perception—most especially the perception of the absence of the woman's penis." J. Laplance and J.-B. Pontalis, *The Language of Psycho Analysis*, trans. Donald Nicholson-Smith (New York: Norton, 1973), p. 118. Although Freud used the term originally in regard to fetishism and the psychoses, he later generalized it somewhat, remarking in his last book that it is common for the infantile ego to ward off "some claim from the *external world* which it feels as painful . . . by *denying* the perceptions that bring to knowledge such a demand on the part of reality." Freud goes on to suggest that the "rejection" of denial is "always supplemented by an

acceptance; two contrary and independent attitudes always arise. . . ." *An Outline of Psycho-analysis* (1940), trans. James Strachey (New York: Norton, 1963), p. 118. That is, the psychodynamics of denial operate dialectically: the vehemence with which perception of the painful reality is rejected results from concurrent knowledge of its existence.

Detached from its strictly Freudian context, "denial" has nevertheless retained most of its psychoanalytic meaning as it has entered the psychological parlance of the "recovery" movement, where the phrase "in denial" refers to an addict's stubborn refusal to accept or even to admit the reality of his or her addiction. Thus an alcoholic in denial is one who will not acknowledge the existence of a drinking problem that is usually all too apparent to everyone else. The force of the alcoholic's denial derives precisely from hidden awareness that there *is* a problem and thus from the fear that something drastic might be done about it—such as separating the drinker from the drink!

6. London's self-deception was dreadfully obvious to such friends as Upton Sinclair: "When *John Barleycorn* was published, Jack sent me a copy and I wrote to thank him. I praised him for his courage and frankness. But to myself I uttered a private prayer—that having gone this far in his understanding of the terrible dangers of drink, he would be able to go the one great step further, and give it up completely. I feared the hint of disaster which seemed implicit in his concluding words of *John Barleycorn.* I feared his insistence that he was not an alcoholic. . . ." *The Cup of Fury* (Great Neck, NY: Channel Press, 1956), pp. 164–65.

7. Tales of reformed drunkards were commonplace in the temperance literature of the nineteenth century. For an example of the genre nearly contemporaneous with *John Barleycorn,* see Joseph H. Francis, *My Last Drink* (Chicago: Modern Press, 1915). Subtitled (with immodesty surpassed only by inaccuracy) "The Greatest Human Story Ever Written," this confessional narrative retraces the decline of a former Chicago alderman "from power and wealth to poverty and prison through drink."

8. When London labels himself an "extremist," it is in the context of his early writing career, when he hectically piled up pages and subsisted on five hours' sleep a night. Throughout *John Barleycorn,* London never does anything by halves. Whether he is smuggling oysters, shoveling coal, ironing laundry, or studying for college, he always drives himself beyond all normal limits of endurance. Such behavior is congruent with London's excessive drinking as well as with his "secret and shameful desires for candy." Implicitly comparing his sweet tooth to his hollow leg, London tells how he stocked up on candy and then indulged "in lonely debauches, on nights when I knew my crew was going to sleep ashore" (p. 97).

9. Orestes M. Brands, *Lessons on the Human Body; An Elementary Treatise Upon Physiology, Hygiene, and the Effects of Stimulants and Narcotics on the Human System* (Boston: Leach, Shewell, and Sanborn, 1883), p. 202. Brands, identified on the title page as the principal of a grammar school in Paterson, New Jersey, explicitly intended this book for "the young student" (p. iii). Alcohol is treated, solemnly, as one of a number of dangerously addictive substances against which children must be forewarned: "Eminent authority in all depart-

ments of science, and in every country, agree in classifying *alcohol, opium, chloral,* and *tobacco* as *narcotic cerebral poisons;* and it has been demonstrated to every observer that the use of any of these begets a morbid appetite, that demands that a greater quantity of it *may* and *must* be used to produce its former effects" (pp. 171–72).

10. Mark Edward Lender and Karen R. Karnchanapee point out that for at least fifty years, between the 1880s and the 1930s, "the drunkard of the schoolroom was the drunkard of the Temperance Tales. 'The drunkard, with his foul breath, his noisy tongue, his foolish and dangerous acts, his bloated face, and reeling gait,' a typical text related, 'is in many communities an everyday warning to young and old. . . .'" Long after repeal of the Eighteenth Amendment, "alcoholic education still contained a heavy temperance strain." " 'Temperance Tales': Antiliquor Fiction and American Attitudes toward Alcoholics in the Late 19th and Early 20th Centuries," *Journal of Studies on Alcohol,* 38 (July 1977), 1366.

11. Vance Thompson, *Drink and Be Sober* (New York: Moffat, Yard, 1915), pp. 108–9.

12. As Roy Rosenzweig points out, saloon drinking in Victorian America was largely limited to the working class: "Those in the middle and upper classes who did drink—and the numbers were probably considerably smaller than among the working class in the late nineteenth century—generally drank at home, private clubs, or expensive hotels." The saloon as an American working-class institution—"a leisure institution," as Rosenzweig says, that was "temporally distinct from work and spatially distinct from home"—was spawned by the rapid rise of industrial capitalism after the Civil War. Increased drinking was made possible by higher incomes and increased leisure time, but these gains were offset by the loss of worker control in an increasingly regulated and mechanized work place. "The Rise of the Saloon," in *Rethinking Popular Culture: Contemporary Perspectives in Cultural Studies,* ed. Chandra Mukerji and Michael Schudson (Berkeley: University of California Press, 1991), pp. 136, 131.

13. Rosenzweig, "The Rise of the Saloon," p. 138.

14. During the "golden age" of the saloon, according to Jack S. Blocker, Jr., "men found a sense of group belonging and, within the group, egalitarianism and an opportunity for self-expression." For many younger men, bar drinking "served as an extended ritual of initiation into manhood. Some men of all classes never completed this rite of passage." *American Temperance Movements: Cycles of Reform* (Boston: Twayne, 1989), p. 68.

15. Rosenzweig, "The Rise of the Saloon," pp. 146–47.

16. These lines conclude "The Ladies," one of Rudyard Kipling's "Barrack-room Ballads," in which a well-travelled soldier recounts his sexual education with a wide variety of women.

17. London once told Upton Sinclair about a sequel to *John Barleycorn,* to be titled *Jane Barleycorn* and written under the pseudonym Jack Liverpool, in which he "was planning to denounce female treachery, a poison as noxious as alcohol. He would express his 'tragic disillusionment and his contempt for woman as a parasite, a creature of vanity and self-indulgence.' " See Georges-Michel Sarotte, *Like a Brother, Like a Lover: Male Homosexuality*

in the American Novel and Theatre from Herman Melville to James Baldwin, trans. Richard Miller (Garden City, NY: Anchor Doubleday, 1978), p. 252. Sarotte is quoting from Sinclair's *Mammonart* (1925).

18. Sandra M. Gilbert and Susan Gubar, *No Man's Land: The Place of the Woman Writer in the Twentieth Century; Volume 1, The War of the Words* (New Haven: Yale University Press, 1988), p. xii.

19. Rosenzweig, "The Rise of the Saloon," p. 144.

20. As Granville Hicks remarks in his classic literary history from a Marxist perspective: "No, London might study socialist books, might give money to the party, might lecture on socialism, might become president of the Intercollegiate Socialist Society, might sign his letters 'Yours for the Revolution,' but he remained very little of a socialist. He was sincere, of course; the proof is in the fact that he engaged in active agitation at a time when he knew he was losing popularity and therefore money. But his socialism never affected his way of looking at life, never touched the basic qualities of his personality, out of which his fiction came." *The Great Tradition: An Interpretation of American Literature since the Civil War,* revised edition (New York: Macmillan, 1935), pp. 192–93.

21. Arguing that "No class of society, even the most abjectly poor, forgoes all customary conspicuous consumption," Thorstein Veblen uses the customs of drinking as an example: "Drunkenness and the other pathological consequences of the free use of stimulants therefore tend in their turn to become honorific, as being a mark, at the second remove, of the superior status of those who are able to afford the indulgence." *The Theory of the Leisure Class* (1899; rpt. New York: Penguin, 1979), pp. 85, 70. The economy of excess implicit in saloon culture may thus be regarded as evidence not of its resistance to, but rather of its implication in, the dominant culture.

22. William James, *The Varieties of Religious Experience: A Study in Human Nature* (1902), ed. Martin E. Marty (New York: Penguin, 1985), pp. 127, 130–31, 162.

23. Joseph Wood Krutch, *The Modern Temper: A Study and a Confession* (1929; rpt. New York: Harcourt, Brace and World, 1956), pp. 16–17, 24–25.

24. Donald W. Goodwin, *Alcohol and the Writer* (Kansas City, MO: Andrews and McMeel, 1988), pp. 1, 4. The idea of an "epidemic" is formulated, of course, within the modern disease concept of alcoholism.

25. Robin Room, "A 'Reverence for Strong Drink': The Lost Generation and the Elevation of Alcohol in American Culture," *Journal of Studies on Alcohol,* 45 (September 1984), 540.

26. In compiling this list, I am indebted to George Wedge, Emeritus Professor of English at the University of Kansas, who for many years has been gathering information about alcoholic writers, American and otherwise. From Wedge's even longer roster of those reputed to have been alcoholic (or to have had drinking problems), I have not included those too obscure to be listed in standard reference works, those who were not native-born Americans, those not known primarily as writers, those who were editors and/or journalists but who are not identified with belle lettres, and those about whom some reasonable doubt

exists as to their drinking habits. I have also stopped at 1920 because information about writers born after that date is still so incomplete. In time, I believe, it will be shown that the "epidemic" of alcoholism continued unabated among American writers born in the first half of the twentieth century.

27. Quoted in Room, "A 'Reverence for Strong Drink,'" p. 543.

28. Frederick J. Hoffman, *The Twenties: American Writing in the Postwar Decade,* revised edition (New York: Free Press, 1962), p. 36.

29. Edmund Wilson, "The Lexicon of Prohibition," in *The American Earthquake: A Documentary of the Twenties and Thirties* (Garden City, NY: Doubleday Anchor, 1958), p. 91.

30. Room, "A 'Reverence for Strong Drink,'" pp. 542–43.

31. Alfred Kazin, "'The Giant Killer': Drink & the American Writer," *Commentary,* 61 (March 1976), 46, 44.

32. Room suggests, on the contrary, that London's Victorian attitudes and his class background distinguish him from such modernists as Hemingway: "*John Barleycorn* is not only a temperance tract—however equivocally so—but also identifies drinking with the world of working men. In *The Sun Also Rises,* drinking has become part of a lifestyle of affluent leisure." "A 'Reverence for Strong Drink,'" p. 545. It is true, of course, that the culture of drinking was appropriated by Hemingway and other middle-class writers, stripped of its working-class features, and refashioned as a form of conspicuous consumption within a modernist economy of excess (see Chapter One). But London, as I have argued, was himself a proto-modernist in his celebration of the alcoholic artist as culture hero.

33. Saul Bellow, "The Thinking Man's Waste Land," *Saturday Review,* 48 (3 April 1965), 20. This essay was adapted from Bellow's speech in acceptance of the National Book Award for *Herzog* (1964).

34. Donald Newlove, *Those Drinking Days: Myself and Other Writers* (New York: Horizon Press, 1981), p. 61.

3: Bulls, Balls, and Booze: *The Sun Also Rises*

1. Mark Spilka, *Hemingway's Quarrel with Androgyny* (Lincoln: University of Nebraska Press, 1990), p. 75.

2. Carol Hemingway Gardner quoted in *The True Gen: An Intimate Portrait of Ernest Hemingway by Those Who Knew Him,* ed. Denis Brian (New York: Grove Press, 1988), p. 27.

3. Quoted in Carlos Baker, *Ernest Hemingway: A Life Story* (New York: Scribner's, 1969), p. 121. As a reporter for the *Star,* Hemingway wrote somewhat gleefully about the ineffective enforcement of Prohibition. See "Smuggling Canadian Whiskey into the U.S." and "Chicago Never Wetter Than It Is Today," in *The Wild Years: Ernest Hemingway,* ed. Gene Z. Hanrahan (New York: Dell, 1962), pp. 68–73.

4. Quoted in Tom Dardis, *The Thirsty Muse: Alcohol and the American Writer* (New York: Ticknor and Fields, 1989), p. 157. "One rule I observed," London wrote. "I never took a

drink until my day's work of writing a thousand words was done. And, when done, the cocktails reared a wall of inhibition in my brain between the day's work done and the rest of the day of fun to come. My work ceased from my consciousness. No thought of it flickered in my brain till next morning at nine o'clock when I sat at my desk and began my next thousand words. This was a desirable condition of mind to achieve. I conserved my energy by means of this alcoholic inhibition." *John Barleycorn* (New York: Century, 1913), p. 276. It appears that Hemingway also relied on "alcoholic inhibition" to regulate his creative rhythms.

5. As London's craving for alcohol became more incessant, he found himself breaking his rule: taking a drink when he was only halfway through his daily stint and, eventually, before he began to write: "But a new and most diabolical complication arose. The work refused to be done without drinking. . . . My brain could not think the proper thoughts because continually it was obsessed with the one thought that across the room in the liquor cabinet stood John Barleycorn. When, in despair, I took my drink, at once my brain loosened up and began to roll off the thousand words" (*John Barleycorn*, pp. 300–301).

6. Hemingway's alcoholism, which has been glancingly discussed in recent biographies by Kenneth Lynn and Jeffrey Meyers, is examined in detail by Tom Dardis in *The Thirsty Muse* and also by Donald W. Goodwin in *Alcohol and the Writer* (Kansas City, MO: Andrews and McMeel, 1988), pp. 50–72. Among those who have denied that Hemingway had a drinking problem was his fourth wife Mary, who was probably referring to Goodwin (or else George Wedge) when she snapped: "Some chickenshit professor who teaches English in Arkansas or Kansas listed him as an alcoholic, without ever having apparently made much of an investigation. It is *so* mistaken. I have been told by mutual friends that Faulkner used to go on week-long benders. Ernest never did that. I only once or twice saw him a little unsteady on his feet—in seventeen years." Quoted in Brian, ed., *The True Gen*, p. 238. On the collusion of Hemingway's biographers in the denial of his alcoholism, see Roger Forseth, "Alcohol and the Writer: Some Biographical and Critical Issues (Hemingway)," *Contemporary Drug Problems*, 13 (Summer 1986), 361–86.

7. Dardis, *The Thirsty Muse*, p. 158.

8. *Ernest Hemingway: Selected Letters, 1917–1961*, ed. Carlos Baker (New York: Scribner's, 1981), p. 365. Michael S. Reynolds does note in passing that "one of the traditional values that takes a beating in *The Sun Also Rises* is moderation in drinking," and he also recognizes that Prohibition is pertinent as a context for the novel. *The Sun Also Rises: A Novel of the Twenties* (Boston: Twayne, 1988), p. 61.

9. Robert Penn Warren, "Ernest Hemingway," in *Selected Essays* (New York: Vintage, 1966), p. 102.

10. Ernest Hemingway, *The Sun Also Rises* (New York: Scribner, 1954), p. 32. Subsequent quotations are taken from this standard paperback edition and documented in the text.

11. On the basis solely of the novel, it is impossible to ascertain the exact nature of Jake's war wound. That has not, of course, deterred critics from speculating—to such an extent that

Hemingway himself felt compelled to set the record straight in letters and interviews. Reynolds summarizes the current consensus: "We never see the wound, but we learn implicitly that Jake has all the sexual drives of a normal man but has none of the physical equipment to satisfy those drives. From this information, we must assume that his testicles are intact and his phallus missing." *The Sun Also Rises: A Novel of the Twenties*, p. 25.

12. In fact, Wheeler first joined the cause as a student at Oberlin College. "The Saloon Must Go," the slogan of the Anti-Saloon League, was the title of a popular temperance song from the nineteenth century:

> I stand for prohibition
> The utter demolition
> Of all this curse of misery and woe;
> Complete extermination
> Entire annihilation
> The Saloon must go.

Quoted in Alice Fleming, *Alcohol: The Delightful Poison* (1975; rpt. New York: Dell, 1979), p. 69.

13. Forseth, "Alcohol and the Writer," p. 378.

14. *John Barleycorn*, p. 77.

15. Absinthe, consisting of alcohol (in very high concentration) flavored with wormwood and other herbs, is legendary for its potency. Hemingway described its "slow, culminating wallop" as making one want "to get up and jump on his new straw hat in ecstasy" or "to shimmy rapidly up the side of the Eiffel Tower." "The Great 'Apéritif' Scandal," in *The Wild Years*, p. 93. The drinking of absinthe involves a certain amount of ritual—the thick, green liquid is usually diluted drop by drop with water—and it became especially popular among artists and writers during the nineteenth century. By 1900, however, absinthe was under attack by the medical establishment for its alleged toxicity; and by 1915, it had been banned in Belgium, Switzerland, Italy, and France. See Jean-Charles Sournia, *A History of Alcoholism*, trans. Nick Hindley and Gareth Stanton (London: Basil Blackwell, 1990), pp. 75–77. Thus Jake Barnes has access only to pernod (imitation absinthe) while he is in Paris. Given the lethal reputation of absinthe, his getting drunk on the real stuff in Spain seems all the more self-destructive. Among Hemingway's other characters, Robert Jordan in *For Whom the Bell Tolls* (1940) has a special fondness for absinthe.

16. Warren, *Selected Essays*, pp. 87, 86.

17. In one of the earliest and best statements of this view, Mark Spilka asserts that although Romero cannot serve as an example to be followed literally—given the differences between his cultural background and that of the expatriates—he "does provide an image of integrity, against which Barnes and his generation are weighed and found wanting. In this sense, Pedro is the real hero of the parable, the final moral touchstone, the man whose code

gives meaning to a world where love and religion are defunct, where the proofs of manhood are difficult and scarce, and where every man must learn to define his own moral conditions and then live up to them." "The Death of Love in *The Sun Also Rises*," in *Ernest Hemingway's The Sun Also Rises*, ed. Harold Bloom (New York: Chelsea House, 1987), p. 37.

18. The earliest draft of the novel suggests that it was originally centered on the corruption of a young bullfighter by a group of drunken expatriates. As William Balassi describes one portion of the manuscript: "Events from the fiesta have forced him [Jake] to reexamine his assumption that drinking is 'quite unimportant'. . . . However unimportant drinking may be for the others, it would cost Nino [the bullfighter] his life." "The Trail to *The Sun Also Rises:* The First Week of Writing," in *Hemingway: Essays of Reassessment*, ed. Frank Scafella (New York: Oxford University Press, 1991), p. 43. See also Balassi, "Hemingway's Greatest Iceberg: The Composition of *The Sun Also Rises*," in *Writing the American Classics*, ed. James Barbour and Tom Quirk (Chapel Hill: University of North Carolina Press, 1990), pp. 125–55.

19. The surviving manuscripts show, as Michael S. Reynolds has convincingly argued, that the seed of the entire novel was this Jamesian epiphany when the Spanish aficionado sees the young bullfighter with a drink in his hand, sitting at a table with a seductively bare-shouldered woman. "False Dawn: *The Sun Also Rises* Manuscript," in Bloom, ed., *Ernest Hemingway's The Sun Also Rises*, p. 132.

20. In reaction against the animosity of male critics, some feminists have attempted to cast Brett in a more positive light. Wendy Martin, for one, argues that Hemingway portrays Brett understandingly: "As she tries to find her way between the Scylla of social constraint and the Charybdis of chaotic freedom, her search for a new direction is not validated by the social world in which she lives. In spite of Hemingway's sympathetic treatment of Brett, much critical reaction has mirrored traditional values: Allen Tate calls her 'hard-boiled'; Theodore Bardake sees her as a 'woman devoid of womanhood'; Jackson Benson says that she is 'a female who never becomes a woman'; Edmund Wilson describes her as 'an exclusively destructive force'; and John Aldridge declares that Brett is a 'compulsive bitch.'" "Brett Ashley as New Woman in *The Sun Also Rises*," in *New Essays on The Sun Also Rises*, ed. Linda Wagner-Martin (Cambridge: Cambridge University Press, 1987), p. 69.

21. In the original opening of the novel—the twenty-five pages of typescript that Hemingway deleted from the galleys on the advice of Fitzgerald—Brett Ashley's background is explained in some detail, including her unhappy second marriage to a "thoroughgoing dipsomaniac" who once tried to kill her. "The Unpublished Opening of *The Sun Also Rises*," *Antaeus*, 33 (Spring 1979), 7. Unlike London, Hemingway never uses the term "alcoholic," but he does share London's Victorian understanding of "dipsomania" as a hereditary or acquired form of insanity. In writing of Brett's violent husband, Hemingway imagines this "dipsomaniac" as a madman who has lost touch with reality by losing control of his craving for drink. To cover what is meant by "alcoholic" in its modern sense, Hemingway normally uses the word "drunk."

22. Aside from details in the novel as published, there is further evidence in the un-published manuscript that Hemingway imagined Brett as a drunkard. Brett was modeled on Lady Duff Twysden, who was addicted to opium as well as to alcohol; and when this character, still under the name "Duff," first appears in the earliest draft, she is tagged "the typical Montparnasse drunk." Hemingway goes on to describe her typical day: she sleeps until noon, drinks in the cafés all afternoon, and then parties every night until two in the morning. "But unlike Pat [later called Mike], no matter how much Duff drinks—and she drinks more than he does—she 'never los[es] her form.' " See Balassi, "The Trail to *The Sun Also Rises*," in Scafella, ed., *Hemingway: Essays of Reassessment*, p. 42.

23. See Scott Donaldson, "Hemingway's Morality of Compensation," *American Literature*, 43 (November 1971), 399–420.

24. Donaldson, "Humor in *The Sun Also Rises*," in Wagner-Martin, ed., *New Essays on The Sun Also Rises*, p. 37.

25. The character of Bill Gorton was inspired by the humorist Donald Ogden Stewart, who accompanied Hemingway to Pamplona in 1925. Early in the first draft of the novel, before he substituted fictional for real names, Hemingway wrote: "Don was the best of the lot and he was on a hilarious drunk and thought every body else was and became angry if they were not." Quoted in Balassi, "The Trail to *The Sun Also Rises*," in Scafella, ed., *Hemingway: Essays of Reassessment*, p. 40. According to Scott Donaldson, Stewart "was almost constitutionally incapable of not amusing people. As Scott Fitzgerald said of him, he 'could turn a Sunday school picnic into a public holiday.' " Humor in *The Sun Also Rises*, in Wagner-Martin, ed., *New Essays on The Sun Also Rises*, pp. 34–35.

26. Arnold E. Davidson and Cathy N. Davidson, "Decoding the Hemingway Hero in *The Sun Also Rises*," in Wagner-Martin, ed., *New Essays on The Sun Also Rises*, p. 95.

27. After quoting this same passage, James W. Tuttleton remarks: "The problem of Hemingway's male characters is how to indicate friendship for each other without its being misconstrued as homosexual affection; and facetious verbal horseplay is the way out of an edgy situation where affection is sensed but the expression of it must be repressed." Tuttleton goes on to note that homosexuality is "invariably a profound evil" in Hemingway's fiction and to wonder if this judgment had a "moral basis." "Hemingway Unbound," *The New Criterion*, 11 (December 1992), 27. Tuttleton has the same difficulty he attributes to Hemingway in knowing how the affection of friendship between men can ever be differentiated cleanly from "homosexual affection"—or in explaining why the affection that is "sensed," if it is not "homosexual," still "must be repressed."

28. Spilka, *Hemingway's Quarrel with Androgyny*, p. 3.

29. Davidson and Davidson, "Decoding the Hemingway Hero," in Wagner-Martin, ed., *New Essays on The Sun Also Rises*, p. 95.

30. Spilka, *Hemingway's Quarrel with Androgyny*, p. 204. Spilka's phrase about Jake's "womanly" desire for Brett comes at the end of a gnarly sentence that begins by rejecting a reading of Jake as covertly homosexual: "I do not mean to imply here that Jacob, a soulful

wrestler with his own physical condition, would also like to make it with bullfighters and other males—that seems to me misleading—but rather that—in accord with the oddly common attraction for men of lesbian lovemaking, the imagining into it that exercises suppressed femininity, and indeed the need for such imagining, such identification with the original nurturing sources of love—he wants Brett in a womanly way."

31. *Ernest Hemingway: Selected Letters*, pp. 204–5.

32. Michael S. Reynolds, "The *Sun* in Its Time: Recovering the Historical Context," in Wagner-Martin, ed., *New Essays on The Sun Also Rises*, pp. 45, 62.

33. Robert McAlmon, *Being Geniuses Together, 1920–1930*, revised edition (1968; rpt. San Francisco: North Point Press, 1984), pp. 328, 171–72. As originally published by McAlmon in England in 1938, *Being Geniuses Together* consisted entirely of his literary memoirs. The later American edition was edited and augmented by Boyle, such that her own autobiographical chapters alternate with his.

34. *Being Geniuses Together*, pp. 169, 171. Boyle's quotation is taken from *The Autobiography of William Carlos Williams* (1951; rpt. New York: New Directions, 1967), p. 51.

35. *The Complete Poems of Emily Dickinson*, ed. Thomas H. Johnson (Boston: Little, Brown, 1960), pp. 98–99.

36. McAlmon eventually died from alcoholism in 1956, five years before Hemingway's suicide. At the end, he exhibited the symptoms of Korsakoff's Syndrome: the severe brain damage, usually involving continuous memory failure, that results from the direct toxicity of alcohol on nervous tissue.

4: The Drunkard's Holiday: *Tender Is the Night*

1. *The Letters of F. Scott Fitzgerald*, ed. Andrew Turnbull (New York: Scribner's, 1963), p. 230.

2. Ernest Hemingway, *A Moveable Feast* (New York: Scribner's, 1964), p. 166.

3. Thomas B. Gilmore, *Equivocal Spirits: Alcoholism and Drinking in Twentieth-Century Literature* (Chapel Hill: University of North Carolina Press, 1987), pp. 109–10. In his discussion of one notorious incident—Irving Thalberg's Hollywood party at which Fitzgerald got drunk, supposedly on just a couple of cocktails, and made a scene for which he was later fired by the producer—Gilmore suggests that Fitzgerald may have been concealing his actual consumption. In order for him to have been as drunk as he was reported to have been, "Fitzgerald must have managed to sneak quick drinks at the party or to be mostly drunk before ever arriving, each of these ploys being familiar to many alcoholics" (p. 194 n.35).

4. Donald W. Goodwin has also suggested that Fitzgerald's "intolerance" for alcohol was "probably a myth": "That Fitzgerald became drunk on small amounts of alcohol is contradicted by numerous accounts of steady consumption of very unsmall amounts. . . . Also, the true alcoholic never does all of his drinking where people can see it; the 'invisible'

drinks must be counted into the total." *Alcohol and the Writer* (Kansas City, MO: Andrews and McMeel, 1988), pp. 40–41.

5. In addition to studies cited in the notes to this chapter, see Arthur Mizener, *The Far Side of Paradise: A Biography of F. Scott Fitzgerald* (Boston: Houghton Mifflin, 1951); James Thurber, "Scott in Thorns," in *Credos and Curios* (New York: Harper and Row, 1962); Nancy Milford, *Zelda: A Biography* (New York: Harper and Row, 1970); Aaron Latham, *Crazy Sundays: F. Scott Fitzgerald in Hollywood* (New York: Viking, 1971); Matthew J. Bruccoli, *Some Sort of Epic Grandeur: The Life of F. Scott Fitzgerald* (New York: Harcourt Brace Jovanovich, 1981); and William Wasserstrom, "The Goad of Guilt: Adams, Scott and Zelda," in *The Ironies of Progress: Henry Adams and the American Dream* (Carbondale and Edwardsville: Southern Illinois University Press, 1984), pp. 162–83.

6. *Correspondence of F. Scott Fitzgerald*, ed. Matthew J. Bruccoli and Margaret M. Duggan (New York: Random House, 1980), p. 243. See also Zelda Fitzgerald's long and poignant letter to Scott from the Swiss clinic where she was being treated in 1930 (*Correspondence*, pp. 245–51); she recounts here many specific instances of his drunkenness and its destructiveness. In a May 1933 session between both Fitzgeralds and Zelda's psychiatrist, she directly blamed Scott's drinking for their marital misery (see Bruccoli, *Epic Grandeur*, pp. 349–53)—a charge that he, of course, denounced.

7. According to Sheilah Graham, who threatened to leave Fitzgerald if he continued to drink, he never touched a drop during the last year of his life; several scholars have echoed this claim. Tom Dardis cites recent evidence to the contrary: on at least one occasion, Fitzgerald apparently took advantage of Graham's absence in order to drink. *The Thirsty Muse: Alcohol and the American Writer* (New York: Ticknor and Fields, 1989), p. 143.

8. Scott Donaldson, *Fool for Love: F. Scott Fitzgerald* (New York: Congdon and Weed, 1983), p. 173.

9. Dardis, *The Thirsty Muse*, p. 124.

10. *As Ever, Scott Fitz—: Letters Between F. Scott Fitzgerald and His Literary Agent, Harold Ober, 1919–1940*, ed. Matthew J. Bruccoli and Jennifer M. Atkinson (Philadelphia: Lippincott, 1972), pp. 209–10.

11. Julie M. Irwin, "F. Scott Fitzgerald's Little Drinking Problem," *The American Scholar*, 56 (Summer 1987), 427.

12. *The Crack-Up*, ed. Edmund Wilson (New York: New Directions, 1945), p. 30.

13. Donaldson, *Fool for Love*, p. 162. See also the mock genealogy prepared for Edmund Wilson late in 1920. As the bud on a family tree that purportedly included Duns Scotus, Mary, Queen of Scots, Walter Scott, Edward FitzGerald (author of *The Rubaiyat of Omar Khayyam*), and Francis Scott Key (the only real ancestor in the lot), F. Scott Fitzgerald is identified simply as "(drunkard)." *Correspondence*, p. 76.

14. *Letters*, pp. 148, 276.

15. Kenneth E. Eble, "Touches of Disaster: Alcoholism and Mental Illness in Fitzgerald's Short Stories," in *The Short Stories of F. Scott Fitzgerald: New Approaches in Criticism*, ed. Jackson R. Bryer (Madison: University of Wisconsin Press, 1982), p. 44.

16. Gilmore, *Equivocal Spirits*, pp. 101, 100.

17. *The Crack-Up*, p. 71. Seabrook's book was *Asylum* (New York: Harcourt Brace, 1935).

18. In the same volume in which the "Crack-Up" essays were collected, Glenway Wescott cast suspicion on Fitzgerald's veracity: "It was not from alcohol, he said, evidently proud of the fact that he had not had any for six months, not even beer. We may be a little doubtful of this protestation; for protestation indeed is a kind of sub-habit of the alcoholic. Six months is no time at all, in terms of the things that kill us." "The Moral of Scott Fitzgerald," in *The Crack-Up*, pp. 327–28.

19. Donaldson, *Fool for Love*, p. 152.

20. Alfred Kazin, "An American Confession," in *F. Scott Fitzgerald: The Man and His Work*, ed. Alfred Kazin (1951; rpt. New York: Collier, 1962), pp. 173–76.

21. Ibid., p. 176.

22. Marty Roth, "'The Milk of Wonder': Fitzgerald, Alcoholism, and *The Great Gatsby*," *Dionysos*, 2 (Fall 1990), 4, 6. In my approach to Fitzgerald, I am generally indebted to Roth's suggestive essay.

23. Matthew J. Bruccoli, *The Composition of Tender Is the Night: A Study of the Manuscripts* (Pittsburgh: University of Pittsburgh Press, 1963), pp. 5, 12.

24. Malcolm Cowley, "Introduction" to *Tender Is the Night: A Romance* (New York: Scribner's, 1951); rpt. in *Critical Essays on F. Scott Fitzgerald's Tender Is the Night*, ed. Milton R. Stern (Boston: Twayne, 1986), p. 109.

25. Roth, "'The Milk of Wonder,'" p. 7.

26. Aside from Roth, the only critics who seem sufficiently aware of alcoholism and its significance in *Tender Is the Night* are Dardis, Gilmore, and Donaldson. Far more typical is Bruccoli's undiscerning reaction (in a study that is generally astute) to Fitzgerald's working title: "*The Drunkard's Holiday* . . . is certainly curious. It is thematically linked with *The World's Fair* [another discarded working title] in that both titles suggest a time of relaxation. Both titles are ironic, but *The Drunkard's Holiday* carries a strong implication of contempt for the hero, who is a sympathetic—even an admirable—figure." *The Composition of Tender Is the Night*, p. 86.

27. D. W. Harding, "Mechanisms of Misery," in Kazin, ed., *Fitzgerald: The Man and His Work*, pp. 100–1. Harding was very self-conscious about the psychological depth of his reading, as if he feared it might be injurious to Fitzgerald; and he ended his review on an apologetic note: "I am prepared to be told that this attempt at analysis is itself childish—an attempt to assure myself that the magician didn't really cut the lady's head off, did he? I still believe there was a trick in it" (p. 102).

28. Bruccoli, *The Composition of Tender Is the Night*, pp. 7, 109.

29. Ibid., pp. 76–78.

30. Arthur Mizener, "*Tender Is the Night*," in Stern, ed., *Critical Essays on Tender Is the Night*, p. 165.

31. Robert Penn Warren, "Ernest Hemingway," in *Selected Essays* (New York: Vintage, 1966), p. 82.

32. *Tender Is the Night* (New York: Scribner's, 1934), p. 129. All other quotations from the novel are taken from this (first) edition and documented in the text. The first and all subsequent editions of *Tender Is the Night* are textually corrupt, and I have therefore checked quoted passages against Matthew J. Bruccoli's list of "Emendations to be Made in the First-Edition Copy-Text" and silently made changes that seem warranted. See Bruccoli, "Material for a Centenary Edition of *Tender Is the Night*," in Stern, ed., *Critical Essays on Tender Is the Night*, pp. 32–57.

33. Gilmore, *Equivocal Spirits*, pp. 102–3.

34. William E. Doherty, "*Tender Is the Night* and the 'Ode to a Nightingale,'" in Stern, ed., *Critical Essays on Tender Is the Night*, p. 154.

35. Abe's initial departure from the Saint Lazare station in Paris is said to take place in July 1925 (see p. 113). After returning with Nicole to the Villa Diana, Dick meets Mrs. Speers on the Riviera in August (see p. 213). Although this meeting comes chronologically only a month after the chaotic scenes that end Book One, it appears many pages later, after the flashback section of Book Two. The continuity between Abe's climactic binge and Dick's incipient alcoholism is much clearer in the "final" version of *Tender Is the Night* that Fitzgerald prepared before his death in 1940, but that did not appear until 1951, under the editorship of Malcolm Cowley. Having decided that the true beginning of the novel was buried in Book Two, Fitzgerald reordered the plot line, making the chronology perfectly linear. The "final" version has its defenders, but most critics believe it to be artistically inferior to the original version, which is the only one available at present. Milton Stern, an advocate of the "final" version, usefully summarizes the textual arguments in "*Tender Is the Night:* The Text Itself," in Stern, ed., *Critical Essays on Tender Is the Night*, pp. 21–31.

36. Lowry quoted in "Introduction" to *The Cinema of Malcolm Lowry: A Scholarly Edition of Lowry's "Tender Is the Night,"* ed. Miguel Mota and Paul Tiessen (Vancouver: University of British Columbia Press, 1990), p. 35. Lowry and his wife Margerie wrote this screenplay from 1949 to 1950, soon after the publication of *Under the Volcano*. See also *Notes on a Screenplay for F. Scott Fitzgerald's Tender Is the Night*, ed. Matthew J. Bruccoli (Bloomfield Hills, MI and Columbia, SC: Bruccoli Clark, 1976).

37. See Mota and Tiessen, eds., *The Cinema of Malcolm Lowry*, pp. 147–69. As the editors point out, Lowry reacted so strongly to the novel that "he effectively declared Fitzgerald a 'family member,' appropriated him as a kind of brother, and got down to work with him, as it were, in writing the *Tender Is the Night* story as Lowry felt it should have been written" (p. 27).

38. Mota and Tiessen, "Introduction" to *The Cinema of Malcolm Lowry*, p. 35.

39. Lowry's new ending was only slightly less melodramatic than the one Fitzgerald himself had co-authored (with Charles Warren) for his own unproduced screenplay. "Summary Movie Treatment for Tender Is the Night" appears as an appendix to Bruccoli, *Epic Grandeur*, pp. 511–23. In the finale of this rather preposterous Hollywood adaptation, obviously written with all eyes on the box office, Dick is happily reunited with Nicole after saving her life and restoring her sanity through emergency brain surgery!

40. *Correspondence,* p. 329.

41. Scott Donaldson, "A Short History of *Tender Is the Night,*" in *Writing the American Classics,* ed. James Barbour and Tom Quirk (Chapel Hill: University of North Carolina Press, 1990), p. 195.

42. Fitzgerald's manuscript is reproduced in Bruccoli, *The Composition of Tender Is the Night,* pp. 154–55. ⟨Angled brackets⟩ enclose Fitzgerald's deletions from the draft. Sarah Gamp is a character in Dickens's *Martin Chuzzlewit.*

43. Quoted in Bruccoli, *The Composition of Tender Is the Night,* p. 132.

44. From manuscript pages reproduced in Bruccoli, *The Composition of Tender Is the Night,* pp. 149–50. Fitzgerald's deletions from the manuscript are shown in ⟨angled brackets⟩.

45. See Bruccoli, *The Composition of Tender Is the Night,* pp. 158, 172.

46. Donaldson, "A Short History of *Tender Is the Night,*" in Barbour and Quirk, eds., *Writing the American Classics,* p. 186.

47. Late in her long life, Barnes claimed that Fitzgerald had "told her the entire story of Gatsby one night at Julius's before he had written a single word." She had known him well, she recalled, but "wished she had known him better." Hank O'Neal, *"Life Is Painful, Nasty & Short . . . In My Case It Has Only Been Painful & Nasty": Djuna Barnes 1978–1981* (New York: Paragon House, 1990), p. 151.

48. Donaldson, *Fool for Love,* pp. 75–76.

49. Donaldson, "A Short History of *Tender Is the Night,*" in Barbour and Quirk, eds., *Writing the American Classics,* p. 185. The "Wanda Brested" scene was first printed in an appendix to Cowley's 1951 "final" edition of *Tender Is the Night.*

50. Bruccoli, *The Composition of Tender Is the Night,* p. 147. For the published version of this passage, see *Tender,* p. 404.

51. Bruccoli, *The Composition of Tender Is the Night,* p. 133.

52. Ibid.

53. Donaldson, "A Short History of *Tender Is the Night,*" in Barbour and Quirk, eds., *Writing the American Classics,* p. 185.

54. Shari Benstock, *Women of the Left Bank: Paris, 1900–1940* (Austin: University of Texas Press, 1986), pp. 27–28.

3: The Infernal Grove: *Appointment in Samarra*

1. Details about O'Hara's life are taken from three excellent studies: Finis Farr, *O'Hara: A Biography* (Boston: Little, Brown, 1973); Matthew J. Bruccoli, *The O'Hara Concern: A Biography of John O'Hara* (New York: Random House, 1975); and Frank MacShane, *The Life of John O'Hara* (New York: Dutton, 1980).

2. *Selected Letters of John O'Hara,* ed. Matthew J. Bruccoli (New York: Random House, 1978), pp. 8–9.

3. Bruccoli, *The O'Hara Concern,* p. 58.

4. MacShane, *The Life of John O'Hara,* p. 45.

5. O'Hara's three biographers have independently portrayed Belle Wylie O'Hara as the sort of person who matches the psychological profile of the "co-dependent." In recent years, this term has been used in psychological literature to describe someone close to an alcoholic whose suffering at the hands of the alcoholic is compensated, within a systemic economy of addiction and family neurosis, by a certain power of control. Belle O'Hara was a true believer in her husband's literary genius, and her wifely devotion, according to Bruccoli, "assumed legendary dimensions" among their friends: "She accommodated herself to his drinking and working habits, protected him from distractions, unobtrusively interposed herself in his professional problems when necessary, and never complained or criticized him in anyone's hearing—even when he was in his black alcoholic moods." Those closest to Belle thought, however, that although she was fiercely loyal to her husband and apparently subservient to his desires, she was actually "in control of the marriage—and that it was what she wanted" (*The O'Hara Concern*, pp. 144–45). O'Hara was most completely dependent on Belle after his binges, when he relied on her tender ministrations to get back on his feet.

6. Farr, *O'Hara: A Biography*, p. 179.

7. *Selected Letters*, p. 240.

8. MacShane, *The Life of John O'Hara*, p. 1.

9. Bruccoli, *The O'Hara Concern*, p. 151.

10. Wolcott Gibbs, "Watch Out for Mr. O'Hara," *Saturday Review of Literature*, 17 (19 February 1938), 10.

11. Quoted in Farr, *O'Hara: A Biography*, pp. 175–76.

12. *Selected Letters*, p. 120.

13. Quoted in Farr, *O'Hara: A Biography*, p. 189.

14. Bruccoli, *The O'Hara Concern*, p. 145.

15. "It Happened Last Night," *New York Post*, 28 March 1946; reprinted in *"An Artist Is His Own Fault": John O'Hara on Writers and Writing*, ed. Matthew J. Bruccoli (Carbondale and Edwardsville: Southern Illinois University Press, 1977), pp. 180–82.

16. Foreword to *Appointment in Samarra* (New York: Modern Library, 1953). In a 1961 letter, O'Hara recalled that "Fitzgerald really didn't like APPOINTMENT IN SA-MARRA or BUTTERFIELD 8, because he was basically a prude. I wish I had saved a letter he wrote me about BUTTERFIELD 8, in which he said something to the effect that sex should be used sparingly, and refused to give Harcourt, Brace a quote for an ad." *Selected Letters*, p. 380. For *Appointment in Samarra*, Fitzgerald did supply a blurb: "John O'Hara's novel indicates the tremendous strides that American writers have taken since the war." Quoted in Bruccoli, *The O'Hara Concern*, p. 110.

17. *Selected Letters*, p. 92.

18. Quoted in MacShane, *The Life of John O'Hara*, pp. 104–5.

19. F. Scott Fitzgerald, *The Crack-Up*, ed. Edmund Wilson (New York: New Directions, 1945), p. 75. In a review of this posthumously published miscellany, O'Hara deplored "The Crack-Up" as an "orgy of self-pity which, characteristically, the magazine *Esquire* and the

critic Edmund Wilson thought was good, but which should have been suppressed at the mailbox." "Scott Fitzgerald—Odds and Ends" (1945), in Bruccoli, ed., *An Artist Is His Own Fault,*" p. 140.

20. "In Memory of Scott Fitzgerald: Certain Aspects" (1941), in *"An Artist Is His Own Fault,"* p. 136.

21. Bruccoli, *The O'Hara Concern,* p. 84.

22. *Selected Letters,* p. 76.

23. *Selected Letters,* p. 84.

24. O'Hara quoted these stanzas, the last two of Blake's poem, in a February 1934 letter; see *Selected Letters,* p. 89.

25. Foreword to *Appointment in Samarra.* Although there is no reason to doubt O'Hara's account of his chance encounter with Maugham's *Sheppey* at Dorothy Parker's apartment, the same legend, with some interesting variations, might have been discovered in Edith Wharton's autobiography, which was serialized in the *Ladies' Home Journal* during 1933 (but not published in book form until June 1934). Wharton heard the "strangely beautiful story" from Jean Cocteau, who claimed to have read it somewhere. In this version, the destined youth, a favorite of the Sultan in Damascus, begs for a horse to escape Death, whom he has just spied in the palace garden. Once the boy has fled for Baghdad, the Sultan upbraids Death for his impudence in threatening so favored a young man: "but Death, astonished, answered: 'I assure your Majesty I did not threaten him. I only threw up my arms in surprise at seeing him here, because I have a tryst with him tonight in Baghdad.'" Aside from naming a different site for the fatal appointment, Cocteau's story differs from Maugham's play in casting Death as a man rather than a woman. See Wharton, *A Backward Glance* (New York: Appleton-Century, 1934), pp. 285–86.

26. Bruccoli, *The O'Hara Concern,* p. 99.

27. In a 1962 letter to Gerald and Sara Murphy, the supposed models for Fitzgerald's Dick and Nicole Diver, O'Hara mocked those who identified the Julian English character with his author: "They said it was of course autobiographical, and it did no good to point out that I had not inhaled carbon monoxide." O'Hara claimed that his characters, like Fitzgerald's, were always composites: "I use the psychological pattern of the real people, then I put them in different locations and times, and cover them up with superficial characteristics, etc." In Julian's case, the real model was "a fellow named [William] Richards, who was definitely not country-club, but had charm and a certain kind of native intelligence, and who, when the chips were down, shot himself [in Pottsville, on 14 February 1933]. I took his life, his psychological pattern, and covered him up with Brooks shirts and a Cadillac dealership and so on, and the reason the story rings so true is that it is God's truth, out of life." *Selected Letters,* pp. 401–2. It may be argued, however, that Julian's drinking habits and the dynamics of his marriage were out of O'Hara's own life.

28. *Selected Letters,* p. 80.

29. Edmund Wilson, "The Boys in the Back Room," in *Classics and Commercials: A*

Literary Chronicle of the Forties (New York: Noonday Press, 1967), p. 24. Arthur Mizener makes a similar point in his "Afterword" to the Signet edition of the novel (New York: New American Library, 1963).

30. James W. Tuttleton, *The Novel of Manners in America* (Chapel Hill: University of North Carolina Press, 1972), p. 198.

31. Robert Emmet Long, *John O'Hara* (New York: Ungar, 1983), p. 52.

32. Matthew J. Bruccoli, "Focus on *Appointment in Samarra:* The Importance of Knowing What You Are Talking About," in *Tough Guy Writers of the Thirties,* ed. David Madden (Carbondale & Edwardsville: Southern Illinois University Press, 1968), p. 135. MacShane agrees that Julian is a charming but insubstantial young man, typical of the "hangover generation" that came of age in the mid-twenties: "young people who grew up accustomed to the good life without having to earn it." Julian's privileged upbringing has left him unequipped to face adversity: "Without any sort of interior life, without values formed through hardship, he has nothing to rely on." *The Life of John O'Hara,* p. 64.

33. Mizener, "Afterword" to *Appointment in Samarra,* p. 211.

34. Long has observed that *"Appointment in Samarra* resembles *The Great Gatsby* in a number of specific respects—the sense of 'corruption' in the society O'Hara depicts, for example, and the manner in which the hero is singled out to pay the penalty for his involvement in this corrupt world. . . . In both novels, a close link is established between sexuality and death; and at the end of *Appointment in Samarra,* Julian is 'sacrificed'—dying alone, as Gatsby dies alone." *John O'Hara,* p. 177 n.4.

35. Sheldon Norman Grebstein, *John O'Hara* (New York: Twayne, 1966), p. 41. The parallels between O'Hara and Fitzgerald should not be exaggerated. O'Hara's style is, after all, far less evocative than Fitzgerald's; and the omniscient narrator of *Appointment in Samarra* maintains such ironic distance from all the characters, including Julian, that the novel has often been regarded as a model of American "naturalism." As Bruccoli observes, "O'Hara's uninvolved point-of-view is his tactic for disciplining his sentimentality." "Focus on *Appointment in Samarra,*" in Madden, ed., *Tough Guy Writers,* p. 135. As a psychic defense against indulgence in either sentimentality or self-pity, O'Hara's narrative detachment was a self-discipline similar to his abstaining from alcohol during the composition of the novel.

36. *Selected Letters,* pp. 344–45. O'Hara went on to compare his work to Fitzgerald's: "GATSBY is a great book, but GATSBY is satirical. APPOINTMENT IN SAMARRA is not satirical; it is, literally, deadly serious. It is not a sarcastic comment on the time; it is *of* the time—and should be done as a motion picture, with every last detail correct." Once a screenwriter, O'Hara knew the ways of Hollywood; and he was so determined to prevent an unfaithful adaptation that he set the discouraging price of a million dollars for the rights to *Appointment in Samarra.* Although there was one television production during the era of live performances (with Robert Montgomery as Julian), no film version has ever been attempted.

37. An exception is John Updike, who remarks in a recent reassessment of the novel, "For

all its excellence as a social panorama and a sketch of a marriage, it is as a picture of a man destroyed by drink and pride that *Appointment in Samarra* lives frighteningly in the mind." "*Appointment in Samarra:* A New Introduction," pamphlet insert to the Book-of-the-Month Club facsimile of the first edition (1988).

38. John O'Hara, *Appointment in Samarra* (New York: Harcourt, Brace, 1934), pp. 293–94. Subsequent quotations are taken from this (first) edition and documented in the text.

39. Lionel Trilling, Introduction to *Selected Short Stories of John O'Hara* (New York: Modern Library, 1956); rpt. in *Speaking of Literature and Society,* ed. Diana Trilling (New York: Harcourt Brace Jovanovich, 1980), pp. 281, 283.

40. In "Imagine Kissing Pete," O'Hara has his narrator, James Malloy, react to Julian's death: "I was shocked and saddened by the English suicide; he was an attractive man whose shortcomings seemed out of proportion to the magnitude of killing himself. He had not been a friend of mine, only an acquaintance with whom I had had many drinks and played some golf; but friends of mine, my closest friends in the world, boys-now-men like myself, were at the beginning of the same kind of life and doing the same kind of thing that for Julian English ended in a sealed-up garage with a motor running. I hated what I thought those next few days and weeks. There is nothing young about killing oneself, no matter when it happens, and I hated this being deprived of the sweetness of youth. And that was what it was, that was what was happening to us." *Sermons and Soda-Water* (New York: Random House, 1960), 2:52. O'Hara called special attention to this passage, as if it had the authorial imprimatur, in his 1960 letter to a Hollywood producer (*Selected Letters,* p. 345).

41. Bruccoli, "Focus on *Appointment in Samarra,*" in Madden, ed., *Tough Guy Writers,* p. 135.

42. *Selected Letters,* pp. 344–45.

43. *Sermons and Soda-Water,* 2:27–28. Before he was revived in these novellas, James Malloy, the most autobiographical of O'Hara's characters, had not appeared in his fiction for over twenty years. Throughout *Sermons and Soda-Water,* Malloy as narrator serves virtually as an authorial spokesman.

44. Later, in a stream-of-consciousness passage from Caroline's point of view, she mentally pleads with the absent Julian: "Are you so dumb blind after four and a half years [of marriage] that you don't know that there are times when I just plain don't feel like having you? Does there have to be a reason for it? An excuse? Must I be ready to want you at all times except when I'm not well? If you knew anything you'd know I want you probably more then [i.e., when she is menstruating] than any other time" (p. 220). Such frankness about sex, which was quite daring in 1934, earned *Appointment in Samarra* the opprobrium of some reviewers, who denounced O'Hara for filthy-mindedness. Although O'Hara's publishers generally went along, they did require the deletion of two passages they considered too explicit. In one of these, Julian and Caroline trade confessions about their "mastication." (This bawdy pun on "masturbation" was allowed to remain in the published text.) The censored passages have been printed in Bruccoli, *The O'Hara Concern,* p. 351 n.3.

45. O'Hara liked to boast that Julian's suicide was the first of its kind in American literature.

46. Caroline, in turn, blames Dr. English: "Your only son. Well, he never liked you. I guess you know that, don't you? So high and mighty and nasty to him when we went to your house for Christmas. Don't think he didn't notice it. You made him do it, not me" (p. 291).

47. Bruccoli, "Focus on *Appointment in Samarra,*" in Madden, ed., *Tough Guy Writers,* p. 136.

48. *English Romantic Poetry: An Anthology,* ed. Harold Bloom (New York: Anchor Books, 1963), 1:38. The phrase "the Infernal Grove" appears twice in the poem: in the stanza quoted and in the penultimate stanza, quoted by O'Hara in a letter (see above).

49. The same restraint applies to Caroline's drinking after she deliberately gets drunk on one occasion—in reaction to being jilted by a man she might have married. Completely "blotto" in Paris, she is taken by her date, a perverted Harvard voyeur, "to a place where a man and a woman—you know?" (p. 147). Fortunately, Caroline suffers a blackout and can't remember anything.

50. Gibbsville is apparently less cognizant of lesbianism. Julian suavely reflects that Mildred Ammermann, whose preoccupation with golf (not to mention her surname) ought to be a dead giveaway, passes unrecognized: "He always had liked Mill anyway. He was fragmentarily glad over again that Mill did not live in New York, for in New York she would have been marked Lesbian on sight. But in Gibbsville she was just a healthy girl. Good old Mill" (p. 95).

6: Transcendence Downward: *Nightwood*

1. Barnes to Barney, 22 April 1966; quoted in Gillian Hanscombe and Virginia L. Smyers, *Writing for Their Lives: The Modernist Women 1910–1940* (London: Women's Press, 1987), p. 105.

2. Andrew Field, *Djuna: The Life and Times of Djuna Barnes* (New York: G. P. Putnam's, 1983), p. 99. In a 1968 letter to a friend, Barnes took dour delight in quoting the opinion of a German critic: "Her work has not fallen into oblivion, it was predestined for it." See Louis F. Kannenstine, *The Art of Djuna Barnes: Duality and Damnation* (New York: New York University Press, 1977), p. 169.

3. Shari Benstock, *Women of the Left Bank: Paris, 1900–1940* (Austin: University of Texas Press, 1986), pp. 231, 233.

4. Amid fierce critical contention over the true nature of Barnes's erotic life, Andrew Field, her only biographer to date, has been denounced by some feminists for his considered opinion that Barnes was "basically heterosexual" (*Djuna,* p. 153).

5. A notable exception is Constance M. Perry, "A Woman Writing Under the Influence: Djuna Barnes and *Nightwood,*" *Dionysos,* 4 (Fall 1992), 3–14.

6. Carolyn Allen, "Writing toward *Nightwood:* Djuna Barnes's Seduction Stories," in *Silence and Power: A Reevaluation of Djuna Barnes,* ed. Mary Lynn Broe (Carbondale &

Edwardsville: Southern Illinois University Press, 1991), p. 54. Allen remarks that "Djuna Barnes' status as a lesbian culture hero has shifted dramatically over the last decade." She has been claimed as a role model, but also disclaimed as a self-hating homophobe. The biographical evidence may be read to support either contention.

7. Of course, women in nineteenth-century America were discouraged from writing as well as from drinking; the absolute number of female writers—at least those who worked successfully enough within the emergent literary marketplace to become visible to later literary historians—was much smaller than it would later be. The cohort of potential drunkards comprised, therefore, far fewer female than male writers. The first significant female American artist to become alcoholic may well have been Isadora Duncan (b. 1878). Since Duncan is known primarily as a dancer, I have excluded her from the list of alcoholic American writers—although she did produce, with editorial assistance, a posthumously published autobiography: *My Life* (New York: Liveright, 1927).

8. Typical of the alcoholic harlot in temperance fiction is the character Loreen in Charles M. Sheldon's enormously popular *In His Steps* (1897). Rescued from the Rectangle (an urban sink hole surrounded by saloons) by two respectable young women who are afire with the Social Gospel, Loreen is redeemed from prostitution as well as drunkenness. But she soon becomes a martyr to the temperance cause: struck down by a heavy bottle thrown from the upper floor of a saloon! At the moment of her death, Sheldon emotionally fixes the blame: "Ye killed her, ye drunken murderers! And yet, O Christian America! who killed this woman? Stand back! Silence, there! A woman has been killed. Who? Loreen. Child of the streets. Poor, drunken, vile sinner! O Lord God, how long? Yes. The saloon killed her. That is, the voters in Christian America who license the saloon. And the Judgement Day only shall declare who was the murderer of Loreen." *In His Steps: "What Would Jesus Do?"* (Chicago: Smith-Andrews, 1899), p. 178.

9. Bruce Holley Johnson, "The Alcoholism Movement in America: A Study in Cultural Innovation," Diss. University of Illinois 1973, p. 178.

10. Andrew Sinclair, *Era of Excess: A Social History of the Prohibition Movement* (New York: Harper & Row, 1964), p. 233. See also Robin Room, "'Should I Surrender?'—Women's Drinking and Courtship in American Movies," paper presented at the annual meeting of the American Psychological Association, August 1991.

11. In his pioneering psychoanalytic study on alcoholism, Karl Abraham followed Freud in postulating "a greater proneness to repression and the forming of resistances" in women than in men and thus "the more passive sexual instinct of the woman." Since, supposedly, the effects of repression constitute a woman's sexual appeal, and since alcohol undoes repression by lowering resistances, a woman who drinks risks the loss of her "charm for men." Abraham concluded, therefore, that "[w]omen who display a strong inclination towards alcohol would probably, on closer observation, always reveal a strong homosexual tendency." "The Psychological Relations Between Sexuality and Alcoholism" (1908), *International Journal of Psycho-Analysis*, 7 (January 1926), 3, 8.

12. Benstock, *Women of the Left Bank,* p. 242.

13. Perry, "A Woman Writing Under the Influence," p. 3.

14. Hanscombe and Smyers, *Writing for Their Lives,* p. 87.

15. According to Mary Lynn Broe, Djuna Barnes was forcibly betrothed at the age of eighteen to Percy Faulkner, the dimwitted, fifty-two-year-old brother of Wald Barnes's mistress. See "My Art Belongs to Daddy: Incest as Exile, The Textual Economics of Hayford Hall," in *Women's Writing in Exile,* ed. Mary Lynn Broe and Angela Ingram (Chapel Hill: University of North Carolina Press, 1989), p. 42.

16. At present, in the absence of a biography more comprehensive and fully documented than Field's *Djuna,* there remain many blanks and uncertainties concerning Barnes's early life. The picture will become clearer, perhaps, with the appearance of *Cold Comfort: A Biographical Portrait of Djuna Barnes in Letters,* ed. Mary Lynn Broe and Frances Mc-Cullough (New York: Random House, forthcoming). Several essays in Broe, ed., *Silence and Power* touch on the sexual complications of Barnes's childhood.

17. Broe, "My Art Belongs to Daddy," in Broe and Ingram, eds., *Women's Writing in Exile,* p. 53. Broe cites letters from Zadel to Djuna that suggest sexual intimacy between them—intimacy that Broe interprets as having been affirmative and supportive rather than negative and exploitative.

18. Field, *Djuna,* p. 177.

19. Quoted in Field, *Djuna,* pp. 176–77. Field adds, "It is clear beyond question that the lives of both his former wife and their son were played out in precise reaction against everything that he was and stood for. Whereas Henry Budington championed the spirit of man ascending, Wald Barnes and then his daughter [Djuna] chose the theme of man bowing down to his animal nature" (p. 177).

20. Field, *Djuna,* p. 156.

21. Quoted in Field, *Djuna,* p. 156.

22. Wood to Barnes, 14 April 1969; quoted in Broe, ed., *Silence and Power,* p. 53.

23. See Field, *Djuna,* p. 220.

24. Hank O'Neal, *"Life Is Painful, Nasty & Short . . . In My Case It Has Only Been Painful & Nasty": Djuna Barnes 1978–1981* (New York: Paragon House, 1990), p. 116.

25. Ibid., p. 86. From the remnants of a long-abandoned book in Barnes's files, O'Neal concludes that her inefficient work habits were of long standing: "She had started the project in 1932 and then started again and again, always beginning from page one. Even then it seemed she had difficulty in beginning a story, poem, or in this case a loosely autobiographical novel, and continuing through to a conclusion. She would begin, type a number of pages, and stop. Then she would repeat the process with minor alterations. The project was never completed" (p. 149).

26. Benstock, *Women of the Left Bank,* pp. 237, 267.

27. According to Field, Barnes did not quit smoking until 1962, at the age of seventy (*Djuna,* p. 236). When James B. Scott interviewed her in April 1971, she offered him sherry

but asserted that she herself had not had a drink in twenty years or smoked a cigarette in eight. "Reminiscences," in Broe, ed. *Silence and Power*, p. 341. Nearly everyone who met Barnes in her later years recalls her prolonged coughing fits; during the late 1970s, when Hank O'Neal was acting as her factotum, she required the installation of oxygen inhalation equipment in her apartment.

28. O'Neal, "*Life Is Painful, Nasty & Short*," p. 13.

29. Quoted in Benstock, *Women of the Left Bank*, p. 257.

30. Field, *Djuna*, p. 198.

31. Review from *Newstatesman and Nation* (17 October 1936); quoted in Jane Marcus, "Mousemeat: Contemporary Reviews of *Nightwood*," in Broe, ed., *Silence and Power*, p. 198. Marcus notes that this reviewer sounds "remarkably like Rebecca West" (p. 197).

32. As a child, Barnes greatly admired Jack London, from whom she once received a reply to a fan letter she had sent him. See O'Neal, "*Life is Painful, Nasty & Short*," p. 46. Members of Barnes's family, including her grandmother, were spiritists; and after London's death in 1916, he became one of "the 'Eaches' or spirits, who used Zadel's body to come through the dead." Broe, "My Art Belongs to Daddy," in Broe and Ingram, eds., *Women's Writing in Exile*, p. 53.

33. Djuna Barnes, *Nightwood* (New York: New Directions, 1961), p. 124. Subsequent quotations from this edition are documented in the text. The novel was first published in England by Faber & Faber in 1936; the first American edition appeared a year later from Harcourt, Brace. Another American edition was issued by New Directions in 1946, as part of its "New Classics Series." At the time, Barnes complained to James Laughlin, founding editor of New Directions, that errors she had identified in the text had not been corrected. *Nightwood* was subsequently reset for the American edition of 1961, which has been frequently reprinted. The published version of the novel comprises only about a third of the final draft, which was drastically cut by Barnes on instructions from T. S. Eliot and other editors at Faber and Faber. A fully collated and properly edited *Nightwood* is badly needed.

34. Mary Lynn Broe, "Introduction," in Broe, ed., *Silence and Power*, p. 7.

35. Barnes herself copied down Moore's jibe, in a note found in her papers and quoted in Broe, ed., *Silence and Power*, p. 155.

36. Field, *Djuna*, pp. 32, 140.

37. Annette Kolodny, "Some Notes on Defining a 'Feminist Literary Criticism,'" in *Feminist Criticism: Essays on Theory, Poetry and Prose*, ed. Cheryl L. Brown and Karen Olson (Metuchen, NJ: Scarecrow Press, 1978), p. 44.

38. Benstock, *Women of the Left Bank*, p. 246.

39. Judith Lee, "*Nightwood:* 'The Sweetest Lie,'" in Broe, ed., *Silence and Power*, pp. 217–18.

40. See Jane Marcus's stunning and influential essay, "Laughing at Leviticus: *Nightwood* as Woman's Circus Epic," in Broe, ed., *Silence and Power*, pp. 221–50. Marcus sees the novel as "a study in *abjection*" in which "by its concentration on the figure of The One Who Is

Slapped, the downtrodden victim, it figures by absence the authoritarian dominators of Europe in the 1930s, the sexual and political fascists" (p. 221).

41. Kenneth Burke, "Version, Con-, Per-, and In-: Thoughts on Djuna Barnes's Novel *Nightwood*," in *Language as Symbolic Action: Essays on Life, Literature, and Method* (Berkeley: University of California Press, 1968), pp. 241, 242, 244, 246. According to O'Neal, Barnes took offense at this essay when it first appeared in 1966. She and Burke, who had been good friends, "quarreled ferociously" and became totally estranged. "*Life Is Painful, Nasty & Short,*" p. xii.

42. Kannenstine, *The Art of Djuna Barnes*, p. 112.

43. See, for example, Benstock: "Definitions of gender and sexuality are shown to be socially produced rather than biologically determined, but the directions of sexual orientation are also discovered to be at odds with social norms. The literary artifact reflects the inversion and subversion of sexual coding through the dislocation and disruption of literary genre." *Women of the Left Bank*, p. 262.

44. Charles Baudelaire, "Get Drunk," in *Paris Spleen* (1869), trans. Louise Varèse (New York: New Directions, 1970), p. 74.

45. James B. Scott, *Djuna Barnes* (Boston: Twayne, 1976), p. 96.

46. Whereas the early criticism on *Nightwood*, which often registered distaste at the decadence of its setting and characters, tended to see Nora sympathetically as the victim of Robin's drunken promiscuity, the recent criticism inflected by feminist theory has inverted this reading and found Robin to be the victim of Nora's unconsciously masculinist mentality. In Benstock's opinion, for instance, Nora inevitably "misreads" Robin because "Robin's behavior, appearance, and efforts to communicate are not inscribed in the societal code to which she is asked to conform." Nora, in fact, "sees Robin as a man would see her: as an object of desire." Thus Nora is unwittingly the agent of her own undoing as well as Robin's: "She becomes the unknowing instrument of the patriarchy. Unaware of the patriarchal crimes against her own nature, she allies herself with her oppressors . . . in trying to 'save' Robin, to make her answer to society's claims." *Women of the Left Bank*, pp. 258, 263.

47. Except on one occasion with Jenny Petherbridge (p. 142), Nora is not shown to drink in the novel—although she tells O'Connor about her brief fling at debauchery and her travels to bars early in their relationship with Robin.

48. Some critics have speculated that the cryptic last section of *Nightwood* depicts sexual contact between Robin and Nora's dog. Barnes vigorously denied that there was any bestiality involved. "The final scene was crucial and it annoyed her that many people thought the girl and the dog were sexually engaged. She told me repeatedly the girl was drunk, the dog confused, and that she had witnessed the scene herself. It involved her friend 'Fitzie' (M. E. Fitzgerald) and her dog Buff." O'Neal, "*Life Is Painful, Nasty & Short,*" p. 104.

49. Benstock, *Women of the Left Bank*, p. 263.

50. Field, *Djuna*, pp. 139, 140.

51. Ibid., pp. 137–38, 145. From an examination of Mahoney's few surviving letters to

Barnes and a comparison of Barnes's fictional version of Mahoney with that of Robert McAlmon in one of his stories, Field concludes, "We are prisoners of the texts we possess, always, and it may well be that Mahoney did indeed possess a manner closer to that of Dr. O'Connor than is evident in those little letters. But on the face of it the evidence suggests that it was McAlmon, not Barnes, who simply transcribed the speech of the real Mahoney, and that from an artistic point of view this was rather limited stuff" (p. 141).

52. The "Simon" and "Irene" identities of Thelma Wood and Djuna Barnes anticipate the "butch-femme" roles that came to prominence in American lesbian bar culture during the 1940s and 1950s. See Sue-Ellen Case, "Towards a Butch-Femme Aesthetic," *Discourse*, 11 (Fall-Winter 1988–89), 55–73; and Elizabeth Lapovsky Kennedy and Madeline D. Davis, *Boots of Leather, Slippers of Gold: The History of a Lesbian Community* (New York: Routledge, 1993).

53. *Selected Letters of Malcolm Lowry*, ed. Harvey Breit and Margerie Bonner Lowry (New York: Capricorn, 1969), pp. 312–13.

7: After the Lost Generation: *The Lost Weekend*

1. Malcolm Lowry, *Dark As the Grave Wherein My Friend Is Laid*, ed. Douglas Day and Margerie Lowry (New York: New American Library, 1968), pp. 22, 24–25. By coincidence, yet another novel centered on an alcoholic's disastrous descent was written in 1944 (although not published until 1950): *Der Trinker* by Rudolf Ditzen, the popular German writer who used the pen name "Hans Fallada." It has recently been reprinted as *The Drinker*, ed. John Willett (Marlboro, VT: Marlboro Press, 1990).

2. *Selected Letters of Malcolm Lowry*, ed. Harvey Breit and Margerie Bonner Lowry (1965; rpt. New York: Capricorn, 1969), p. 64.

3. Ignored even in such likely places as Chester E. Eisinger's comprehensive survey, *Fiction of the Forties* (Chicago: University of Chicago, 1963), Jackson's work has drawn limited attention from gay literary historians for its pioneering treatment of homosexuality, particularly in *The Fall of Valor*. See Roger Austen, *Playing the Game: The Homosexual Novel in America* (Indianapolis: Bobbs-Merrill, 1977); Georges-Michel Sarotte, *Like a Brother, Like a Lover: Male Homosexuality in the American Novel and Theatre from Herman Melville to James Baldwin*, trans. Richard Miller (Garden City, NY: Anchor Doubleday, 1978); and Felice Picano, Introduction to *The Fall of Valor* (New York: Arbor House, 1986). For a biographical sketch of Jackson, see John W. Crowley, "Recovering the Author of *The Lost Weekend*: Notes on Charles Jackson," *Dionysos*, 5 (Winter 1994).

4. Bruce Holley Johnson, "The Alcoholism Movement in America: A Study in Cultural Innovation," Diss. University of Illinois 1973, pp. 233–34, 387 n.67. As outlined in 1935, the year before Jackson's admission to Bellevue, Jolliffe's ambitious research program was "to consist of a substantial number of case histories focusing on physiological, psychological, and sociological variables. The initial stage of the project was to be a thorough review of the

literature including all European and American publications for the past century." This review was ultimately done by E. M. Jellinek, who was to become the leading authority on the modern disease concept of alcoholism.

5. Charles Jackson, *The Lost Weekend* (New York: Farrar and Rinehart, 1944), p. 149. Subsequent quotations from the novel are taken from this (first) edition and documented in the text. Birnam owns a complete set of Fitzgerald's books, which he has lavishly rebound "in calf or morocco or levant" as a "kind of personal tribute to the writer he so dearly loved" (p. 148). Don recalls that after reading *Tender Is the Night,* he had been so eager to talk to its author that he had "telephoned all over the Atlantic seaboard till he finally located Fitzgerald at Tuxedo; and the man had said: 'Why don't you write me a letter about it? I think you're a little tight now'" (pp. 149–50).

6. Edmund Wilson, "The Twilight of Drink and the Poetic Drama," *The New Yorker,* 19 (5 February 1944), 78.

7. Half fearing that it might happen, Sigbjørn Wilderness has told his wife "that should another book be published on that theme—not on that mere theme, but which entered as tremendously far as he flattered himself he was going into the calamitous suffering drink could cause to the drinker—he would kill himself." Lowry, *Dark As the Grave,* p. 23.

8. Jackson, a literary autodidact, created a notably bookish character. In addition to Mann, Birnam alludes to or quotes from such writers as Shakespeare, Burns, Tennyson, Poe, Dostoevsky, Chekhov, Fitzgerald, and Joyce.

9. This is one of many references in the novel to *Macbeth.* Birnam (changed from "Burnham" in the manuscript of "The Long Weekend") probably owes his name to Great Birnam Wood; and in describing his fictitious family to Gloria, the bar hostess, he claims that his sons are called Malcolm and Donaldbain (p. 79). Even Macbeth's prophetic witches appear, in the guise of the three crones who haunt Don's dream in Part Four (p. 159).

10. Wilson, "The Twilight of Drink," p. 78.

11. Roger Forseth, "'Why Did They Make Such a Fuss?': Don Birnam's Emotional Barometer," *Dionysos,* 3 (Spring 1991), 12.

12. Johnson suggests that the "ideas presented in *The Lost Weekend* were generally unfamiliar to the American people." As evidence, he cites a *New York Times* review of the film in which Bosley Crowther refers to Don Birnam as a "dipso": "Although the term 'alcoholic' occurs once in the script, it was not part of the vernacular in 1945. The word 'dipsomaniac' was much more familiar. It is also significant that Crowther places the word 'illness' in quotes when he refers to this condition." According to Johnson, the first use in the *New York Times* of the term "alcoholic" occurred on 13 September 1943, just four months before the publication of Jackson's novel. "The Alcoholism Movement in America," pp. 387 n.68, 139 n.34.

13. Ibid., p. 148. Johnson asserts that by the mid-1960s, "those who had not yet brought their opinions into line with this new point of view were forced to contend with the fact that their ideas were inconsistent with practically all of the statements on this subject emanating

from the centers of national culture" (p. 148). Johnson bases this conclusion on his review of literature produced by various institutions responsible for the dissemination of public discourse: religious organizations, medical associations, state and federal governments, the judicial system, corporations, magazines, encyclopedias, and dictionaries.

14. Jack S. Blocker, Jr., remarks, "Viewed in historical perspective, Alcoholics Anonymous represents a flowering among middle-class and upper-class men of the self-help tradition that flourished primarily within the ranks of working-class men from the early nineteenth century to the early twentieth century." *American Temperance Movements: Cycles of Reform* (Boston: Twayne, 1989), pp. 142–43. Blocker goes on to point out a connection between the self-help impulse among workers and periods of pronounced economic instability and/or technological change. Alcoholics Anonymous was founded, of course, in the midst of the Great Depression, when economic anxieties and real hardships were more widely shared than ever before in America by middle-class and even upper-class men.

15. See Blocker, *American Temperance Movements*, p. 141. Given the anonymous and decentralized nature of the fellowship, membership figures for Alcoholics Anonymous are notoriously difficult to determine accurately. All estimates, based on statistics provided by the General Service Office of A.A. itself, are inevitably crude and unreliable—indicative only of a general order of magnitude.

16. Genevieve Parkhurst, "Drinking and Alcoholism," *Harper's Monthly Magazine, 177* (July 1938), 159. The medical expert interviewed by Parkhurst is not identified.

17. Johnson, "The Alcoholism Movement in America," pp. 183, 427. Ernest Kurtz points out that when *Alcoholics Anonymous* (the so-called "Big Book") was being assembled during the late 1930s, the homogeneity of current A.A. membership made it difficult to furnish any variety in the part devoted to personal narratives. "The problem was met by editing to accent different phases of the drinkers' common experience," he explains. It was also decided that the story of Bill D., the first person recruited for A.A. by Bill W. and Doctor Bob, would not be published: "His 'credentials,' in fact the usual ones for 'getting the program' in these early years, were apparently too blatant: highly respectable upper middle-class background, above average education, intensive youthful religious training which had since been rejected, and former social prominence recently nullified by such behavior as his assault on two nurses." *Not-God: A History of Alcoholics Anonymous* (Center City, MN: Hazelden, 1979), pp. 73–74.

18. Blocker, *American Temperance Movements*, p. 146. One early critique of the "disease" paradigm was mounted during the 1960s by the radical psychiatrist Thomas S. Szasz. See "Alcoholism: A Socio-Ethical Perspective," *Western Medicine Medical Journal, 7* (December 1966), 15–21. The attack has since been taken up by a variety of alcohol researchers and has now reached the level of popularization. See, for instance, Stanton Peele, *Diseasing of America: Addiction Treatment Out of Control* (1989; rpt. Boston: Houghton Mifflin, 1991); and Stanton Peele and Archie Brodsky, *The Truth About Addiction and Recovery: The Life Process Program for Outgrowing Destructive Habits* (New York: Simon and Schuster, 1991).

19. See the evasive preface to Jellinek's book, which finally appeared in 1960, years after

he had established his reputation as the premier scientific exponent of the disease paradigm. Jellinek's convoluted prose may be read as symptomatic of the ambivalence he had developed about the ideas that had made him famous: "It goes against my grain to use the expression disease concept—the proper wording would be disease conception. But the publisher's objection that conception sounds awkward must be admitted. . . . Strictly speaking, alcoholism is a concept; so is disease. But that alcoholism is a disease is a viewpoint and thus a conception. Nevertheless I have bowed to the prevalent usage of concept, especially for the title of this book. Indeed, alcoholism itself is only a part issue—but this book is limited to the disease concept issue." *The Disease Concept of Alcoholism* (New Haven, CT: College and University Press, 1960), p. ix. For signs of Jellinek's dis-ease with the disease concept(ion), see also pp. 11–12, 158–59, 165–66.

20. Johnson, "The Alcoholism Movement in America," p. 328. Johnson points to important ideological differences between Mann and Jellinek. Because Mann ardently advocated the A.A. doctrine that "the physiological basis for chronic inebriety was a scientifically established fact," she was "frequently annoyed by statements made by representatives of the Yale Center which, in her opinion, cast doubts on the scientific validity of the medical model." Although some of these statements by Jellinek "make it clear that he was skeptical of the validity of the disease concept of alcoholism," and although he knew that "the medical model was unsubstantiated by empirical findings of any kind," he nevertheless, for humanitarian reasons, "went along with Marty Mann's crusade and . . . he was the prime instigator of almost all of the major efforts to promote this idea during the 1930s" (pp. 292–93).

21. Kurtz, *Not-God,* pp. 120, 294 n.26. Wilder's letter to A.A. headquarters is dated 3 July 1944. Rinehart's letter to Wilson is dated 20 December 1943.

22. Initially rejected by Hollywood as far too depressing for successful adaptation, *The Lost Weekend* was then championed by Billy Wilder and his partner Charles Brackett, who wrote the screenplay and convinced Paramount to make the film against the studio's better judgment. Although the filming of *The Lost Weekend* was finished by the end of 1944, release was delayed indefinitely after sneak preview audiences "were unanimously of the opinion that the movie was putrid, disgusting, boring." Maurice Zolotow, *Billy Wilder in Hollywood* (New York: Putnam's, 1977), pp. 132–33, 139. After New York critics reacted favorably at a private screening, Paramount relented; the movie finally opened, nearly a year late, on 16 November 1945. Although the script was generally faithful to the novel, there was one significant departure: the Hollywood ending, written by Jackson himself at the request of Wilder and Brackett, who were under pressure from the studio to provide an upbeat finale. Whereas the novel closes darkly, with Birnam ready for another bender, the movie ends happily as Don suddenly gives up the booze and starts to work on the novel that his drunkenness has blocked for years.

23. S. D. B. [Selden D. Bacon], "A Student of the Problems of Alcohol and Alcoholism Views the Motion Picture, *The Lost Weekend,*" *Quarterly Journal of Studies on Alcohol,* 6 (December 1945), 402–5. In 1963, after he had become Director of the Rutgers Center of

Alcohol Studies (the successor to the Yale Center), Bacon provided the imprimatur of the Alcoholism Movement for a new edition of *The Lost Weekend*. In a preface, he claimed for the book "a unique position in American literature" by virtue of its being "one of those literary rareties: a novel which has exerted a profound influence on the field with which it deals." Although *The Lost Weekend* was not, in Bacon's opinion, solely responsible for the triumph of a more constructive public attitude toward alcoholism—i.e., the triumph of the disease concept—it had "achieved something far beyond the capacity of any organization or scientist. It made it possible for the first time for large numbers of Americans to identify with the alcoholic." *The Lost Weekend*, Time Reading Program Special Edition (New York: Time, 1963), p. xv.

24. Daniel Brower, "An Opinion Poll on Reactions to 'The Lost Weekend,'" *Quarterly Journal of Studies on Alcohol*, 7 (March 1947), 596–98.

25. Jackson first made contact with A.A. when he was invited to address an open meeting of the Hartford group in November 1944. This event was reported in what was then A.A.'s recently founded journal: "Charles Jackson Speaks at Hartford A.A.," *The A.A. Grapevine*, 1 (January 1945), 3.

26. *The Grapevine* reported that Jackson "said he was indebted to A.A. for one of the novel's most telling points. He referred to the phrase he used in the book which says that, for the alcoholic, 'one drink is too many and a hundred not enough.'" "Charles Jackson Speaks at Hartford A.A.," p. 3.

27. Karl Abraham, "The Psychological Relations Between Sexuality and Alcoholism" (1908), *International Journal of Psycho-Analysis*, 7 (January 1926), 6, 7, 4.

28. Robert P. Knight, "The Dynamics and Treatment of Chronic Alcohol Addiction," *Bulletin of the Menninger Clinic*, 1 (September 1937), 234–41 passim. On Knight's significance to American psychiatry, see "Robert P. Knight: By Way of a Memoir (1972)," in Erik H. Erikson, *A Way of Looking at Things: Selected Papers From 1930 to 1980*, ed. Stephen Schlein (New York: Norton, 1987), pp. 733–38.

29. Edward A. Strecker and Francis T. Chambers, Jr., *Alcohol: One Man's Meat—* (New York: Macmillan, 1938), p. 110.

30. Edmund Bergler, "Contributions to the Psychogenesis of Alcohol Addiction," *Quarterly Journal of Studies on Alcohol*, 5 (December 1944), 446. Bergler, who treated many patients for "writer's block" (a term he invented and popularized), developed a comprehensive and controversial theory about the nature of creativity: *The Writer and Psychoanalysis* (Garden City, NY: Doubleday, 1950). Bergler's book, which received wide and sometimes hostile notice, repeated many points from his 1944 article and helped to spread the idea that homosexuality and alcoholism were related—even though Bergler carefully qualified this claim.

When Malcolm Cowley entered the debate over *The Writer and Psychoanalysis*, he ignored these qualifications in summarizing Bergler's idea of the "orally regressed psychic masochist": "Such is the mechanism that—according to Dr. Bergler—underlies writing, alcoholism, and homosexuality. Since all these are types of oral regression, 'there is nothing remarkable in the fact that they are frequently found in combination, or that the combination of writing and alcoholism is even more frequently observed.'" *The Literary Situation* (New York: Viking 1954), pp. 134–35.

Bergler, who has been called "the most important analytic-theorist of homosexuality in the 1950s," gained notoriety for his view that "homosexuals are essentially disagreeable people . . . [displaying] a mixture of superciliousness, false aggression, and whimpering, . . . subservient when confronted with a stronger person, merciless when in power, unscrupulous about trampling on a weaker person." See Kenneth Lewes, *The Psychoanalytic Theory of Male Homosexuality* (New York: Simon and Schuster, 1988), p. 15.

31. Carney Landis, "Theories of the Alcoholic Personality," in *Alcohol, Science and Society: Twenty-nine Lectures with Discussions as Given at the Yale Summer School of Alcohol Studies,* ed. Howard W. Haggard (New Haven, CT: Quarterly Journal of Studies on Alcohol, 1945), pp. 134–35.

32. Karl A. Menninger, *Man Against Himself* (1938; rpt. New York: Harcourt, Brace, 1959), p. 157. In the typescript of *The Lost Weekend,* held by the Dartmouth College Library, there is an echo (later deleted) of Menninger's pronouncement that "alcohol addiction can be thought of not as a disease, but as a suicidal *flight from* disease, a disastrous attempt at the self-cure of an unseen inner conflict, aggravated but not primarily caused (as many think) by external conflict" (p. 147).

33. Neither this important passage nor the related one quoted below appears in the original typescript of *The Lost Weekend;* Jackson later expanded Birnam's interior monologue to include his agonized thoughts about homosexuality and alcoholism. The nurse, who was called "George" in the early versions of the novel, was renamed "Bim," perhaps as an in-joke: Jackson's brother Frederick, who was openly gay, was familiarly known as "Boom." In line with the strict censorship that governed Hollywood in the 1940s, every trace of the novel's homosexual theme vanished in the Paramount screenplay. In the film, Bim is played by Frank Faylen as a malevolent character, more sadistic than seductive.

34. Although Jackson publicly distanced himself from Don Birnam when the novel first appeared, he later acknowledged that *The Lost Weekend* was largely autobiographical: "Only two minor incidents are pure invention: He did not pawn his girl's leopard jacket to get money for whiskey, and he did not stand up the hostess of his favorite bar during an alcoholic lapse of memory. The rest—the desperations, delirium tremens, nightmares and bitter introspection and remorse—are from life. . . ." "Editors' Preface" to *The Lost Weekend,* Time Reading Program Special Edition, p. xi.

35. In interviews during 1944, Jackson explained that his narrative intention had been to examine a particular character with a drinking problem rather than to offer any solution to the problem of alcoholism in general; *The Lost Weekend* was a slice of life, not a clinical tract. Jackson also insisted that Birnam's case was not hopeless: "Don Birnam must save himself. . . . Until he wants to stop drinking, no help from anyone will cure him. I have suggested

throughout the book that he has character left. He has it within himself to work it out—that remorse is what he's going to build from—but at the end of the book he still isn't ready." "Mary Morris Goes to See the Author of 'The Lost Weekend,'" *New York World-Telegram*, 10 March 1944, pp. m10–m11; clipping in the Charles Jackson Papers, Dartmouth College Library.

36. *Current Biography 1944*, ed. Anna Rothe (New York: H.W. Wilson, 1945), p. 326.

37. "Thomas Randall" is the pseudonym of a writer who wished to remain anonymous in accordance with A.A. traditions. Although Randall apparently died in 1958, his anonymity is still being respected by his publisher, Charles Scribner's Sons. Perhaps the first American novel to detail the inner workings of A.A., *The Twelfth Step* remains the best depiction of the vicissitudes of early sobriety. It is also an interesting period piece about gender tensions and pressures for conformity during the 1950s.

38. An anti-type to these novels is June Arnold's *Sister Gin* (1975), whose relationship to the recovery narrative is similar to that of *Nightwood* to the drunk narrative. Like Djuna Barnes, Arnold deliberately inverts the generic conventions followed by male writers in order to explore links between alcoholism and lesbianism.

39. See Robin Room, "Alcoholism and Alcoholics Anonymous in U.S. Films, 1945–1962: The Party Ends for the 'Wet Generations,'" *Journal of Studies on Alcohol*, 50 (July 1989), 368–83. *Come Fill the Cup* and *Come Back, Little Sheba* were based, respectively, on the novel by Harlan Ware (New York: Random House, 1952) and the play by William Inge (New York: Random House, 1950). *I'll Cry Tomorrow* was adapted from the confessional autobiography (New York: Frederick Fell, 1954) of the popular singer Lillian Roth. J. P. Miller's screenplay for *Days of Wine and Roses* was later novelized by David Westheimer (New York: Bantam, 1963).

40. Published originally in 1939, *Alcoholics Anonymous* was reissued in 1955 and 1976. Although the main body of the text has remained virtually unchanged from the first to the third editions, the "Personal Stories" section has been revised to reflect the changing demographics of the membership. See Kurtz, *Not-God*, p. 132.

41. Room, "Alcoholism and Alcoholics Anonymous," p. 380.

42. Donald Newlove, *Those Drinking Days: Myself and Other Writers* (New York: Horizon Press, 1981), pp. 71, 48.

43. Fitzgerald, *The Last Tycoon: An Unfinished Novel* (1941; rpt. New York: Scribner's, 1969), p. 163.

Index

Abraham, Karl, 61, 149, 160n. 10, 183n. 11
Absinthe, 47, 49, 64, 170n. 15
Addiction, 4–5, 9–18 passim, 22–23, 24, 56, 79, 118, 119, 122, 138, 146, 150, 161n. 13, 161–62n. 18, 162n. 19, 164–65n. 5, 165–66n. 9, 172n. 22. *See also* Alcoholism
Agee, James, 39
Aiken, Conrad, 39
Alcoholics Anonymous (A.A.), 138, 144, 147, 148, 156–57, 189nn. 14, 15, 17, 190n. 20, 191nn. 25, 26, 193n. 37
Alcoholics Anonymous ("Big Book"), 156, 189n. 17, 193n. 40
Alcoholism, x, 4–5, 18, 22–24, 35–42 passim, 65, 68–69, 116–18, 131, 143–48, 149, 154–57, 160n. 10, 160–61n. 11, 161n. 13, 161–62n. 18, 163n. 29, 171n. 21, 173–74n. 4, 188n. 12, 191–92nn. 30. *See also* Addiction, Delirium tremens, Denial, Dipsomania, Disease concept, Drinking practices, Inebriation, Intemperance

Alcoholism Movement, 144–48, 155–56, 188–89n. 13, 190–91n. 23
Aldridge, John, 171n. 20
Allen, Carolyn, 182–83n. 6
American Temperance Society, 2, 5, 160n. 8
American Temperance Union, 5
Anderson, Sherwood, 38
Anti-Saloon League, 46, 60, 61, 170n. 12
Archbald, Margaretta, 93, 98
Arnold, June: *Sister Gin*, 193n. 38

Bacon, Selden D., 147, 190–91n. 23
Balassi, William, 171n. 18
Baldwin, James, x
Bardake, Theodore, 171n. 20
Barnes, Djuna, 39, 86, 114, 115–34, 177n. 47, 182nn. 2, 4, 184nn. 15, 16, 17, 19, 25, 184–85n. 27, 185nn. 32, 33, 35, 186nn. 41, 48, 186–87n. 51, 187n. 52, 193n. 38; *Antiphon, The*, 121; *Nightwood*, 116, 118, 121–34, 155,

Barnes, Djuna (*cont.*)
185n. 33, 186nn. 46, 47, 48, 193n. 38;
Ryder, 130
Barnes, Wald, 118, 119, 184nn. 15, 19
Barney, Natalie Clifford, 86, 115, 122
Barry, Philip, 39
Bateson, Gregory: *Steps to an Ecology of Mind,* 164n. 33
Baudelaire, Charles, 125
Beard, George M., 11, 15, 17
Beecher, Lyman, 3
Bellow, Saul, 41; *Herzog,* 168n. 33
Benchley, Robert, 36, 39, 99
Benson, Jackson, 171n. 20
Benstock, Shari, 88, 116, 118, 121–22, 129, 186nn. 43, 46
Bergler, Edmund, 150; *Writer and Psychoanalysis, The,* 191–92n. 30
Berridge, Virginia, 5, 161–62n. 18
Berryman, John, 36, 39; *Recovery,* 156
Bierce, Ambrose, 38
Bishop, Elizabeth, 39
Blackmur, R. P., 39
Blake, William, 98, 110
Blocker, Jack S., Jr., 161n. 13, 162–63n. 25, 166n. 14, 189n. 14
Bodenheim, Maxwell, 39
Bogan, Louise, 39
Bowles, Jane, 39
Boyle, Kay, 63–64, 173n. 33
Brackett, Charles, 190n. 22
Brands, Orestes M.: *Lessons on the Human Body,* 165–66n. 9
Broe, Mary Lynn, 118, 123, 184nn. 15, 16, 17
Brooks, Romaine, 86
Broun, Heywood, 38
Bruccoli, Matthew J., 71, 74, 87, 93, 95, 97, 99, 100, 102, 110, 175n. 26, 176n. 32, 178n. 5, 180n. 35
Budington, Henry Aaron, 119, 184n. 19; *Man Makes His Body,* 119

Burke, Kenneth, 39, 125, 186n. 41
Burns, Robert, 188n. 8
Byron, Lord (George Gordon), 141

Cain, James M., 39
Cape, Jonathan, 136
Capone, Al, 96
Cass, Lewis, 11
Chandler, Raymond, 36, 38
Chatterton, Thomas, 141
Cheever, John, 39; *Falconer,* 156
Chekhov, Anton, 188n. 8
Civil War, 6, 35, 61, 166n. 12
Cocteau, Jean, 179n. 25
Codependence, 178n. 5
Come Back, Little Sheba (film), 156, 193n. 39
Come Fill the Cup (film), 156, 193n. 39
Cook, George Cram, 38
Cowley, Malcolm, 39, 72, 176n. 35, 177n. 49, 191–92n. 30
Cozzens, James Gould, 39
Crane, Hart, 36, 39
Crosby, Harry, 39, 63
Crowther, Bosley, 188n. 12
cummings, e. e., 36, 39
Cunard, Nancy, 39

Dardis, Tom, x, 44, 67–68, 162n. 23, 169n. 6, 174n. 7
Darwin, Erasmus, 3
Davidson, Arnold, 60, 62
Davidson, Cathy N., 60, 62
Days of Wine and Roses (film), 156, 193n. 33
Delirium tremens, 4, 121, 123, 139, 192n. 34
Denial, 20, 24, 32, 63, 65, 66–67, 70–71, 74, 83, 89, 99, 107, 116, 139–40, 148, 153, 154, 164–65n. 5, 165n. 6, 169n. 6, 175n. 18
Depression, Great, 98, 102–3, 137, 189n. 14
De Voto, Bernard, 39
Dickens, Charles: *Martin Chuzzlewit,* 177n. 42

Dickinson, Emily, 64

Dietrich, Marlene, 152

Dipsomania, 4, 22–24, 44, 55, 93, 171n. 21, 188n. 12

Disease concept (of alcoholism), x, 4–5, 6–7, 8, 22–24, 35, 68–69, 104, 143–46, 155–56, 161n. 13, 161–62n. 18, 163n. 29, 167n. 24, 167–68n. 26, 187–88n. 4, 188n. 12, 189n. 18, 189–90n. 19, 190n. 20, 190–91n. 23, 192n. 32

Doherty, William E., 78

Donaldson, Scott, x, 58, 67, 70, 81, 84, 86, 87, 172n. 25, 175n. 26

Dostoevsky, Feodor, 16, 188n. 8; *Gambler, The,* 16

Dowson, Ernest, 141

Dreiser, Theodore, 14, 15–16, 17, 38; *Sister Carrie,* 15–16

Drinking practices, 1–2, 26, 35, 37, 40, 69, 117–18, 159n. 1, 159–60n. 2, 162–63n. 25, 166n. 12, 167n. 21, 183n. 7. *See also* Treating

Drunk narrative, x, 41, 44, 67, 116, 118, 125, 133, 140–42, 155–57, 193n. 38

Dunbar, Paul Laurence, 38

Duncan, Isadora, 183n. 7

Dunne, Finley Peter (Mr. Dooley), 38

Eble, Kenneth E., 70

Edwards, Griffith, 5, 161–62n. 18

Eisinger, Chester E.: *Fiction of the Forties,* 187n. 3

Eliot, T. S., x, 34, 123, 185n. 33; *Waste Land, The,* 34, 41–42

Ellis, Havelock, 112

Emerson, Ralph Waldo, 64

Esquire, 67, 70, 178–79n. 19

Fallada, Hans (Rudolf Ditzen): *The Drinker,* 187n. 1

Faulkner, Percy, 184n. 15

Faulkner, William, x, 36, 39, 44, 169n. 6

Faylen, Frank, 192n. 33

Fearing, Kenneth, 39

Feminism, 21, 27–28, 88, 116–25 passim, 128–29, 171n. 20, 182n. 4, 186n. 46

Field, Andrew, 119, 123, 124, 130–31, 145, 182n. 4, 184nn. 16, 19, 184–85n. 27, 186–87n. 51

FitzGerald, Edward: *Rubaiyat of Omar Khayyam, The,* 174n. 13

Fitzgerald, F. Scott, ix, x, 36, 39, 44, 63, 65–89, 96–97, 98, 99, 101, 110, 114, 139, 157, 171n. 21, 172n. 25, 173n. 3, 173–74n. 4, 174nn. 6, 7, 174n. 13, 175nn. 26, 27, 178n. 16, 180nn. 35, 36, 188nn. 5, 8; *Beautiful and Damned, The,* 70; "Crack Up, The," 70–71, 175n. 18, 178–79n. 19; "Family in the Wind," 70; *Great Gatsby, The,* 66, 71, 100, 177n. 47, 180nn. 34, 36, 188n. 5; Pat Hobby stories, 67; *Regular Fix, A,* 67; "Shadow Laurels," 67; *Tender Is the Night,* 67–68, 70, 71–89, 96–97, 100, 102, 110, 132, 133, 139, 142, 155, 175n. 26, 176nn. 32, 35, 39, 177n. 49, 179n. 27, 188n. 5; *This Side of Paradise,* 40, 97

Fitzgerald, Zelda, 66–67, 68, 73, 86, 174n. 6

Flexner, Stuart Berg, 160n. 8, 160–61n. 11

Forel, Oscar, 66

Forseth, Roger, xi, 46, 143

Fortune, 137

Francis, Joseph H.: *My Last Drink,* 165n. 7

Freud, Sigmund, 19, 27, 77, 149, 150, 164–65n. 5, 183n. 11

Freytag-Loringhoven, Else von, 119

Friedman, Susan Stanford, 88

Gates, David: *Jernigan,* 156

Gender, x, 10, 13, 19, 25, 26–28, 34, 41, 53, 56–57, 60–62, 84–87, 88–89, 112–14, 117–18, 124, 129–30, 131, 153–54, 162–63n. 25, 166n. 14, 183n. 7, 186n. 43, 193nn. 37, 38

Gibbs, Wolcott, 39, 94

Gilbert, Sandra M., 27

Gilmore, Thomas B., x, 70, 77, 173n. 3, 175n. 26

Gold, Ivan: *Sams in a Dry Season,* 156

Goodwin, Donald W., x, 35, 169n. 6, 173–74n. 4

Gordon, Caroline, 39

Graham, Sheilah, 67, 174n. 7

Grebstein, Sheldon N., 100

Greenwich Village, 37, 115, 119, 121

Gubar, Susan, 27

Guggenheim, Peggy, 122

Gustafson, Zadel Barnes, 118–19, 184n. 17, 185n. 32

Haggard, Howard W., 145

Hammett, Dashiell, 36, 39

Harding, D. W., 73–74, 175n. 27

Harte, Bret, 38

Hartley, Marsden, 119

Hecht, Ben, 39

Heggen, Thomas, x, 39

Hellman, Lillian, 39

Hemingway, Ernest, ix, x, 36, 39, 43–64, 65, 66, 69, 76, 86, 92, 114, 115, 129, 130, 139, 142, 168n. 32, 169–70n. 11, 172nn. 25, 27, 173n. 36; *Farewell to Arms, A,* 75–76; *For Whom the Bell Tolls,* 170n. 15; *Garden of Eden, The,* 62; *Moveable Feast, A,* 65; *Sun Also Rises, The,* 40, 44–63, 88, 95, 114, 115, 117, 130, 142, 155, 168n. 32, 169n. 8, 169–70n. 11, 170n. 15, 170–71n. 17, 171nn. 18, 19, 20, 21, 172nn. 22, 25; *Wild Years, The,* 168n. 3, 170n. 15

Hemingway, Mary Welsh, 169n. 6

Herald Tribune (New York), 93

Hicks, Granville, 39, 167n. 20

Hoffman, Frederick J., 37, 88

Hollywood, 67, 95, 135, 138, 146–47, 156, 173n. 3, 176n. 39, 180n. 36, 190n. 22, 192n. 33

Homophobia, 48, 60–62, 84–87, 88–89, 114, 125, 133, 152–54, 172n. 27

Homosexuality, 57, 60–62, 86–87, 89, 113–14, 125, 130–31, 133, 138, 148–54 passim, 172n. 27, 172–73n. 30, 187n. 3, 191–92n. 30, 192n. 33. *See also* Lesbianism

Hoover, Herbert, 103

Hotchner, A. E., 44

Howells, W. D., 5–17, 161n. 16, 163n. 31, 164n. 37; *Annie Kilburn,* 162n. 19; *Hazard of New Fortunes, A,* 8; *Lady of the Aroostook, The,* 5–7, 9, 19, 162n. 22; *Landlord at Lion's Head, The,* 9–16; *Modern Instance, A,* 7–8, 9, 10, 12, 162nn. 20, 22; *Quality of Mercy, The,* 162n. 19; *Rise of Silas Lapham, The,* 8, 162n. 22; *Son of Royal Langbrith, The,* 162n. 19

Huneker, James Gibbons, 38

Huss, Magnus, 4

I'll Cry Tomorrow (film), 156, 193n. 39

Inebriation (inebriety), 3–5, 22–24, 53, 117, 137, 146, 155, 160n. 8, 190n. 20. *See also* Intemperance

Inge, William, 39; *Come Back, Little Sheba,* 193n. 39

Intemperance, 1–5, 7, 8, 10, 15, 24, 53, 68–69, 117, 159n. 1, 160n. 8. *See also* Inebriation

Irwin, Julie M., 68

Jackson, Charles, x, xi, 14, 39, 135–55, 187–88n. 4, 188nn. 5, 8, 190n. 22, 191nn. 25, 26, 192n. 34, 192–93n. 35; *Fall of Valor, The,* 138; "Farther and Wilder," 155; *Lost Weekend, The,* 135–44, 146, 147, 148–55, 157, 188nn. 5, 8, 9, 12, 190n. 22, 190–91n. 23, 191n. 26, 192nn. 32–34, 192–93n. 35; *Outer Edges, The,* 138; *Second-Hand Life, A,* 138

Jackson, Frederick, 137, 192n. 33

Jackson, Rhoda Booth, 137
Jackson, Shirley, 39
James, William, 33–34, 163n. 31
Jeffers, Robinson, 38
Jellinek, E. M., 145, 146, 161n. 13, 187–88n. 4, 190n. 20; *Disease Concept of Alcoholism, The*, 189–90n. 19
Johnson, Bruce H., 144, 145, 160n. 10, 160–61n. 11, 188n. 12, 188–89n. 13, 190n. 20
Jolliffe, Norman, 137, 187–88n. 4
Jones, James, x
Joyce, James, 188n. 8
Jung, Carl G., 19

Kafka, Franz: *Trial, The*, 102
Kannenstine, Louis F., 125
Karnchanapee, Karen R., 166n. 10
Kazin, Alfred, 40–41, 71, 73
Keats, John, 141
Keeley, Leslie E. (Keeley Cure), 9, 162n. 23
Kees, Weldon, 39
Kenner, Hugh, 88
Kerouac, Jack, 37
Key, Francis Scott, 174n. 13
Kipling, Rudyard: "Ladies, The," 27, 61
Knight, Robert P., 149, 150, 191n. 28
Kolodny, Annette, 124
Korsakoff's syndrome, 173n. 36
Krafft-Ebing, Richard von, 112
Krutch, Joseph Wood: *Modern Temper, The*, 34–35
Kurtz, Ernest, 146

Ladies' Home Journal, 179n. 25
Lamarckianism, 15
Landis, Carney, 150
Lardner, Ring, 36, 38, 65
Laughlin, James, 185n. 33
Lawrence, D. H.: *Fantasia of the Unconscious*, 84
Lears, T. J. Jackson, 14

Lee, Judith, 124
Lemon, Courtnay, 119
Lender, Mark E., 159–60n. 2, 166n. 10
Lesbianism, 57, 61, 62, 83–84, 85–86, 89, 116, 118–23 passim, 131, 133, 152, 172–73n. 30, 182n. 50, 182–83n. 6, 183n. 11, 187n. 52, 193n. 38. See also Homosexuality
Levine, Harry Gene, 4, 17, 159n. 1, 161n. 13, 162–63n. 25, 163n. 29
Lewis, Sinclair, x, 36, 38
Liebling, A. J., 37, 39
London, Charmian, 20, 21, 41
London, Jack, vi, 19–42, 44, 53, 57, 61, 66, 69, 93, 114, 121, 129, 133, 165n. 8, 167n. 20, 168n. 32, 168–69n. 4, 169n. 5, 171n. 21, 185n. 32; *Jane Barleycorn*, 57, 166–67n. 17; *John Barleycorn*, vi, 19–34, 41, 46–47, 53, 57, 58, 88, 123, 155, 160–61n. 11, 168n. 32, 168–69n. 4, 169n. 5
Long, Robert Emmet, x, 100, 180n. 34
Lost Generation, The, 34–42 passim, 59, 63, 115, 117, 135
Lost Weekend, The (film), 135–36, 144, 146–47, 188n. 12, 190n. 22, 192n. 33
Lowell, Robert, 37, 39
Lowry, Malcolm, 80, 88, 132–33, 135–36, 140, 144, 176nn. 36, 37, 39; *Dark as the Grave Wherein My Friend Is Laid*, 135–36, 188n. 7; "Tender Is the Night" (screenplay), 80, 176nn. 36–37; *Under the Volcano*, 80, 132–33, 135, 136, 140
Lowry, Margerie, 176n. 36
Lynn, Kenneth, 169n. 6

MacArthur, Charles, 39
MacShane, Frank, 93, 180n. 32
Mahoney, Dan, 130–31, 186–87n. 51
Mailer, Norman, x
Mann, Marty, 144, 190n. 20
Mann, Thomas, 137, 142, 155, 188n. 8; *Death in Venice*, 141; *Magic Mountain, The*, 137

Marcus, Jane, 185n. 31, 185–86n. 40
Marquand, John P., 36, 39
Marquis, Don, 38
Martin, James K., 159–60n. 2
Martin, Wendy, 171n. 20
Massachusetts Society for the Suppression of Intemperance, 2
Masters, Edgar Lee, 38
Maugham, Somerset: *Sheppy,* 99, 179n. 25
McAlmon, Robert, 39, 63–64, 86, 115n. 33, 173n. 36, 186–87n. 51; *Being Geniuses Together,* 63–64, 173n. 33
McCullers, Carson, 39
Mencken, H. L., 38
Menninger, Karl: *Man Against Himself,* 150, 192n. 32
Meyers, Jeffrey, 169n. 3
Michaels, Walter Benn, 16–17
Milland, Ray, 135
Millay, Edna St. Vincent, 36, 39, 117
Miller, J. P.: *Days of Wine and Roses* (film), 193n. 39
Miller, Joaquin, 38
Miller, Jonathan: *Body in Question, The,* 163n. 29
Misogyny, 26–27, 46, 61, 88, 113, 129–30, 171n. 20
Mizener, Arthur, 75, 100, 179–80n. 29
Modern Temper, The, 34–35, 41, 63, 75, 102, 132, 134, 155, 157
Modernism, ix, x, 14, 15, 17–18, 28, 33, 34–35, 40–42, 44, 48, 69, 75–76, 77, 80, 88, 95, 99, 102, 116, 117–18, 125, 130–36 passim, 140–42, 154–55, 168n. 32
Montgomery, Robert, 180n. 36
Moore, Marianne, 123–24, 185n. 35
Murphy, Gerald, 179n. 27
Murphy, Sara, 179n. 27

Nassau Literary Magazine, The, 67
Nation, Carry, 43

National Committee for Education on Alcoholism (N.C.E.A.), 144, 145–46
Negri, Pola, 152
Nemerov, Howard, 39
Neurasthenia, 11, 14
New Republic, The, 40
New York Times, The, 188n. 12
New Yorker, The, 94, 95, 96
Newlove, Donald, x, 37, 42, 157; *Drunks, The,* 156
Nietzsche, Friedrich, 30, 31, 33

Odets, Clifford, x, 39
O'Hara, Belle Wylie, 93, 94, 95, 178n. 5
O'Hara, Helen Petit, 93, 97–98
O'Hara, John, x, 36, 39, 91–114, 121, 178n. 5, 178–79n. 19, 180nn. 34, 35, 36, 181n. 40, 182n. 45; *Appointment in Samarra,* 93, 96, 97, 98–114, 155, 178n. 16, 179n. 27, 180n. 32, 180nn. 34, 35, 36, 180–81n. 37, 181n. 44, 182nn. 45, 46, 49, 50; *Butterfield 8,* 93, 99, 178n. 16; *From the Terrace,* 101; "Imagine Kissing Pete," 103, 181n. 40; *Pal Joey,* 95–96; *Sermons and Soda Water,* 181n. 43
O'Hara, Katharine Barnes, 94
O'Hara, Martin, 91
O'Hara, Patrick, 91, 92
O'Hara, Thomas, 98, 99
Olson, Charles, 36, 39
O'Neal, Hank, 121, 122, 184n. 25, 184–85n. 27, 186n. 41
O'Neill, Eugene, 36, 38, 119

Parker, Dorothy, x, 36, 39, 117
Partisan Review, The, 137
Peele, Stanton, 189n. 18
Pegler, Westbrook, 103
Perkins, Maxwell, 65, 69, 81, 84
Perry, Constance M., 118, 182n. 5
Pickford, Mary, 123

Poe, Edgar Allan, 35, 36, 38, 66, 96, 141
Porter, Katherine Anne, 39, 79, 117
Porter, William Sidney (O. Henry), 38
Powell, Dawn, 39
Prohibition, 3, 5, 6, 19, 21, 35, 37, 40, 45–46,
    53, 69, 91, 94, 102, 103, 104, 117, 125, 127,
    145, 159–60n. 2, 161nn. 13, 16, 168n. 3,
    169n. 8, 170n. 12. See also Temperance
Psychoanalysis, 19, 148–50, 152, 153, 154,
    160n. 10, 164–65n. 5, 183n. 11, 191–
    92n. 30

Randall, Thomas: Twelfth Step, The, 156,
    193n. 37
Rawlings, Marjorie Kinnan, 39
Recovery movement, 155–56, 164–65n. 5
Recovery narrative, 155–56, 193n. 38
Reynolds, Michael S., 63, 169n. 8, 169–
    70n. 11, 171n. 19
Riley, James Whitcomb, 38
Rinehart, Stanley M., 147
Robinson, E. A., 36, 38
Roethke, Theodore, 36, 39
Room, Robin, 35, 40, 156, 168n. 32
Roosevelt, Franklin Delano, 103
Rorabaugh, W. J., 2
Rosenzweig, Roy, 25, 26, 30, 166n. 12
Roth, Lillian: I'll Cry Tomorrow, 193n. 39
Roth, Marty, 71, 72, 175n. 26
Runyon, Damon, 38
Rush, Benjamin: Inquiry into the Effects of
    Ardent Spirits, 4

Saloons, 25–26, 28, 29, 43, 46, 113, 117,
    166nn. 12, 14, 167n. 21, 170n. 12, 183n. 8
Saroyan, William, x, 39
Saturday Evening Post, The, 65, 74, 164n. 1
Schorer, Mark, 39
Schulberg, Budd, ix–x
Schwartz, Delmore, 39
Scott, James B., 127, 184–85n. 27

Scott, Natalie Anderson: Story of Mrs.
    Murphy, The, 156
Scott, Walter, 174n. 13
Scott, Winfield Townley, 39
Scribner's Magazine, 81
Seabrook, William, 38, 70; Asylum, 175n. 17
Shakespeare, William, 75, 188n. 8; Mac-
    beth, 188n. 9
Shaw, Irwin, x, 39
Sheldon, Charles M.: In His Steps, 183n. 8
Sinclair, Andrew, 117
Sinclair, Upton, 165n. 6, 166–67n. 17
Smith, Robert Holbrook (Dr. Bob), 144,
    189n. 17
Social Darwinian, 11, 14–16, 21, 23, 153,
    163n. 29
Something to Live For (film), 156
Spencer, Herbert, 11, 15
Spengler, Oswald, 67, 75, 84, 132; Decline of
    the West, The, 76, 87, 140
Spilka, Mark, 62, 170–71n. 17, 172–73n. 30
Stafford, Jean, 39
Stasz, Clarice, 20, 164n. 1
Stearns, Harold, 39
Steinbeck, John, x, 36, 39
Sterling, George, 38
Stern, Milton, x, 176n. 35
Stevens, Wallace, 36, 38
Stewart, Donald Ogden, 39, 172n. 25
Stoddard, Charles Warren, 38
Szasz, Thomas S., 189n. 18

Tarkington, Booth, 38
Tate, Allen, 171n. 20
Teetotalism, 3, 8, 43, 54, 62, 91, 129
Temperance, 2–5, 11, 19, 23, 26, 40, 43, 45–
    46, 53, 83, 91, 117, 118, 119, 144, 145, 156,
    159–60n. 2, 160n. 8, 162–63n. 25, 165n. 7,
    166n. 10, 168n. 32, 170n. 12, 183n. 8. See
    also Prohibition
Tennyson, Alfred, 188n. 8

Thalberg, Irving, 173n. 3
Thomson, James: "City of Dreadful Night, The," 41
Thoreau, Henry David, 35
Thurber, James, 39, 94
Tolstoy, Leo: *Anna Karenina*, 110
Toronto Star, The, 44, 168n. 3
Treat, Roger: *Endless Road, The*, 156
Treating, 30, 53, 58, 113, 151
Trilling, Lionel, 102
True Womanhood, Cult of, 13, 117, 162–63n. 25
Trumbo, Dalton, 39
Tuttleton, James W., 100, 172n. 27
Twain, Mark, 162n. 20
Twysden, Lady Duff, 172n. 22

Updike, John, 180–81n. 37

Veblen, Thorstein: *Theory of the Leisure Class, The*, 17–18, 160–61n. 11, 164n. 37, 167n. 21, 168n. 32
Voice in the Mirror, The (film), 156

Walsh, Ernest, 39
Ware, Harlan: *Come, Fill the Cup*, 193n. 39
Warren, Charles, 176n. 39
Warren, Robert Penn, 45, 51, 75–76
Webster, Noah, 3, 160n. 8
Wedge, George, x, 167–68n. 26, 169n. 6
Wescott, Glenway, 175n. 18
West, Nathanael, x, 39
West, Rebecca, 185n. 31
Westheimer, David: *Days of Wine and Roses*, 193n. 39

Wharton, Edith, 179n. 25
Wheeler, Wayne B., 46, 60, 170n. 12
White, E. B., 39
White Logic, The, vi, x, 20–21, 33–34, 41, 42, 45, 64, 75, 77, 102, 109, 118, 123, 132, 133, 134, 140, 142, 155, 157
Wilde, Dolly, 86
Wilde, Oscar, 86
Wilder, Billy, 135, 147, 190n. 22
Wilder, Thornton, 39
Williams, Tennessee, x, 36, 39
Williams, William Carlos, 63–64; *Autobiography*, 64, 173n. 34
Wilson, Earl, 95–96
Wilson, Edmund, 36, 37, 39, 40, 100, 139, 143, 147, 171n. 20, 174n. 13, 178–79n. 19
Wilson, William Griffith (Bill W.), 144, 147, 189n. 17
Wolfe, Thomas, 36, 39
Women's Christian Temperance Union (W.C.T.U.), 23, 46, 117
Wood, Thelma, 119–20, 123, 125, 130, 131, 187n. 52
Woollcott, Alexander, 38
World War I, 35, 37, 43, 49, 74, 77, 87–88, 102, 117, 124, 160–61n. 11
Wright, Alfred M., 95

Yale Center for Studies of Alcohol, 144–47 passim, 150, 190n. 20, 190–91n. 23
Yates, Richard: *Disturbing the Peace*, 156
Young Men's Christian Association (Y.M.C.A.), 25–26